OXFORD TEXTUAL PERSPECTIVES

The Idea of the Book and the Creation of Literature

The Idea of the Book and the Creation of Literature

STEPHEN ORGEL

OXFORD
UNIVERSITY PRESS

OXFORD
UNIVERSITY PRESS

Great Clarendon Street, Oxford, OX2 6DP,
United Kingdom

Oxford University Press is a department of the University of Oxford.
It furthers the University's objective of excellence in research, scholarship,
and education by publishing worldwide. Oxford is a registered trade mark of
Oxford University Press in the UK and in certain other countries

Published in the United States of America by Oxford University Press
198 Madison Avenue, New York, NY 10016, United States of America

British Library Cataloguing in Publication Data
Data available

Library of Congress Control Number: 2022937325

ISBN 978-0-19-287153-4 (hbk.)
ISBN 978-0-19-287158-9 (pbk.)

DOI: 10.1093/oso/9780192871534.001.0001

Printed and bound in the UK by
TJ Books Limited

For John Mustain

SERIES EDITOR'S PREFACE

Oxford Textual Perspectives is a series of informative and provocative studies focused upon texts (conceived of in the broadest sense of that term) and the technologies, cultures, and communities that produce, inform, and receive them. It provides fresh interpretations of fundamental works, images, and artefacts, and of the vital and challenging issues emerging in English literary studies. By engaging with the contexts and materiality of the text, its production, transmission, and reception history, and by frequently testing and exploring the boundaries of the notions of text and meaning themselves, the volumes in the series question conventional frameworks and provide innovative interpretations of both canonical and less well-known works. These books will offer new perspectives, and challenge familiar ones, both on and through texts and textual communities. While they focus on specific authors, periods, and issues, they nonetheless scan wider horizons, addressing themes and provoking questions that have a more general application to literary studies and cultural history as a whole. Each is designed to be as accessible to the non-specialist reader as it is fresh and rewarding for the specialist, combining an informative orientation in a landscape with detailed analysis of the territory and suggestions for further travel.

Elaine Treharne and *Greg Walker*

PREFACE

This book is based on a course I created at Stanford in the early 1990s in the history of the book. The course was initially designed to tempt students away from their computers and into the library, and was taught in the Rare Book Room, first in collaboration with the Classics librarian the late David Sullivan, and subsequently, for more than two decades, with John Mustain, the Curator of Rare Books. It quickly became apparent that the siren call of the Internet was not the greatest impediment to historical scholarship facing modern students: their fascination with old books and excitement at being able to handle them were palpable. But a significant component of the course involved comparing works in modern editions with the original texts those versions purported to represent, and we all soon realized how much was necessarily lost, or sometimes misrepresented, even in what were nominally facsimiles, and even in the photographic reproductions of the indispensable Chadwyck-Healey database Early English Books Online (EEBO). The point was not to condemn these changes, but to be aware of them and to learn how to take into account the inevitable transformations of history.

One frequently hears it claimed that with the availability of EEBO, which includes substantially every book published in England or for the English market before 1700, rare book libraries are no longer necessary for the study of English literature. This claim is simply inaccurate: to begin with, English Renaissance libraries were by no means limited to books published in England, which in fact comprised only a very small part of the literary resources available to early modern British writers. With a readership for much of whom Latin was a second language, most works of philosophy, history, and science—indeed most reference works—were in Latin and published on the continent. Moreover, EEBO's photographs were digitized from microfilms, and they reproduce impeccably what is on the microfilms, including, of course, all spots, blotches, and other defects. Since the microfilms are in black and white, the digitizations render all marks as tonally equivalent. A handwritten correction is not distinguishable as such, and an ink spot or a flyspeck is easily taken for a mark of punctuation. Nor do the digitized microfilms provide any information beyond that revealed by the typography: there is no way of examining the paper to see water-marks and chain lines, which are essential for understanding how the book is put together and for detecting inserted sheets and recognizing forgeries. And of course, on the computer all books are the same size: the heft of a folio and the fragility of a duodecimo are not reproducible.

John Carter's *ABC For Book Collectors*, in its several revisions since 1952, has been an indispensable resource. Dennis Duncan and Adam Smyth's excellent collection *Book Parts*, which codifies the idea of the material book, unfortunately appeared too late to be of use in the course, but it would have been required reading, and I am indebted to it at several points here. I am happy to be able finally to acknowledge many years of conversations with the late Marion Trousdale, a superb scholar and dear friend, who introduced me to the poetry of Abraham Fraunce. For help on particular points I am indebted to Brenda Silver, David Halperin, Angus Gowland, and the late David Sachs. Benjamin L. Albritton, Stanford's current Curator of Rare Books and Classics Librarian, has been unfailingly generous and helpful. I am grateful to Elaine Treharne and Greg Walker, the general editors of Oxford Tex-tual Perspectives, for their enthusiasm for the project, to my editors Hannah Doyle and Emma Varley for their expert guidance, and to the two anonymous and genial Press readers, most of whose suggestions for revision I have followed. I have learned much from many years of exemplary students in the class, of whom I can name only a few: Jonathan Fetter-Vorm, Stephanie Adams-Santos, Robin Whitson-Burns, Ryan Zurowski, Randy Johnson, Garth Kimbrell, Bridget Whearty, Ian Bickford, Britten Heller, Luke Barnhart, Brian Umana, Rachel Hamburg, Jason Vartikar, Bojan Srbinovski, Christina Zempel, Killeen Hanson. The dedication to John Mustain acknowledges both a long and fruitful collaboration and a great deal of admiration and affection.

CONTENTS

LIST OF ILLUSTRATIONS

A NOTE ON QUOTATIONS

In quotations, u, v, i, j, and w have been normalized, and contractions have been expanded; otherwise, quotations are given as they appear in the editions cited. In the case of early books that do not include page numbers, citations are to signature numbers. Signatures are the marks placed by the printer at the beginning of each gathering (or quire) to show how the book is organized. The marks are usually letters or combinations of letters, but they may also be symbols, such as asterisks or pilcrows (paragraph signs). Thus sig. A2^r means the first side (*recto*) of the second leaf of the gathering marked A. The second side, or *verso*, would be A2^v. Shakespeare quotations are from the New Pelican editions, edited by Stephen Orgel and A. R. Braunmuller.

1

Introduction

Books have been, for several millennia, the material embodiment of knowledge and culture—not the only embodiment (there are works of art, architecture, diagrams, scientific formulae), but for us, an essential one for any kind of knowledge involving texts. Texts, however, do not need to be books—they are not even necessarily written. The oldest poems were composed to be recited, and only written down centuries later. Cicero composed his orations in his head, and had them put in writing only after he had delivered them, as a way of preserving them. Most of Montaigne's essays were dictated. As Roger Stoddard has observed, throughout history authors have never written books, they have created texts, not always by writing, which were turned into books by scribes, editors, printers, and publishers,[1] who then required a distribution system, the book trade, for the books to reach purchasers and readers. The book is actually quite distant from the author.

When texts become books they are material objects, manufactured at a particular time and, however subsequently mediated by interpretation, embedded within that time. Literary interpretation, unless it disregards history entirely (which it often does), is at least partly a

[1] Roger E. Stoddard, "Morphology and the Book from an American Perspective," *Printing History* 9.1 (1987), p. 4. The observation has become a commonplace of book history, but Stoddard's is the earliest version I have found.

The Idea of the Book and the Creation of Literature. Stephen Orgel, Oxford University Press.
© Stephen Orgel 2023. DOI: 10.1093/oso/9780192871534.003.0001

form of archeology. This is the book's historicity, the way it is situated in history. The history of the book has become a separate discipline. It had to become a separate discipline because much of the time literary history ignores it. I begin with an example of how it matters. George Herbert's *The Temple* was first published in 1633 in a slim duodecimo, a small volume of less than 200 pages, easily slipped into a pocket or purse—a true *vademecum*: you could always have it with you. It retained this format, despite increasingly elaborate typographic and pictorial embellishments, throughout its many seventeenth-century editions. The standard modern scholarly edition, however, the Oxford English Texts version of F. E. Hutchinson, is a massive volume of 680 pages weighing 3.3 pounds. Nowhere in the compendious commentary is it acknowledged that the work is misrepresented by the modern format, that the original book's portability, modesty, and discreetness were elements of its meaning and a factor in its reception.

The disregard of historicity extends to the editing of the modern edition. "Easter-wings" looks quite straightforward as a poem (Figure 1.1), though the imagery evoked by the title is more manifest as it appears in the edition of 1633 (Figure 1.2), where it is clearly two sets of wings—the seventeenth-century typography both clarifies and adds an element of playfulness to the verse.[2]

But if we look at it that way, it is not clear that we understand how to read it. If we turn the book so the text becomes legible, what we assumed was the second stanza has become the first stanza. It makes sense either way, but do we even know that it is a two-stanza poem? In the 1633 edition it looks like two separate poems, each titled *Easter-wings*. There is no reason why this should not be the case: there are two poems in the volume called *Jordan*, three called *Love*, five called *Affliction*, and elsewhere in the book when a poem runs over onto the next page, the title is not repeated as it is here. What is also evident here is that throughout the volume pilcrows (paragraph symbols) are used to indicate new poems, not new stanzas. In fact, *Easter-wings* makes sense in either order or as two separate poems. There is, however, a

---

[2] For a richly detailed analysis of the original typography, see Randall McLeod (as Random Cloud), "FIAT *f*LUX," in Randall McLeod, ed., *Crisis in Editing: Texts of the English Renaissance* (New York: AMS Press, 1994), pp. 61–172.

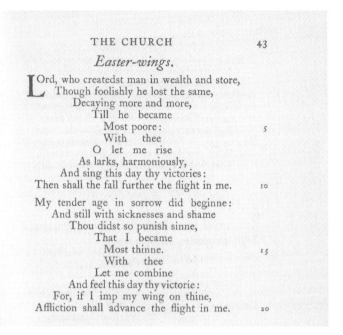

THE CHURCH 43

Easter-wings.

LOrd, who createdst man in wealth and store,
    Though foolishly he lost the same,
        Decaying more and more,
            Till he became
                Most poore: 5
                With thee
            O let me rise
        As larks, harmoniously,
    And sing this day thy victories:
Then shall the fall further the flight in me.   10

My tender age in sorrow did beginne:
    And still with sicknesses and shame
        Thou didst so punish sinne,
            That I became
                Most thinne.   15
                With thee
            Let me combine
        And feel this day thy victorie:
    For, if I imp my wing on thine,
Affliction shall advance the flight in me.   20

FIGURE 1.1   The modern text of "Easter-wings," from F. E. Hutchinson, *The Works of George Herbert* (Oxford: Clarendon Press, 1941).

manuscript of *The Temple* prepared by a scribe, but with corrections in Herbert's own hand; in it the work appears in progress, on facing pages, with many revisions, and is clearly two poems designed to face each other. The modern typography ignores the poem's history, and simply closes down all the other options.[3]

A modern edition will inevitably address modern readers; even in the 1633 editions (there were two in that year) the presentation of the poem is quite different from that of Herbert's manuscript. Every age recreates what it conceives as its classic poetry. But it is worth asking how we got from Herbert's poem to ours. Why, in the preparation of the standard modern scholarly edition, was it assumed that the format was

---

[3] For the various iterations of the work, including the two manuscript versions, the one cited and a scribal fair copy, see https://www.ccel.org/h/herbert/temple/Easterwings. html#W (accessed January 17, 2022).

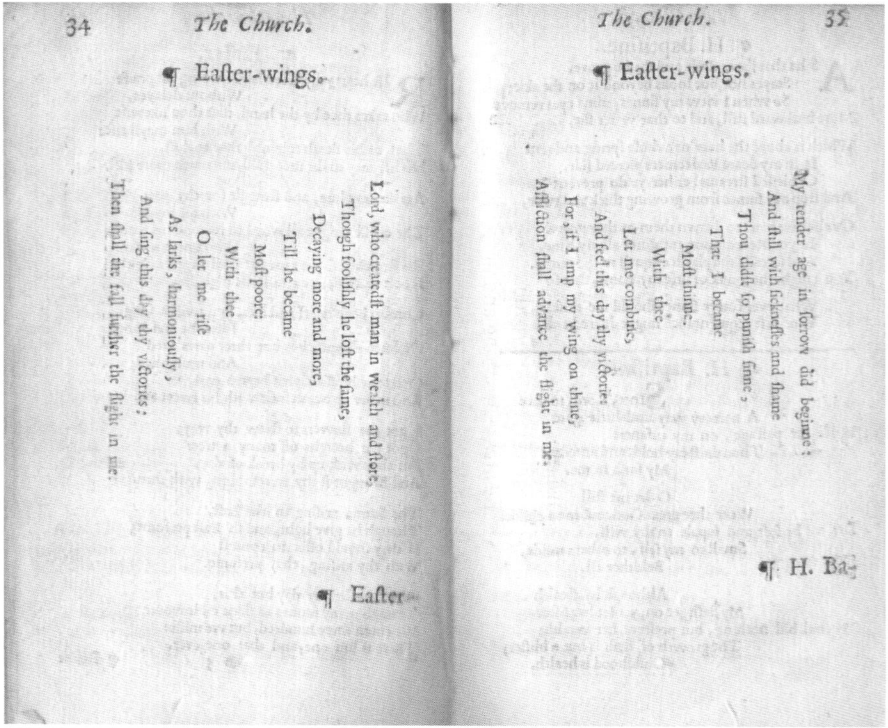

FIGURE 1.2   "Easter-wings" in the text of 1633, and all seventeenth-century printed editions.

irrelevant? Presumably the vertical typography was too playful for Hutchinson's academic text; but is the playful format not part of the meaning? Clearly it was in London in 1633, but by 1941 in Oxford had ceased to be. What kind of information, what range of meaning, then, do books preserve? The answer will change according to the time and place. In this particular case, the issue would have been what had to be censored out of the poem's presentation—censored is a strong term, but *Easter-wings* has surely been deliberately misrepresented: devotional poetry is not supposed to be playful; neither is scholarship. Hutchinson claimed he was basing his text on the manuscript (hence no vertical typography), but even this is not true: in both manuscripts (there are two, the one already cited and a scribal fair copy of the final text), as in all the early editions through the eighteenth century, *Easter-wings* is two poems, not one.

Still, books change from era to era, and any new edition necessarily involves a process of translation. Shakespeare in the original editions has for several centuries been, for most readers, basically unreadable, and not only because of the archaic spelling and unfamiliar typography, but because so much needs to be explained: we have, culturally, forgotten so much that in Shakespeare's time was common knowledge. The translation renders these ancient texts legible; but it also transforms them into something that speaks to us rather than to a world 400 years in the past. Even the earliest Shakespeare texts are not in any sense "original"—they are printed texts, not Shakespeare holographs, though several of them appear to derive from Shakespeare manuscripts—but they are as close as we can come to what the actors, transcribers, and editors were working with. It is only through attending to the early texts that we can have a sense of what has been lost, or, as in the case of *Easter-wings*, suppressed. At the same time, although books do certainly conserve the historicity of texts, that historicity itself keeps changing: it changes as we do, as what we attend to does, as what we mean by history does, and what we want it to account for and explain does, as what we acknowledge to constitute an explanation does, and most of all, as what we want out of Herbert or Shakespeare or literature itself does.

The idea of literature includes an idea of permanence—this is often credited to the print revolution, but that is surely incorrect. Horace saw his poetry as more lasting than bronze, *aere perennius*, 1500 years before Gutenberg; Shakespeare claimed his sonnets circulating in manuscript would preserve his love even to the edge of doom. But most writing, in whatever form, scribal, printed, even carved in stone, has been utterly ephemeral—only seven of Sophocles's 120 plays survive; only fragments of Sappho; a tiny percentage of Elizabethan drama remains. On the other hand, ephemera were precisely what kept printers in business: while the typesetting slowly proceeded on the monuments of early printing, the same presses were turning out innumerable broadsheets, pamphlets, decrees, proclamations, prayers, ballads, accounts of battles, festivals, funerals, lurid stories: these paid the bills. During times of crisis, polemical pamphlets filled the bookstalls in huge numbers and were swiftly replaced by the replies they generated. The pamphlets were characteristically unstable, full of changes of mind, often sent to the press incomplete, often attacked or refuted before they were even published. They were also almost instantly outdated; for the publisher, the creation of a continuing market for instantaneous refutation was the pamphlet's greatest virtue.

The book in such cases was less a product than a process, part of an ongoing dialectic. But the critical element in that process, from the point of view of history—and the reason the book trade has a history at all—was the very small group of purchasers who collected and preserved those ephemera, the bibliophiles who focussed not on the obviously valuable but on the seemingly worthless. A single collector, a single connoisseur of the worthless, can be the agent of history—for example George Thomason, who for twenty years collected every polemical scrap relating to the English Civil War and Commonwealth, and thereby created a value for those ephemera and an invaluable archive for the future, the Thomason Tracts, about 22,000 items, now in the British Library.

Publishers of course also from the beginning had a vision of permanence, an idea of cultural capital—it is not accidental that the first printed book was the Bible. The dissemination of ephemera paid for the creation of the Great Book. And yet great books often were not good business—the Bible soon became a best seller, but not soon enough to save Gutenberg from bankruptcy; most of the first edition of the Aldine Press's masterpiece the *Hypnerotomachia Poliphili* remained unsold; the Shakespeare first folio took nine years to sell out, and the second and third folios took thirty-one and twenty-two years respectively; *Moby Dick* and *The Scarlet Letter* sold very poorly, and only became essential classics of American literature in the next century. Literature, at least in its inception, has often been a losing proposition. Classic texts have never, moreover, been permanent, if by that we mean unchanging. Every new edition improves, amends, alters—a Koberger Bible is not the same as a Gutenberg Bible; the second Shakespeare folio corrects errors in the first folio, as the third and fourth folios amend the first and second; and every subsequent Shakespeare edition purports to improve on the previous ones. No text is ever final—even a text that is never reprinted will be read differently, in effect revised, by different readers.

What do we want out of reading? When books were scrolls, the format assumed that the norm of reading was consecutive; you started at the beginning and read through to the end. But the history of reading is a history of changing modes of attention.[4] The transition from scroll to codex (a codex is the modern form of book, with pages attached at one edge) is a transition from continuous to discontinuous reading—as Peter Stallybrass puts it, the history of the book is the history of the bookmark—and the Bible is a central example.[5] The material reality of the Torah, a huge double scroll, would seem to preclude a discontinuous reading. It is all but impossible to read the book any other way than consecutively. And yet the rabbis, over many centuries, produced a commentary that demanded the most discontinuous of readings, a code of ethics that depended on the constant comparison of widely separated passages. They assumed that the scripture was amenable to any amount of reordering and recontextualization, and the study of the sacred texts included as an essential element the development of a prodigious memory. The Christian Bible, through its narrative structure, seems no less to demand consecutive reading: it runs from Genesis to Apocalypse, beginning at the beginning and ending with, or even a little after, the end.

But the material history of the sacred texts positively inhibits such a reading. John Locke said that "Scripture crumbles into verses, which quickly turn into independent aphorisms."[6] The difference between fifteenth- and seventeenth-century Bibles, in Figure 1.3, is instructive.

---

[4] For an account of the material history of literacy in classical culture, see Stephanie Ann Frampton, *Empire of Letters* (New York: Oxford University Press, 2019).

[5] Peter Stallybrass, "Books and Scrolls," in Jennifer Anderson and Elizabeth Sauer, eds., *Books and Readers in Early Modern England* (Philadelphia: University of Pennsylvania Press, 2002), p. 42.

[6] John Locke, *A Paraphrase and Notes on the Epistles of St. Paul* (1733), p. vii. Cited in Stallybrass, p. 50.

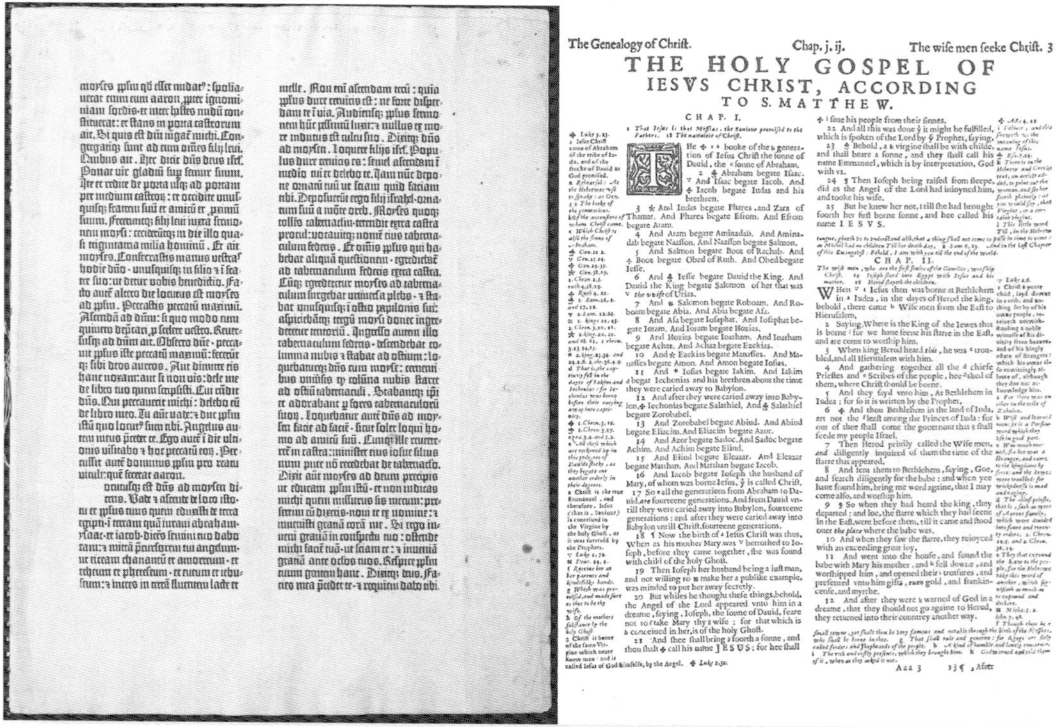

The Genealogy of Christ. Chap. j. ij. The wise men seeke Christ. 3

THE HOLY GOSPEL OF IESVS CHRIST, ACCORDING TO S. MATTHEW.

CHAP. I.

He booke of the generation of Iesus Christ the sonne of Dauid, the sonne of Abraham.
2 Abraham begate Isaac. And Isaac begate Iacob. And Iacob begate Iudas and his brethren.
3 And Iudas begate Phares, and Zara of Thamar. And Phares begate Esrom. And Esrom begate Aram.
4 And Aram begate Aminadab. And Aminadab begate Naasson. And Naasson begate Salmon.
5 And Salmon begate Booz of Rachab. And Booz begate Obed of Ruth. And Obed begate Iesse.
6 And Iesse begate Dauid the King. And Dauid the King begate Salomon of her that was the wife of Urias.
7 And Salomon begate Roboam. And Roboam begate Abia. And Abia begate Asa.
8 And Asa begate Iosaphat. And Iosaphat begate Ioram. And Ioram begate Hozias.
9 And Hozias begate Ioatham. And Ioatham begate Achaz. And Achaz begate Ezekias.
10 And Ezekias begate Manasses. And Manasses begate Amon. And Amon begate Iosias.
11 And Iosias begate Iakim. And Iakim begat Iechonias and his brethren about the time they were caried away to Babylon.
12 And after they were caried away into Babylon, Iechonias begate Salathiel. And Salathiel begate Zorobabel.
13 And Zorobabel begate Abiud. And Abiud begate Eliacim. And Eliacim begate Azor.
14 And Azor begate Sadoc. And Sadoc begate Achim. And Achim begate Eliud.
15 And Eliud begate Eleazar. And Eleazar begate Matthan. And Matthan begate Iacob.
16 And Iacob begate Ioseph the husband of Mary, of whom was borne Iesus, ÿ is called Christ.
17 So all the generations from Abraham to Dauid are fourteene generations. And from Dauid vntill they were caried away into Babylon, fourteene generations: and after they were caried away into Babylon vntill Christ, fourteene generations.
18 ¶ Now the birth of Iesus Christ was thus, When as his mother Mary was betrothed to Ioseph, before they came together, she was found with child of the holy Ghost.
19 Then Ioseph her husband being a iust man, and not willing to make her a publike example, was minded to put her away secretly.
20 But whiles he thought these things, behold, the Angel of the Lord appeared vnto him in a dreame, saying, Ioseph, the sonne of Dauid, feare not to take Mary thy wife: for that which is conceiued in her, is of the holy Ghost.
21 And shee shall bring foorth a sonne, and thou shalt call his name IESUS: for hee shall saue his people from their sinnes.
22 And all this was done ÿ it might be fulfilled, which is spoken of the Lord by ÿ Prophet, saying,
23 Behold, a virgine shall be with childe, and shall beare a sonne, and they shall call his name Emmanuel, which is by interpretation, God with vs.
24 ¶ Then Ioseph being raised from sleepe, did as the Angel of the Lord had inioyned him, and tooke his wife.
25 But he knew her not, till she had brought foorth her first borne sonne, and hee called his name IESUS.

CHAP. II.

WHen Iesus then was borne at Bethlehem in Iudea, in the dayes of Herod the King, behold, there came Wise men from the East to Hierusalem,
2 Saying, Where is the King of the Iewes that is borne? for we haue seene his starre in the East, and are come to worship him.
3 When king Herod heard this, he was troubled, and all Hierusalem with him.
4 And gathering together all the chiefe Priestes and Scribes of the people, hee asked of them, where Christ should be borne.
5 And they sayd vnto him, At Bethlehem in Iudea: for so it is written by the Prophet,
6 And thou Bethlehem in the land of Iuda, art not the least among the Princes of Iuda: for out of thee shall come the gouernour that shall feede my people Israel.
7 Then Herod priuily called the Wise men, and diligently inquired of them the time of the starre that appeared,
8 And sent them to Bethlehem, saying, Goe, and search diligently for the babe: and when yee haue found him, bring me word againe, that I may come also, and worship him.
9 So when they had heard the king, they departed: and loe, the starre which they had seene in the East, went before them, till it came and stood ouer the place where the babe was.
10 And when they saw the starre, they reioyced with an exceeding great ioy,
11 And went into the house, and found the babe with Mary his mother, and fell downe, and worshipped him, and opened their treasures, and presented vnto him gifts, euen gold, and frankincense, and myrrhe.
12 And after they were warned of God in a dreame, that they should not go againe to Herod, they returned into their countrey another way.

Aaa 3

FIGURE 1.3 A page of the Gutenberg Bible and a page of the Geneva Bible. The Gutenberg page is reproduced courtesy of the Department of Special Collections, Stanford University Libraries.

Gutenberg's page, on the left, has no verse markers; some copies have running heads to indicate what book of the Bible you are reading, but that information was put in by hand.[7] A century and a half later, the Geneva Bible page, on the right, looks like an annotated school text. The annotations are designed as guides to reading, but it is increasingly assumed that the reader will be a lay person who requires guidance; that the text—even the text of the Bible—is not enough. Increasingly, also, the Bible looks less and less like a whole continuous work, more and more like a compilation of exerptable fragments; and these, of course, could be used to bolster widely varying positions in theological debates.

The history of reading has some significant consequences for modern notions of the norms of reading. Is continuity really the norm? Consecutive reading is certainly an essential mode of attention if we are undertaking to follow a narrative or a logical argument. But reading has always had many other ends. Suppose we are reading for wisdom. Then the extraction of dicta might very well be our primary purpose, and separable nuggets of philosophy would take precedence over narrative or logical coherence. Consider the history of the "ut pictura poesis" crux in Horace's *Ars Poetica*:

> Ut pictura poesis; erit quae, si propius stes,
> te capiat magis, et quaedam, si longius abstes...[8]

[As with painting, so with poetry: there are those which will impress you more if you stand near them, and others, if you stand farther away...]

"Ut pictura poesis" means literally that poetry is like painting. But in what way? Sir Philip Sidney, following a tradition of many centuries, took it to mean that poetry and painting had essential qualities in common, and that poetry was, as Simonides put it in the fifth century BC, "a speaking picture"—this assumption, with classical authority behind it, informs a great deal of Renaissance aesthetic theory. If we read Horace's dictum in context, however, we will find that it means nothing of the sort. All it says is that just as some paintings are designed to be viewed from afar, and therefore presumably need not be scrupulous about detail, and some are designed to be closely scrutinized, and

---

[7] Reproduced courtesy of the Department of Special Collections, Stanford University Libraries, catalog number KA1454 .B5 F CB.

[8] Line 361.

must be composed with meticulous attention to detail, so it is with poetry. The only similarity claimed for the two arts has to do with the necessity for both poet and artist to keep the purpose of the work of art in mind.

Does this mean that Sidney was ignorant of the context—had he not read the rest of the passage? No doubt he had; but in his defence, we might observe that the phrase as a dictum actually makes better sense than the phrase in context: modern attempts to derive a useful critical principle from the phrase require a great deal of interpretive lattitude.[9] Horace seems to argue that some poems need not be as carefully written as other poems. Can this be right? What poems? Long poems versus short poems, epics on the one hand and lyrics on the other? Did Virgil not need to worry about details? (It is difficult to come up with untendentious examples—perhaps the Roman equivalents of rap lyrics and sonnets, whatever these might be; poetry that is immediately pleasing, versus poetry that repays close attention.) In any case, the only way to claim that Sidney's reading of this passage is incorrect is to argue that Horace did not mean it to be read that way. This is doubtless true, but surely no critic would want to limit the possibilities of reading to those defined by the author's intentions—an especially problematic move when the example is the Bible.

There are, of course, many books that are not designed to be read consecutively; books are not only literature: they are dictionaries, en-cyclopedias, almanacs, handbooks of all sorts. Most modern books of information depend for their usefulness not on their narrative coher-ence or the persuasiveness of their argument, but on the capaciousness of their indexes. We go to them to find what we are looking for, and the coherence is that of the reader's narrative, not the author's.

Constructing readers

If readers construct books, books also construct readers. Formats keep changing. We know what a book is because the title page tells us, but initially, books did not have title pages. Why did these develop, and

---

[9] E.g., Wesley Trimpi, "The Meaning of Horace's *Ut Pictura Poesis*," *Journal of the Warburg and Courtauld Institutes*, 36 (1973), pp. 1–34.

what information do they convey? Whitney Trettien writes that the history of the title page "neatly illustrates the impact of print."

> Simply put, before the advent of movable type, books did not have title pages; within fifty years of print's emergence, they did. The story of how books developed from medieval manuscripts with no title page, to incunables with a simple label-title, to printed books coming with a title page as standard, seems to index every technological shift in the history of printing.... The title page is the site of a book's self-presentation to its potential audience, where it informs readers about a text by in-forming—moulding into structured information—the facts of its production. This process of bibliographic encoding is full of friction. On the one hand, the book trade needs readers (and authorities) to trust its products, and the architecture of the title page serves a critical role in generating confidence in a text. On the other, precisely because it functions in this way, the title page is susceptible to manipulation by printers and publishers eager to advertise a book's contents, skirt regulations, and bypass censors.[10]

The development of the title page has everything to do with the creation of marketability, that is, with the book trade.

Figure 1.4 shows the opening page of the first printed edition of Chaucer's *Canterbury Tales*, published by William Caxton around 1477—this is the first page you see in the book; there is no title page, and indeed, no title. Caxton's second edition of the work, in Figure 1.5, published in 1483, still has no title page, but now includes a preface (the two pages in the image are recto and verso of the same leaf). Chaucer's name appears nine lines down, identified as a great philosopher and refiner of the English language. The information that the book you are reading is *The Canterbury Tales* comes two-thirds of the way down the page. On the next page you learn that this is a better text than that of Caxton's earlier edition—this is, of course, the whole point of the preface, but it takes a while to get there. The largest name on the page is Caxton's at the bottom—the poetry is Chaucer's, but the book is Caxton's. And then on the facing page (Figure 1.6) the poem begins. As in the earlier edition, it has no title, but now it has a section-heading, *Prologue*.

---

[10] Whitney Trettien, "Title Pages," in Dennis Duncan and Adam Smyth, eds., *Book Parts* (Oxford: Oxford University Press, 2019), pp. 41–2.

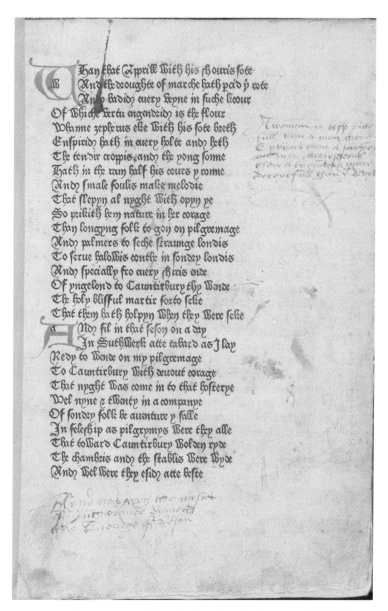

FIGURE 1.4   Opening page of Caxton's *Canterbury Tales*, 1476–7. British Library 167.c.26.

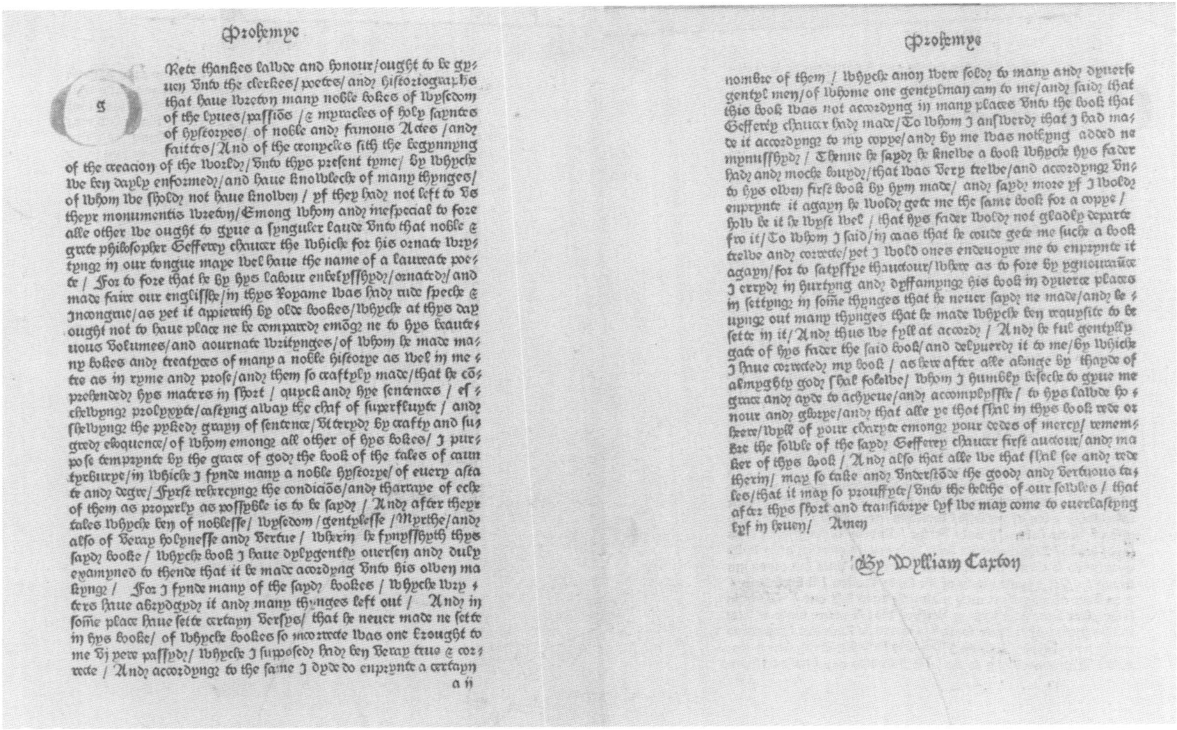

Prohemye

G

Rete thankes lawde and honour/ought to be gy-
uen vnto the clerkes/poetes/and historiographs
that haue wreton many noble bokes of wysedom
of the lyues/passiōs/& myracles of holy sayntes
of hystoryes/ of noble and famous Actes /and
faittes/And of the cronycles sith the begynnyng
of the creacion of the world/vnto thys present tyme/ by whyche
we ben dayly enformed/and haue knowleche of many thynges/
of whom we shold not haue knowen / yf they had not left to vs
theyr monumentis wreton/Emong whom and inespecial to fore
alle other we ought to gyue a synguler laude vnto that noble &
grete philosopher Gefferey chaucer the whiche for his ornate wry-
tyng in our tongue maye wel haue the name of a laureate poe-
te / For to fore that he by hys labour enbelysshyd/ornated/and
made faire our englisshe/in thys Royame was had rude speche &
Incongrue/as yet it appiereth by olde bookes/whyche at thys day
ought not to haue place ne be compared emōg ne to hys beaute-
uous volumes/and aournate writynges/of whom he made many bokes and treatyces of many a noble historye as wel in me-
tre as in ryme and prose/and them so craftyly made/that he cō-
prehended hys maters in short / quyck and hye sentences / es-
chewyng prolyxyte/castyng away the chaf of superfluyte / and
shewyng the pyked grayn of sentence/vttered by crafty and sugred eloquence/of whom emonge all other of hys bokes/ I purpose temprynte by the grace of god the book of the tales of caun-
tyrburye/in whiche I fynde many a noble hystorye/of euery asta-
te and degre/Fyrst rehercyng the condiciōs/and tharraye of eche
of them as properly as possyble is to be sayd / And after theyr
tales whyche ben of noblesse/ wysedom /gentylesse /Myrthe/and
also of veray holynesse and vertue / wherin he fynysshyth thys
sayd booke / whyche book I haue dylygently ouersen and duly
examyned to thende that it be made acordyng vnto his owen ma-
kyng / For I fynde many of the sayd bookes / whyche wry-
ters haue abrydgyd it and many thynges left out / And in
some place haue sette certayn versys/ that he neuer made ne sette
in hys booke/ of whyche bookes so incorrecte was one brought to
me vj yere passyd/ whyche I supposed had ben veray true & cor-
recte / And accordyng to the same I dyde do enprynte a certayn
a ij

Prohemye

nombre of them / whyche anon were sold to many and dyuerse
gentyl men/of whome one gentylman cam to me/and said that
this book was not accordyng in many places vnto the book that
Gefferey chaucer had made/To whom I answerd that I had made it accordyng to my copye/and by me was nothyng added ne
mynusshyd / Thenne he sayd he knewe a book whyche hys fader
had and moche louyd/that was very trewe/and accordyng vnto hys owen first book by hym made/ and sayd more yf I wold
enprynte it agayn he wold gete me the same book for a copye /
how be it he wyst wel / that hys fader wold not gladly departe
fro it/To whom I said/in caas that he coude gete me suche a book
trewe and correcte/yet I wold ones endeuoyre me to enprynte it
agayn/for to satysfye thauctour/where as to fore by ygnouraūce
I erryd in hurtyng and dyffamyng his book in dyuerce places
in settyng in somme thynges that he neuer sayd ne made/and le-
uyng out many thynges that he made whyche ben requysite to be
sette in it/And thus we fyll at accord / And he ful gentylly
gate of hys fader the said book/and delyuerd it to me/by whiche
I haue corrected my book / as here after alle alonge by thayde of
almyghty god shal folowe/ whom I humbly beseche to gyue me
grace and ayde to achyeue/and accomplysshe/ to hys lawde honour and glorye/and that alle ye that shal in thys book rede or
here/wyll of your charyte emonge your dedes of mercy/ remem-
bre the sowle of the sayd Gefferey chaucer first auctour/and ma-
ker of thys book / And also that alle we that shal see and rede
therin/ may so take and vnderstōde the good and vertuous ta-
les/that it may so prouffyte/vnto the helthe of our sowles / that
after thys short and transitorye lyf we may come to euerlastyng
lyf in heuen/ Amen

By Wylliam Caxton

FIGURE 1.5 Opening pages of Caxton's *Canterbury Tales*, 1483. British Library G.11586.

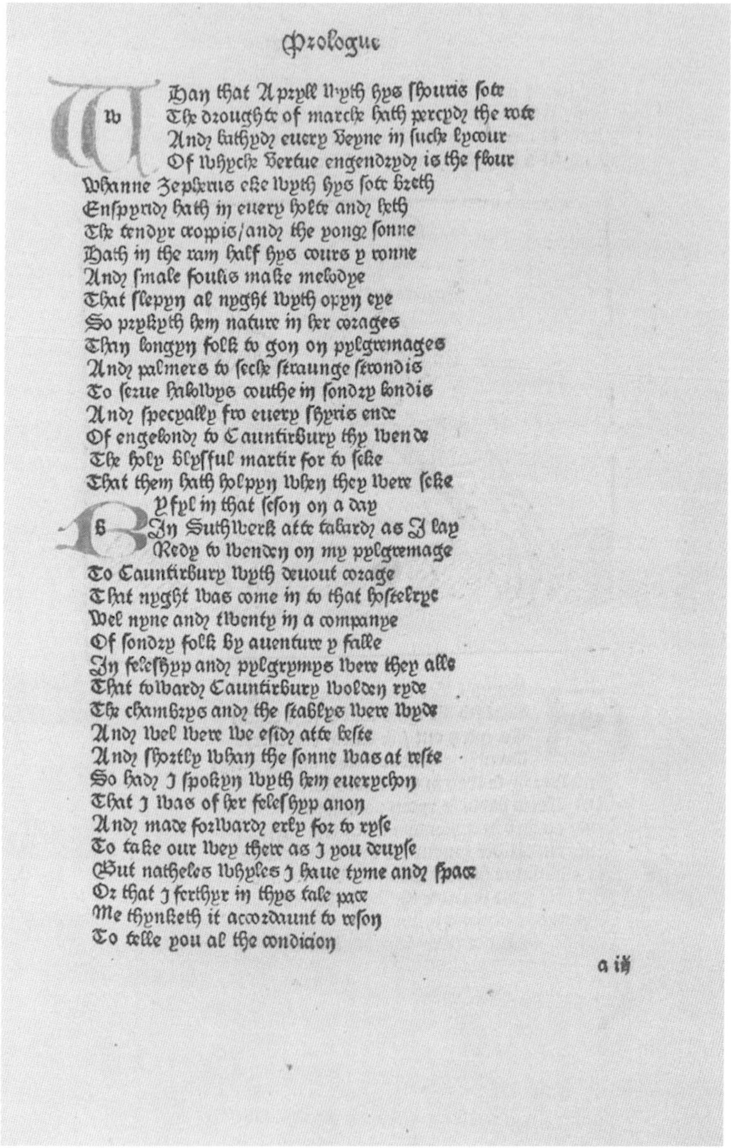

Prologue

Whan that Aprill with hys shouris soote
The droughte of marche hath percyd the rote
And bathyd euery veyne in suche lycour
Of whyche vertue engendryd is the flour
Whanne zephyrus eke with hys soote breth
Enspyryd hath in euery holte and heth
The tendyr croppis / and the yong sonne
Hath in the ram half hys cours y ronne
And smale foulis make melodye
That sleppyn al nyght with oppyn eye
So prykyth hem nature in her corages
Than longyn folk to gon on pylgremages
And palmers to seche straunge strondis
To serue halolwys couthe in sondry londis
And specyally fro euery shyris ende
Of engelond to Cauntirbury thy wende
The holy blyssful martir for to seke
That them hath holppyn when they were seke

Byfyl in that seson on a day
In Suthwerk atte tabard as I lay
Redy to wenden on my pylgremage
To Cauntirbury wyth deuout corage
That nyght was come in to that hostelrye
Wel nyne and twenty in a companye
Of sondry folk by auenture y falle
In felishyp and pylgrymps were they alle
That toward Cauntirbury wolden ryde
The chambrys and the stablys were wyde
And wel were we esyd atte beste
And shortly whan the sonne was at reste
So had I spokyn wyth hem euerychon
That I was of her felishyp anon
And made forlwardz erly for to ryse
To take our wey there as I you deuyse
But natheles whyles I haue tyme and space
Or that I ferther in thys tale pace
Me thynketh it accordaunt to reson
To telle you al the condicion

a iij

FIGURE 1.6 Opening of the *Prologue* in Caxton's *Canterbury Tales*, 1483. British Library G.11586.

By 1498 Wynkyn de Worde's edition of *The Canterbury Tales*, in Figure 1.7, includes what we would recognize as a title page—now, anyone can tell what the book is without reading it. It is a very modest beginning, but it represents a significant transformation in how the relation of books to readers is conceived. Unbound sheets in the bookseller's shop were labeled; but to make the label part of the book, to make it not only what sold the book but what then encapsulated the book's identity, was really a huge change (even now antiquarian books missing their title pages have lost a large percentage of their value). And then develop tables of contents, chapter headings, glosses, notes, indexes—what, following Gérard Genette, we call paratexts (the French is *seuils*, thresholds): we still have some sense that they are not really part of the book.[11]

Paratexts are thresholds in the sense that they are ways into the book, guides to the material; but over the years what sort of information has the potential buyer required to turn her or him into a reader?—women become increasingly visible as readers and book collectors from the sixteenth century on. To begin with, not necessarily the author's name, which for a modern reader would be a primary attraction. Despite the fact that by the early seventeenth century Shakespeare's name was sufficiently famous to sell a number of books with which in fact he had no connection, most of the early quartos of his own plays were issued anonymously. Shakespeare's name first appears on the title page of a play in the 1598 quarto of *Love's Labour's Lost*—he had been writing plays for seven or eight years at that point, and both *Venus and Adonis* and *The Rape of Lucrece,* which include his name (though not on their title pages), were selling well. Would his name on the 1597 quartos of *Romeo and Juliet, Richard II*, and *Richard III* not have attracted purchasers? But what the title pages advertise are the acting companies—*Romeo and Juliet* adds the information that the play is, like *Love's Labour's Lost,* excellent conceited (that is, very witty and poetical) and was played with great applause. But there is nothing about the

---

[11] Gérard Genette, *Seuils* (Paris: Editions du Seuil, 1987). English translation by Jane E. Lewin, *Paratexts: Thresholds of Interpretation* (Cambridge: Cambridge University Press, 1997). Dennis Duncan and Adam Smyth, eds., *Book Parts* includes valuable discussions of a wide variety of paratexts, including dust jackets, frontispieces, tables of contents, etc.

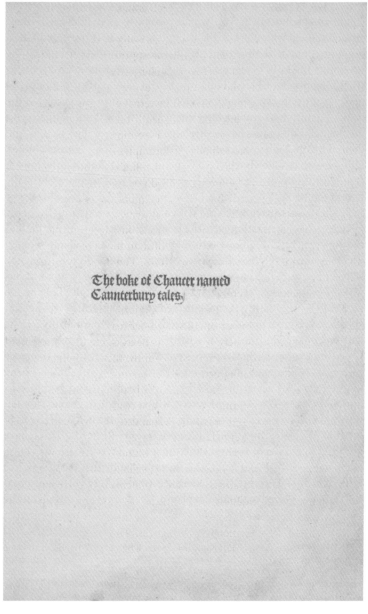

FIGURE 1.7 Title page of Wynkyn de Worde's *Canterbury Tales*, 1498. British Library.

witty, successful author: plays were not yet literature; moreover, literature could still be anonymous.[12]

For Shakespeare in print, 1598 was the watershed: in that year in addition to *Love's Labour's Lost,* his name appears on new editions of the two Richard plays, and thereafter regularly (though not invariably) on the title pages of his plays and poetry, as well as on those of some other people's. But in general, the author remains an elusive character in book publishing well into the seventeenth century. Sometimes the concealment is deliberate, of course, for example in satires and polemics. But consider some less obvious examples.

Figure 1.8 shows the title pages of the first editions of Sidney's *Astrophil and Stella* and Donne's collected poems. The initials tell you that the author is somebody important, too important to want his name revealed (that is, not simply a professional writer); but if you belong to the right social or intellectual circle, you will know whom the initials stand for. The mystery, then, flattered those in the know, and assured other readers that the book was prestigious. The title page of the first two editions of Robert Burton's *Anatomy of Melancholy* (1621, 1624) offered purchasers a different sort of nominal tease. Here the name of the author is given only as "Democritus Junior," hence an epigone of the pre-Socratic philosopher-scientist Democritus, who postulated the existence of atoms, and thereby got to the heart of matter.

The engraved title page commissioned for the third edition (1628), in Figure 1.9, even includes a portrait of Burton, but nothing identifying him. Burton's name appears nowhere in the book. Surely not everyone knew who "Democritus Junior" was, but that really was not important: what attracted a purchaser was a large, handsome, obviously learned work, eventually with a very elaborate engraved title page. The obvious pseudonym served as both a claim of profundity and an intriguing puzzle. This vast treatise is not without its element of playfulness.

But let us consider paratexts: Burton's *Anatomy* is encyclopedic, but consulting it for information is a daunting task. Burton supplied the book with an elaborate synoptic outline, but this gives little help, not least because it includes no page references. This is a case where an encyclopedic index would seem called for. The 1621 first edition has

---

[12] Lukas Erne cites some important exceptions and interestingly complicates the claim in *Shakespeare as Literary Dramatist* (Cambridge: Cambridge University Press, 2003).

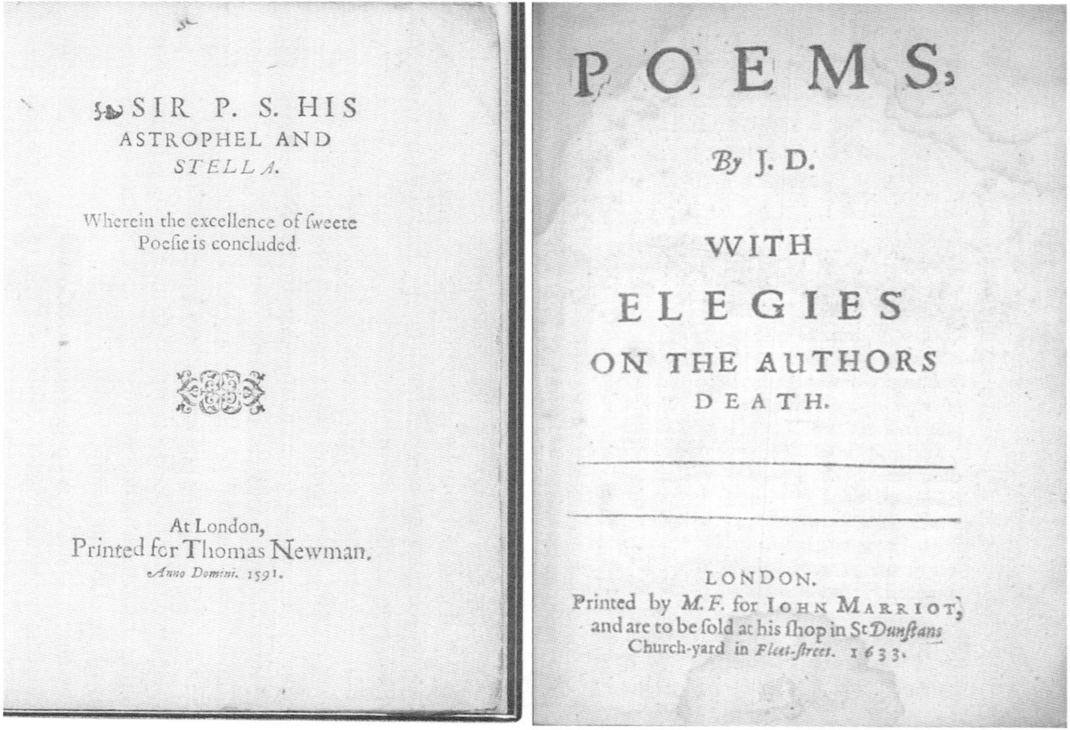

FIGURE 1.8 Title pages of Sidney and Donne first editions.

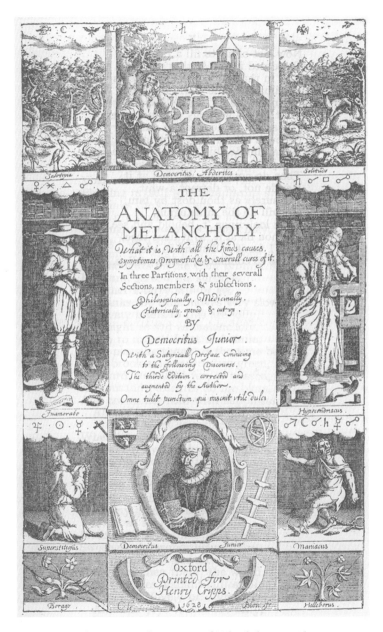

FIGURE 1.9 Robert Burton, *The Anatomy of Melancholy*, 1628, title page.

none. The 1624 second edition was "corrected and augmented by the author"—the improvements involved a promotion from quarto to folio and a good deal of new material, but still no mention of the author's name. An index is now provided, but it is singularly erratic and vague: characteristic entries under A include "All are melancholy" and "All beautiful parts attractive in love"; under B, "Best site of an house" and "Black eyes best." Though bugloss wine is said in the text to be effective in curing leprosy, leprosy is not indexed, and bugloss appears only in an entry for "borage and buglosse." Examples could be endlessly multiplied: what are readers expected to use this index for? Nor, as the work went through its many revisions, was the index revised: there are some additional entries, but the seventh edition of 1660 has substantially the same index as the second edition, with only the page numbers adjusted.

In contrast, continental scientific texts often have splendid indexes, which were clearly felt to constitute a significant part of the book's value; these were generally placed before the text, not at the end. But the English seem to have had more resistance to serious indices than continental publishers: for example, both Helkiah Crooke's compendious medical encyclopedia the *Mikrokosmographia* (1615, 1618, 1631, 1634, 1651) and Plutarch's great biographical compendium the *Lives* in Sir Thomas North's translation (1579, 1595, 1603, 1612, 1631, 1657), were issued without indexes. It is probably the half-hearted quality of Burton's index that is most striking, as if the publisher is asking, how do you make an index?[13]

Moreover, as the Burton example reveals, even when books acknowledge the value of an index, there is no agreement about the proper form for the references: how to list things, what needs to be cross-referenced, what, indeed, constitutes an adequate reference; no agreement, that is, about how readers are expected to construe what they are looking for. Here are some samples from the index to the 1550 edition of Edward Halle's chronicle *The Union of the Two Noble and Illustre Families of Lancastre and Yorke,* which covers English history from Henry IV to the Tudors (the first edition, published in 1548, had no index). "Abell, ffetherstone and Powell, executed in Smithfield for treason" appears under both Abell and ffetherstone, but not under Powell. "Abbot of

---

[13] For a compendious and witty overview, see Dennis Duncan, *Index, A History of the* (London: Allen Lane, 2021).

Jerney hanged at Tiburn" appears under Abbot but not under Jerney. "Acte made in Spain called Premetica" is listed under Acte but not under Premetica. The index is, however, consistent about the listing of proper names: Anne Bulleyn is under Anne, not Bulleyn; Stephen Gardiner is under Stephen. This is standard sixteenth-century practice; so Juliet asks "Wherefore art thou Romeo?," not "Wherefore art thou Montague?": if she were looking for him in a sixteenth-century index, she would look under R.

Even when the index was recognized as essential to the book, its utility was another matter. Thomas Wilson's *Arte of Rhetorick* in its 1567 first edition includes an index keyed to the book's folio numbers, not to page numbers (each folio consists of two pages, recto or front and verso or back); a reference to the recto of folio 57 would be numbered 57,1, and a reference to the verso would be 57,2. This is an accurate and useful index. But the identical index is reprinted in the 1584 edition, and that book is foliated with *page* numbers, not folio numbers, rendering the index largely useless. Why then is the old index included? Presumably simply because the format seems to require it: handbooks need indexes, or at least, need to look as if they have indexes. That is why we find so many books with marginal subject headings written in by their owners. Readers require guides; and this I imagine was how the strange Burton *Anatomy* index was compiled, out of some reader's marginal subject headings.

Illustration

One obvious way of making books more attractive to a purchaser, and more valuable to an owner, was to decorate and illustrate them: the consumer is the end point of the book trade. When books were manuscripts, they were expensive to produce. They were not only texts, they were valuable commodities, and even utilitarian manuscripts were decorated. Figure 1.10 is the first page of a school text, a thirteenth-century Ovid.[14]

---

[14] Reproduced courtesy of the Department of Special Collections, Stanford University Libraries, catalog number MSS CODEX M0414 CB.

FIGURE 1.10   Opening page of a thirteenth-century Ovid manuscript. Courtesy of the Department of Special Collections, Stanford University Libraries.

There is no title; it starts at the top with a bit of commentary. This was a working copy; it has students' marginal and interlinear notes. It is not a grand book; the scriptorium used vellum of odd sizes and with some damage, but even this schoolbook has some lovely rubrication. Connoisseurs made their manuscripts significantly more valuable by having them elaborately embellished. The embellishment was generally commissioned by the purchaser; the finished book was a complex collaboration of publisher, scribe, purchaser, and artist. The first owner of such a book would have been actively involved in its production.

Illustrations can be an essential element in many kinds of books—bestiaries, herbals and such—but in medieval examples they are often more imaginative than informative: this has everything to do with what we want books to tell us, what we want out of reading; most of all, what kinds of possessions we consider them. The imagery in books often has a life of its own—manuscripts regularly include little vignettes, often jokey and sometimes obscene, hiding in the decorative foliage, even in the margins of psalters and saints' lives. Recreation, fun, everyday life takes place in the margins.

Medieval bestiaries regularly involve a combination of taxonomy and fantasy, but very little observation: Figure 1.11 shows a turtle from a fourteenth-century manuscript, by an artist who had probably read a description, but had apparently never seen one.

Herbals present a different sort of case: for hundreds of years herbals simply copied the images from earlier herbals—one would think this would be self-defeating, since the whole point of an herbal is to teach readers to recognize plants. But these herbals are not practical hand-books, they are celebrations of the infinite variety of the natural world, and their images are not realistic, they are imaginative responses to descriptions. Two herbals published in Mainz in 1484 are the first printed ones to be naturalistic, based on observation. Figure 1.12 shows the image of a mandrake from *Hortus Sanitatis*, 1491, an old-style herbal, and the mandrake in John Gerard's *Herbal or generall historie of Plantes*, 1633. These two examples encode quite different types of information.

Certain kinds of books would seem to require images based on observation: books that tell you how to do things, like build fortifications or make topographic surveys. And starting in the mid-sixteenth

FIGURE 1.11   Jacob van Maerlant, *Der Naturen Bloeme*, Utrecht, *c.*1340–50. Tortuca (turtle); miniature from folio 110v. KB KA 16; Koninklijke Bibliotheek, Den Haag.

century such books do have illustrations that look very realistic; but it is doubtful that they are, in any practical sense; builders and surveyors learn not by reading books, but by being trained by other builders and surveyors. This soon becomes a source of wit—Figure 1.13 is an illustration from a 1696 *Art of Swimming,* showing how to cut your toenails while in the water: this is obviously not a practical handbook.

The book also shows how to swim without moving your arms, though it is not explained why you would need to do that. The pictures are embellishments for an entertaining book. There are some exceptions, such as architectural treatises; and travel books are increasingly based on observation—in Figure 1.14 Venice in the Nuremberg Chronicle is full of recognizable buildings—but it is often difficult to tell how much images like this are based on observation and how much on the traditions of illustration (rather in the way the first photographic illustrations were doctored to look like paintings).

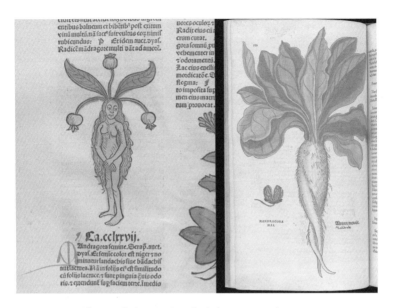

FIGURE 1.12   The mandrake root from herbals in 1491 and 1633.

FIGURE 1.13   Melchisédech Thévenot, *L'Art de Nager* (1696), figure xviii.

Figure 1.15 is a watercolor of a native American dance by the artist John White, who accompanied Sir Walter Ralegh's first expedition to North Carolina.

White obviously sees the natives as savages. Note the three women at the center; there is nothing elegant or romanticized about them.

FIGURE 1.14 *Liber Cronicarum* (The Nuremberg Chronicle), 1493, view of Venice.

FIGURE 1.15 John White, American natives dancing. British Museum.

FIGURE 1.16 Theodore de Bry, American natives dancing, from Thomas Hariot, *A Briefe and True Report of the New Found Land of Virginia* (1590), figure xviii. Folger Shakespeare Library.

Figure 1.16 is the engraving made from the watercolor by Theodore de Bry, an illustration for Thomas Hariot's published account of the expedition, *A Briefe and True Report of the New Found Land of Virginia* (1590). The women are now classically beautiful, their pose reminiscent of the three Graces.

The embellishment of printed books began as soon as printing began. To begin with, there was a great deal that the press did not do, and that readers needed to add by hand—titles, running heads, page numbers, chapter divisions. The additions could be elegant, but they were also necessary to make the book usable. Other kinds of embellishment had nothing to do with utility. Books were expensive, and connoisseurs often treated printed works like illuminated manuscripts—the decorative additions both testified to the book's value and added to it.

Figure 1.17 is a page of a 1483 Venetian Aristotle—this is a printed book that has been decorated by hand. What was revolutionary about printing was its ability to produce multiple copies, hundreds or even

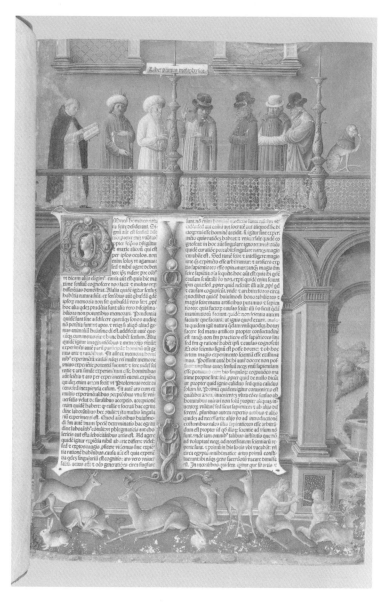

FIGURE 1.17   Aristotle, *Opera*, Venice, 1483, opening of vol. 2 (The Morgan Library & Museum, New York. PML 21194–95. Purchased by J.P. Morgan, Jr.)

thousands, of a single book. But after this book left the press, it was turned into a unique object at great effort and expense. Why would one do this to a copy of Aristotle? The embellishment says that Aristotle is the prince of philosophers, that his works are a treasure deserving an appropriately rich setting. What is omitted, of course, is any sense that the book is intended to be read. If the aristocratic owner wanted a splendid Aristotle because he revered philosophy and was a student of Aristotle, this was not the Aristotle he studied. This is a book to admire, not read. The history of books as objects has yet to be written.[15]

Early printers characteristically left space at the beginning of sections for the initial letters to be put in by hand, indicating the letter with a small roman capital. Figure 1.18 is a 1504 Horace Epistles in which the handwork on the initial letter T of Troiani has not been done.[16] There is a clear sense of something missing, a hole in the printed page; but this is somebody's working copy, and all the handwork is in the margins. This owner has made the book far more uniquely his own than the opulent connoisseur who so lavishly embellished his Aristotle.

Books are most strikingly imbricated in history when we have the evidence of contemporary readers at work. In Figure 1.19, a sixteenth-century reader interacts with his or her copy of the 1587 edition of Holinshed's *Chronicles*. The book has been splendidly decorated by an early owner with the heraldic shields of the warriors and statesmen who appear in the narrative, beautifully painted and gilded. The shields were so precious an addition that a subsequent owner sliced a number of them out, presumably to be pasted in an album—the marginalia took on a value of their own, independent of the book. And however offensive we find the excisions, an outrage committed on the body of the book, they are, like the shields themselves, part of both the book's history and its historicity, testifying to the changing notion of what kind of repository the book was, and what in it was valuable. The remaining shields were trimmed in a subsequent rebinding—by that time they had lost their value entirely, even as

---

[15] But see, for a start, David McKitterick, *The Invention of Rare Books* (Cambridge: Cambridge University Press, 2018), chapter 2: "Books as Objects."

[16] Reproduced courtesy of the Department of Special Collections, Stanford University Libraries, catalog number KA1504 .H67 CB.

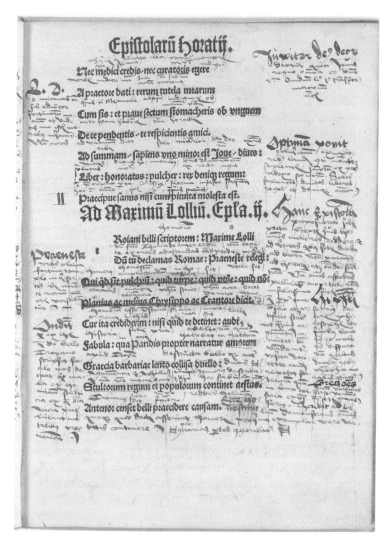

FIGURE 1.18 Page from Horace, *Epistles*, 1504. Courtesy of the Department of Special Collections, Stanford University Libraries.

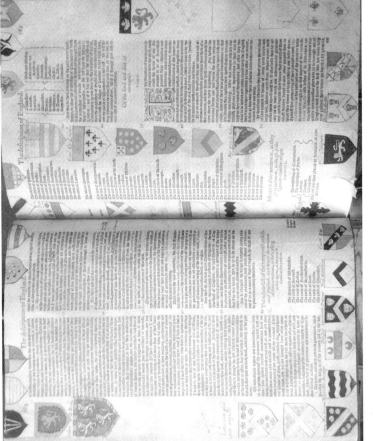

FIGURE 1.19 Raphael Holinshed, *Chronicles*, 1586, heraldic shields added by hand.

an adornment to the volume. For the series of owners of this book, what was relevant to the reading of Holinshed went through significant changes, and the work performed by the margins changed accordingly.[17]

Moreover, the same text may mean different things to different readers—this is hardly a radical contention. The question, and it is always an open one, is how far the meaning is inherent in the text; and, if it is inherent, how far it is determined by the author; and, if it is, how far we can know the author's intention, or even whether the author's intention has any relevance at all. And is the meaning of a work several hundred years old the same now as its meaning when it was new—to what extent are meanings transhistorical? It is not that there are no answers to such questions, but the answers keep changing according to what we want literature to tell us and what we want out of reading, and according to what at any moment will constitute a sufficient answer. In fact, if we try to historicize early modern texts, the issue of the author's intention becomes especially complicated, since the author is often little more than a name, sometimes not even that, and must be deduced or even constructed out of the text.

Or inserted into the text, or the text revised to suit it. As soon as Shakespeare's name became a marketable commodity it was attached not only to his works, but to poems and plays by less famous writers, producing a factitious historicity, but also testifying to how important the claim of historicity had become. Books preserve Shakespeare's historicity, and that was what sold the books. And since that historicity was increasingly what was meant by "Shakespeare," the plays and poems were subject to any amount of revision and interpretation to produce an acceptable, marketable Shakespeare— hence John Benson's 1640 edition of the sonnets, which provides gendered titles and substitutes female for male pronouns to undo the chronicle of love for another man. Where exactly *is* Shakespeare in that?

---

[17] A more detailed discussion of the book is in my *The Reader in the Book* (Oxford: Oxford University Press, 2015), pp. 11–13.

Constructing the author

The book market has also constructed authors in changing ways. Increasingly a frontispiece portrait became essential as the author, rather than the publisher or the patron, moved to the center of the text. Chaucer's name was radically unobtrusive in the earliest printed editions. There is a portrait of Chaucer in the Ellesmere manuscript, the grandest of the early Chaucer manuscripts, but he is merely one of the pilgrims—it is included because there are portraits of all the pilgrims. But in the 1602 edition of Chaucer, the author, in Figure 1.20, oversees his book: there are in addition a genealogy, a biography, and Chaucer's family coats of arms.

Such an image exemplifies a significant transformation in the function of illustration, realizing the author, not the narrative. Similarly, the title-page portrait in the Shakespeare folio is now so famous that it seems normative, but it is actually quite a new idea, and Ben Jonson, in his commendatory poem facing it, advises you to ignore it: "reader, look/ Not on his picture, but his book." The picture, Jonson says, captures nothing of what is distinctive about Shakespeare, the wit, the intelligence, everything that is expressed in the writing. Jonson did not want his portrait in his own folio. Instead, he commissioned the elaborate allegorical title page in Figure 1.21, anatomizing his place in relation to classical drama, with his name at the center of a triumphal arch.

But readers wanted portraits. So the 1640 Jonson second folio, published three years after his death, has as its frontispiece Figure 1.22, Robert Vaughan's engraved version of the only surviving painting of Jonson done during his lifetime, Abraham van Blyenberch's portrait of the poet from around 1621 (see Figure 3.1). Adaptations of this portrait continued to confront readers in editions of Jonson throughout the century; and by the end of the century bibliophiles began adding the Vaughan engraving to their copies of the first folio, as if something were missing. Antiquarian book dealers now often advertise perfectly complete copies of the Jonson 1616 folio as "lacking the portrait." This may be simply ignorance; but it also reflects what purchasers for several hundred years have wanted the Jonson folio to be.

What we do to books is an index to what we want out of them, and it is a rare case in which we want simply entertainment or information.

FIGURE 1.20 Geoffrey Chaucer, *Workes*, ed. Thomas Speght, 1602, portrait of Chaucer.

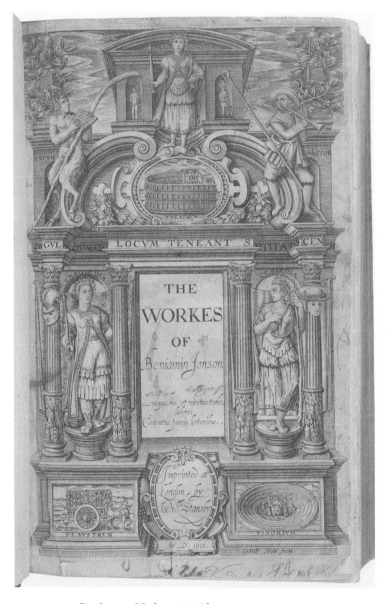

FIGURE 1.21   Ben Jonson, *Workes*, 1616, title page.

FIGURE 1.22   Robert Vaughan, portrait of Ben Jonson, *c*.1627.

Milton says in *Areopagitica* that "books are not absolutely dead things"[18]—not absolutely, that is, but relatively dead, dead without the life imbued in them by readers. Hence, Milton argues, books must not be censored before publication: they must be allowed to reach readers or else they are truly dead. And marginalia and embellishments are commonplace because even in the hands of a reader the book was never self-sufficient, it always needed something that could only be supplied by the reader—understanding, commentary, explanation, decoration, something to help us remember it, or even simply doodles, something to make it ours, something to make it not absolutely dead.

[18] *Areopagitica* (1644), p. 4.

| 2 |

Some Plays

In a sense, books are most alive when they are texts for performance. I begin with two topics: Shakespeare in the theater, and Shakespeare and the text. These subjects would normally be conceived as involving a set of alternatives—the performance versus the book, actors and audiences versus texts and readers, most basically perhaps, the drama as the property of the theatrical company, endlessly subject to their revisions and reinterpretations, versus the drama as the property of the author, a text determined and fixed by his or her authority, directly addressed to an audience without the mediation (and the inevitable misrepresentation) of actors and directors. And this dichotomy is certainly part of the point: Shakespeare was a man of the theater, who identified his interests with those of the playhouse spectators, and apparently had little or no interest in a reading public for his plays.

If we take this line, we will argue that there is a sense in which the history of Shakespeare scholarship, which since the time of the first folio has been concerned with establishing authentic texts, fixing them and interpreting them correctly, has misrepresented the true nature of the plays, and of Shakespeare's intentions for them: the folio editors claim to preserve in that great volume "the true original copies," which are declared to be the only correct (but more precisely, the only authorized) versions of the plays. For Shakespeare as man of the theater, however, the text was not fixed; it changed as the actors' sense of the occasion and the audience changed, from season to season

The Idea of the Book and the Creation of Literature. Stephen Orgel, Oxford University Press.
© Stephen Orgel 2023. DOI: 10.1093/oso/9780192871534.003.0002

and even in some cases from performance to performance. The text
for a dramatist like Shakespeare was only where the play started, not
its final version at all, which transpired only in the performance.
H. R. Woudhuysen puts the case succinctly: "the text of a play is not
the play itself, but a set of directions for how it might be reconstituted
or performed."[1] There is a good deal of truth in this, and it is the line
that much recent writing on the subject has taken; but it also simplifies
matters, and in significant ways misrepresents them. Here I shall be
arguing both for and against it. Something certainly happens to a play
when it turns into a book; but perhaps there is more of the book in the
drama than it has been in the interests of theater to acknowledge.[2]

To begin with, we need to account for the fact that plays were
preserved and ultimately printed at all. Only a small percentage of
ancient drama survives, but that was never dismissed as popular entertainment. It was transcribed into often splendid manuscripts, and from
the earliest years of printing was edited and published in very grand
editions. Vernacular drama was obviously less prized, but the fact that
by the early sixteenth century plays in English were being published
indicates that there was an audience of readers for them. Clearly there
was some confusion about who those readers might be—were they
actors who needed scripts, audiences who wanted mementos of plays
they had seen, potential audiences who had been unable to see a
performance and wanted to reconstruct the play in their heads, or
simply readers for whom drama, like any other written form, was a
source of recreation and wisdom? By the seventeenth century, when
vernacular drama was being collected and issued in carefully edited,
lavishly produced folios, the question of whether plays were books was
effectively moot: plays were modern classics.

But let us begin where plays begin. Drama begins with a script—
something written by hand, the work, that is, of a writer, not of a
printer and publisher. The term always denoted something written by
hand; its use specifically for the text of a play apparently dates only

---

[1] H. R. Woudhuysen, "Editors and Texts, Authorities and Originals," in Lukas Erne
and Margaret Jane Kidnie, *Textual Performances* (Cambridge: Cambridge University
Press, 2004), p. 40.
[2] For a shrewd and detailed overview, see Claire M. L. Bourne, *Typographies of
Performance in Early Modern England* (Oxford: Oxford University Press, 2020).

from the nineteenth century. In the sixteenth and seventeenth centuries the text of a play in the theater, for example the prompter's copy or the copy that was submitted to the censor, was "the book of the play." The actors did not receive the whole play, but only their parts with the cue lines. The play was, then, more than its book or a collection of parts: play-books or scripts are realized, parts made whole, in performances; the performance is the play, and unlike its text, every iteration is different—hence the censor's standard, unenforceable stipulation that the actors speak no more than the script. Moreover, published quartos of plays are not simply reproductions of the script: to make a script publishable required an editor, at the very least to standardize the presentation, and in many cases to introduce revisions and additional material to adapt the play to an audience of readers rather than spectators (there is an especially clear case in *The Spanish Tragedy*, discussed below). That editor would not necessarily, or usually, have been the author. The book is not the play.

It is significant, therefore, that Renaissance plays so often turn to written discourse, letters, documents, and books, as the precipitating or clinching elements for action: the bond with the devil signed in blood in *Doctor Faustus*, the ambiguous message in *Edward II* that sends both the king and Mortimer to their deaths, Tiberius's long, insinuating letter to the senate in *Sejanus* that causes the favorite's downfall, the forged letters left for Malvolio to find or shown to Gloucester by Edmund, Macbeth's dissembling letter to Lady Macbeth about meeting the witches, the documents found in Roderigo's pocket that confirm Iago's perfidy, Goneril's villainous letters discovered at the end of *King Lear*, the bad love poems written by the courtiers in *Love's Labour's Lost* or pinned on trees by Orlando in *As You Like It*, the book that enables Prospero's magic and that he eventually drowns, or at least says that he will do so. *Hamlet* provides a particularly striking example: when Hamlet saves his own life, destroys Rosencrantz and Guildenstern, usurps his uncle's authority and by implication his throne, he does all these things not by any stage heroics, but by forging a royal letter. Moreover, none of this crucial action takes place on stage; we do not even see the letter being forged. What we see instead is Horatio reading aloud from a letter which Hamlet has written to him about it. On the stage these most critical incidents of the play, including the encounter with the pirates and the consequent transformation of the dilatory hero into a man of action, are conveyed simply by Horatio reading the letter.[3]

The drama here returns to its origins in the script; actors do not perform actions, they recite lines, and whatever acting they do is determined by the script—the life of the play is in its text. There is in *Hamlet* a paradigm for the drama of its age, which increasingly registers a profound awareness not only of the authority of the script, and of script, but also of the status of the drama's own action as a text. In fact, Hamlet himself worries about the disruptive possibilities of improvisation during the performance, warning the visiting players:

> let those that play your clowns speak no more than is set down for them, for there be of them that will themselves laugh, to set on some quantity of barren spectators to laugh too, though in the meantime some necessary question of the play be then to be considered.
>
> (3.2. 37–42)

This was a real danger: the clown embodied a good deal of what was popular about theater. Seeing a play is a social event, and in the Elizabethan playhouse involved a great deal of interaction between the audience and the actors, especially the clowns. Much of the clowns' performance was improvised, but playwrights increasingly took Hamlet's line and undertook to remain in control of the action by incorporating the clown's role into the script—in the folio version of *King Lear*, which is substantially shorter than the quarto version, the only role that is actually increased is that of the fool. In the first quarto of *Hamlet*, Hamlet even adds several examples of disruptive jokes by the clown.[4]

Hamlet is both playwright and actor, and his play continually, at critical moments, in effect deconstructs itself, declaring that it is taking place in a playhouse, being performed by actors, not an action but a performance, alluding constantly to the fact that it is a play. *Hamlet* is probably Shakespeare's most self-reflexive drama. This is, obviously, a

---

[3] Jonathan Goldberg, "Hamlet's Hand," *Shakespeare Quarterly* 39.3 (Autumn, 1988), pp. 307–27, gives a brilliant analysis of the significance of writing in the play and in the period.

[4] For a superb analysis of the changing role of the clown, see Richard Preiss, *Clowning and Authorship in Early Modern England* (Cambridge: Cambridge University Press, 2014).

theatrical strategy as well as a textual one, both part of the action, and a way of breaking through it. The hero is presented as a figure who invests a great deal in the stage, not simply as entertainment, but as therapy and a way to knowledge. The arrival of the players seems to galvanize him; actors are, he says, "the abstract and brief chronicle of the time" (2.2.464); they "hold the mirror up to nature, to show virtue her own feature, scorn her own image, and the very age and body of the time his form and pressure" (3.2.21–4). These are, moreover, not offered simply as philosophical musings. The central device in his own schemes against the king, the crucial means of confirming the ghost's story, is the production of a play.

Here is what he says about it:

> I have heard that guilty creatures sitting at a play
> Have by the very cunning of the scene
> Been struck so to the soul that presently
> They have proclaimed their malefactions.
> For murder, though it have no tongue, will speak
> With most miraculous organ. I'll have these players
> Play something like the murder of my father
> Before mine uncle. I'll observe his looks.
> I'll tent him to the quick. If 'a do blench,
> I know my course...
>   The play's the thing
> Wherein I'll catch the conscience of the king.
>
>   (2.2.575)

The assumptions this makes about the nature of theater have a long history. To begin with, the notion that the way to get the king to confess is to present him with an imitation of his own crime is obviously related to the claim that what actors do is "hold the mirror up to nature." All theater, then, is a mirror; what we see in it is ourselves. We may think of mirrors as harmless, at worst indulgences of our vanity, but in the play they have much more powerful implications. When Hamlet goes to see his mother after the play scene, he says that he will "set you up a glass / Where you may see the inmost part of you" and the queen replies—to the modern eye quite illogically unless an actor invents some stage business to account for the line—"What wilt thou do? Thou wilt not murder me?" (3.4.19–21) and calls for help. (Garrick at this point pulled out his dagger, and held up the blade as a mirror.) Mirrors are threats, and can precipitate violent and dangerous actions; and the result of setting up this glass is the murder of Polonius behind the arras, or, as Hamlet thinks, the murder of the king.

Somewhere far behind Hamlet's mirror must be Aristotle's dictum that drama is an imitation of an action. Aristotle and Hamlet mean something different by imitation, however: for Aristotle, the action being imitated is something that never happened—drama is, as we would say, an imitation-action, with no original behind it. It is not a representation, but a presentation. In this respect it is a lie, and this made theater problematic for a number of ancient writers, most significantly Plato—though not for Aristotle, who argued in effect that there are good reasons for telling lies, and the creation of drama is one of them.

The idea that the theatrical mirror is dangerous has a very long and complex history; the antitheatrical movement has been exhaustively traced by Jonas Barish.[5] By the Renaissance, the problematic character of theater's kind of imitation had got inextricably mixed up with a number of biblical prohibitions—against images, against cross-dressing— but the subtext was a clear sense of the theater's powerfully seductive attractiveness. Antitheatrical writers always assume that the seductions of theater are irresistible, though the sort of danger it represents is ambiguously and often contradictorily described. Love scenes on stage are said to be so exciting that they inevitably result in inflaming the audience to lust and rape—audiences are assumed to be incapable of seeing through the action to its meaning, however morally intended, or even to the fact that it is not real. On the other hand, the fact that women on the Elizabethan stage were played by boys is often claimed to serve as an incitement to homosexual passion in the audience—in this case, the spectator is incapable of responding to the representation, the boy as a woman, but can only see through it. These are contradictory positions, but both are maintained, sometimes as part of the same argument, by a number of polemicists.

There are surprisingly few English defenders of the stage to answer the polemical attackers. The reason for this may be simply that few

[5] *The Anti-Theatrical Prejudice* (Berkeley: University of California Press, 1981).

people took the attacks seriously, that the antitheatrical movement was a great deal less effective than it looks from our vantage point with nothing but writers like Stephen Gossen and William Prynne to go by. But an odd aspect of the movement is that both attackers and defenders seem to share all the basic assumptions—Hamlet's prediction about the effects of theatrical imitation on Claudius is conceding a good deal.

The most elaborate defense of theater in Shakespeare's time was the playwright Thomas Heywood's *Apology for Actors*. This is a rag-bag of arguments on behalf of his profession, some of them rather desperate, but all of them in some way essential to both sides of the debate. The largest, and in some ways the most striking, claim has to do with what goes on in a theater (it is not, as we shall see, a play). Here is a description of a Roman theater:

> the Basses, Columnes, Pillars, and Pyramides were all of hewed Marble, the coverings of the stage, which wee call the heavens (where upon any occasion their Gods descended) were Geometrically supported by a Giant-like *Atlas*,... in which an artificial Sunne and Moone of extraordinary aspect and brightnesse had their diurnall, and nocturnall motions; so had the starres their true and coelestial course; so had the spheares, which in their continual motion made a most sweet and ravishing harmony: Here were the Elements and planets in their degrees, the sky [i.e., sphere] of the *Moone*, the sky of *Mercury, Venus, Sol, Mars, Jupiter and Saturn*; the starres, both fixed and wandering: and above all these, the first mover or *primum mobile*, there were the 12 signes; the lines Equinoctiall and Zodiacal, the Meridian circle, or Zenith, the Orizon circle, or Emisphere, the Zones torrid & frozen, the poles articke & antarticke, with all other tropickes, orbs, lines, circles, the *Solstitium* & all other motions of the stars, signes, & planets. In briefe, in that little compasse were comprehended the perfect modell of the firmament, the whole frame of the heavens, with all grounds of Astronomical conjecture.[6]

Theater here is a triumph of human ingenuity and craftsmanship and a model of the universe. What it is not is a setting for drama: this theater does not require plays to make it what it is. But if there *were* a play on such a stage, it too would be a model, by analogy, of human

---

[6] *An Apology For Actors* (1612), sigs. D2^{v}–D3^{r}.

behavior—it would hold the mirror up to human nature, as the theater holds the mirror up to the cosmos.

Why is this conception of theater so compelling for Heywood—why is it offered as a better argument in favor of theater than, say, the claim that Seneca teaches us morals? Another way of putting the question is to ask why we want models: they give us the illusion that we control our world, and perhaps even help us to do so. The account of ancient theater is pure fantasy, but the fantasy is not unique to Heywood. It is shared by much of his culture, including Shakespeare's theatrical company, in their decision to name their playhouse the Globe. All the world's a stage. The metaphor takes on an important legal force in Thomas Hobbes's *Leviathan*, discussing the concept of a person:

> The word Person...in latine signifies the *disguise*, or *outward appearance* of a man, counterfeited on the Stage; and sometimes more particularly that part of it, which disguiseth the face, as a Mask or Vizard: and from the Stage, hath been translated to any Representer of speech and action, as well in Tribunalls, as Theaters. So that a *Person* is the same that an *Actor* is, both on the Stage and in common conversation; and to *Personate* is to Act, or *Represent* himselfe, or an other.[7]

Since Hobbes's commonwealth is made up of persons, "all the world's a stage" becomes a political metaphor as well as a theatrical one. The central element is the role that individuals play within the society—this is the *persona*—and to conceive of society in that way is to conceive of it as a theater.

What about Hamlet's more strategic notion that the play will "catch the conscience of the king"? Somewhere behind this must be Aristotle's principle of catharsis, which holds that drama has a purgative effect. The passage from *The Poetics* in which this is asserted is brief and obscure, and it has been much debated. It says literally that "drama effects through pity and terror purgation of the like"—that pitiable and terrible events (not the emotions of pity and terror, but the things in the play that arouse these emotions) purge events of a similar nature. Gerald Else has persuasively argued that Aristotle is talking here not about the effect of drama on the audience but about the structure of the

---

[7] *Leviathan* (1651), p. 80.

play: the terrible events that precipitate tragedy—the murder of Laius by Oedipus, or of Agamemnon by Clytemnestra and Aegisthus—are purged by the terrible sufferings of the protagonist. It is the world of the play, Thebes or Athens, that is thereby purified, not the audience.[8]

But from the earliest Renaissance commentators onwards, it has generally (though not invariably) been assumed that the purgation takes place in the audience, that it is the spectators who are purged by their response to the terrifying events of the drama. Especially for Italian Renaissance theorists (who were much more favorably disposed towards the stage than their English counterparts) this became a powerful argument in favor of the utility of theater to the health of the state, and was one of the commonest reasons given for why princes should subsidize the stage. English claims tend to be more modest, though Heywood does base his concluding arguments on the assumption that drama is genuinely therapeutic, and even manages to produce a few examples to prove the point. One of these concerns a woman who had murdered her husband and, seeing a play about a similar crime, was driven to confess in a paroxysm of repentant guilt. As an instance demonstrating the value of theater this is so specialized as to be fairly desperate, though it is certainly a case of Aristotelian catharsis taking place in the audience, pitiable and terrible events purging events of a similar nature, and it must be the sort of example Hamlet has in mind when he talks about the response of guilty creatures sitting at a play.

One could stop here, and say that Hamlet's assumptions have been accounted for. But it is not at all clear from the action that Hamlet is right about the effects of the play within the play. Actors and directors have to interpolate a good deal of stage business to make *The Murder of Gonzago* work the way Hamlet says it is supposed to do. The dumb show presents a perfectly clear mirror of Claudius's crime, but if the king blenches, the text gives no indication of the fact. Some directors have Claudius not paying attention at this point; others have him

---

[8] Gerald Else, *Aristotle's Poetics: The Argument* (Cambridge, MA: Harvard University Press, 1963), pp. 225–32, 423–47. For a summary of the arguments against Else's position, see Stephen Halliwell, *Aristotle's Poetics* (London: Duckworth, 1986), p. 355. See also Francis Sparshott, "The Riddle of Katharsis," in Eleanor Cook et al., eds., *Centre and Labyrinth* (Toronto: University of Toronto Press, 1983), pp. 14–37. For the history of the concept in the Renaissance, see my essay "The Play of Conscience" in Stephen Orgel, *The Authentic Shakespeare* (New York: Routledge, 2002), pp. 129–42.

struggle to control his dismay; most productions simply cut the dumb show entirely. Of course, it is also possible to maintain that Claudius is not upset because the play does not in fact mirror his crime: the ghost is lying, abusing Hamlet, as he says, to damn him. This was argued with great energy by Sir Walter Greg in 1917, and though J. Dover Wilson wrote a rebuttal that has been generally thought to settle the matter, Greg did call attention to some aspects of the play scene that remain very problematic.[9]

Is Hamlet correct about what happens in the play scene? Since the king does not get upset at the dumb show, what does he get upset at? After a long discussion of the ethics of widows remarrying, the Player Queen swears that she will never do so after the death of her husband:

> Both here and hence pursue me lasting strife,
> If, once a widow, ever I be wife!

(3.2.218–19)

Hamlet seems more moved by this than either the king or the queen; he interrupts to ask Gertrude how she likes the play, and she gives a sensible and famous reply, "The lady doth protest too much, methinks." Nothing implies any feeling of guilt on her part, though the drama has certainly provided a mirror of her own history. The king, however, asks Hamlet "Have you heard the argument? Is there no offense in it?"—this must mean, in the context of widows remarrying, no offense to the queen. It is Hamlet who then turns the discussion to the question of poison and murder. The play proceeds with the entrance of the murderer, whom Hamlet identifies as "one Lucianus, nephew to the king." There is a little obscene talk between Hamlet and Ophelia—Shakespeare obviously believes, like all the enemies of theater, that seeing plays provokes lust—and then Lucianus commits the murder, Hamlet gives another bit of commentary, and finally the king rises and flees.

Is Claudius running from the mirror of his own crime? Or is he running from the clear threat to his throne and his life that the play

[9] W. W. Greg, "Hamlet's Hallucination," *The Modern Language Review*, 12.4 (October, 1917) p. 419; J. Dover Wilson, "The Parallel Plots in 'Hamlet'," *The Modern Language Review*, 13.2 (April, 1918), pp. 129–56.

implies: Hamlet himself has told him that this is a play about the murder of a king by his nephew. The play is certainly a mirror; but is it a mirror of the king's guilt or of Hamlet's intentions? At the very least, we would have to say that it is both: Hamlet may have revealed the king, but he has certainly revealed himself as well. The scene shows the mirror of theater reflecting the playwright's mind as much as the spectator's.

Mischief

Hamlet opens with that creakiest of Elizabethan stage devices, a ghost. Initially, the apparition is taken very seriously; Horatio doubts the report of it but is convinced by "the sensible and true avouch / Of mine own eyes" (1.1.56–8)—he is a pragmatist and an empiricist, and the ghost is in fact really there. The problems at this point are metaphysical ones, not physical ones: what *is* this apparition; is it a ghost or "a goblin damned"; and when Hamlet finally gets it to speak with it, what is the quality of its evidence, can it be trusted?

But in fact, though the ghost determines the disastrous course of Hamlet's action throughout the play, as the play proceeds Hamlet takes it less seriously than the other witnesses. Hamlet's empiricism is more complicated than Horatio's, and his seeing the ghost brings into the play a whole range of issues that are certainly disruptive, and even, in significant ways, both eminently theatrical and antidramatic. Consider lines like "well said, old mole! Canst work i'th'earth so fast?," "art thou there, truepenny?," "you hear this fellow in the cellarage" (1.5.153–4); and all the racing around in order to avoid the ghost under the stage— why does Hamlet want to avoid the ghost at this point? Critics and editors have tried in vain to accommodate such moments to the gravity of the dramatic occasion. But they are metatheatrical bits, bringing into the action an awareness of the ghost not as a horrific apparition but as a familiar theatrical device, and of the ramparts of Elsinore Castle as a stage with a "cellarage." The effect, at this highly charged moment, is to reveal the hero as a particularly slippery character—one who slips in and out of character with disconcerting ease—and to assert a very clear kind of control over the play on the part of somebody, though whether that somebody is the playwright or the actor nobody without a script (that is, nobody in Shakespeare's audience) would be able to say.

Hamlet later complains about clowns improvising, and thereby obfuscating "some necessary question of the play." Surely that is the feel of these moments on the battlements: to an audience without access to the text, they will look as if the actor is improvising, mocking the play and the author. Hamlet is here doing what he later objects to—the hero becomes the clown, and, for a gag, disrupts the action by treating the ghost, that most "necessary question of the play," as simply a familiar stage device. Which side is the audience going to be on here? Audiences are generally on the side of mischief: theater, after all, appeals to the carnivalesque aspects of our nature. But as readers, we know that these passages, in fact, are not improvised; they are in the script. Why does the author at this moment invoke a compact between actor and audience against himself? And the question gets even trickier when we remember what editors and critics, in their primary concern for the text, are most likely to forget: that Shakespeare was as much an actor as an author: these moments reveal, at the very least, a divided loyalty.

The mischief extends beyond the theatrical, too: Hamlet's "old mole," "truepenny," "ha ha, boy, say'st thou so?," and so forth, will also violate an audience's notions of the decorum appropriate to addressing one's father and one's king, to say nothing of the ghost of these personages. For a deeply patriarchal and hierarchical society, this side of theater must for some spectators have been especially liberating, allowing them to do vicariously what they had always wanted but never dared to do.

We know that there was an earlier *Hamlet* play on the stage in the 1590s. Shakespeare's use of the old *Hamlet* (long credited to Thomas Kyd because of its putative similarity to *The Spanish Tragedy*, but now widely considered to be an early version of the play by Shakespeare)[10] argues extraordinary self-consciousness, particularly about the theater. One central element of the *Hamlet* of 1601 that is simply not

---

[10] Terri Bourus, *Young Shakespeare's Young Hamlet* (London: Palgrave Macmillan, 2014)—following, notably, Andrew Cairncross, *The Problem of Hamlet: A Solution* (London: Macmillan, 1936)—makes a persuasive case for the first quarto of *Hamlet* being the ur-*Hamlet* referred to as early as 1589, a view shared by, among others, Harold Bloom, Hardin Craig, Peter Alexander, and myself.

recoverable is his audience's awareness of the popular old drama, the essential context for those moments when the stage illusion is deliberately broken to force on the attention of the spectator the dramatic background, the theatrical medium and even its supernatural gimmickry. If we keep this sort of theatrical background in mind, some parts of the play come much more clearly into focus. The old *Hamlet* is characterized by Thomas Nashe in his preface to Robert Greene's *Menaphon*, published in 1589:

> English *Seneca* read by candle light yeeldes manie good sentences, as *Bloud is a begger*, and so foorth; and, if you intreate him faire in a frostie morning, he will affoord you whole *Hamlets*, I should say handfulls of tragical speaches.[11]

Like Kyd's *Spanish Tragedy*, with which it was contemporary, this *Hamlet* must have been a warhorse of a play, with blood-curdling rhetoric, and it would have been continually revived and revised—it appears again in Henslowe's records in 1594. In 1601 Henslowe paid Ben Jonson to write new speeches for a revival of *The Spanish Tragedy*, perhaps precisely to cash in on the success of Shakespeare's revised revenge drama.

Here is the first quarto's version of Hamlet's "rogue and peasant slave" soliloquy—I focus here on the first quarto, which is more in touch with the theatrical realities of the play than the second quarto, the basis of the standard modern text:

> Why what a dunghill idiote slave am I?
> Why these Players here draw water from my eyes:
> For Hecuba, why what is Hecuba to him, or he to Hecuba?
> What would he do and if he had my losse?
> His father murdred, and a Crowne bereft him,
> He would turne all his teares to droppes of blood,
> Amaze the standers by with his laments,
> Strike more then wonder in the judiciall eares,
> Confound the ignorant, and make mute the wise.
> Indeed his passion would be generall.
> Yet I like to an asse and John a Dreames,

---

[11] Preface to Greene's *Menaphon*, in G. Gregory Smith, ed., *Elizabethan Critical Essays* (Oxford: Oxford University Press, 1904 and many reprints), Vol. 1, p. 312.

Having my father murdred by a villaine,
Stand still, and let it passe, why sure I am a coward:
Who pluckes me by the beard, or twites my nose,
Give's me the lie I'th throate downe to the lungs,
Sure I should take it, or else I have no gall,
Or by this I should a fatted all the region kites
With this slaves offell, this damned villaine,
Treacherous, bawdy, murderous villaine:
Why this is brave, that I the sonne of my dear father,
Should like a scalion, like a very drabbe
Thus raile in wordes....[12]

This is a soliloquy, and like Hieronymo's passionate soliloquies in *The Spanish Tragedy* it gives us a good sense of how different that theatrical device was on the Elizabethan stage from what it is on ours. When in modern productions Hamlet declares himself a rogue and peasant slave, he does so as if he is thinking aloud—in the beautiful 1948 film, Laurence Olivier did not even speak his soliloquies; they were recited as voice-overs while the actor appeared on the screen lost in thought. But Shakespeare's Hamlet harangues and berates, "like a very drabbe" railing in words; not meditating, but arguing and inveighing, an orator directly addressing the audience, persuading them of the tragic issues of his drama and the justice of his cause.

The book of the play

Whatever we think about the degree of contamination of the original text that Q1 represents, it embodies some version of the play that lies behind the classic text so familiar to us; and only the first quarto text is short enough to have been performed complete in the Elizabethan theater. The three versions of *Hamlet* in the first two quartos and the folio obviously embody many others, all of them palimpsests of versions and revisions. We also need to bear in mind that the book of a

---

[12] *The Tragicall Historie of Hamlet* . . . (1603) [i.e., *Hamlet* Q1], sigs. E4ᵛ–F1ʳ. There are analyses of the Q1 version of the "To be or not to be" soliloquy in Robert Weimann, *Author's Pen and Actor's Voice* (Cambridge: Cambridge University Press, 2000), pp. 19–22, and in Seth Lerer, "'A Scaffold in the Marketplace': Bad *Hamlet*, Good Romans, and the Shakespearean Idiom," *Anglia* 122 (2004), pp. 376–7.

play is not the play. There is a significant difference between a book and a script; and the script is not the play either. The performers turn it into a play, and its text therefore is not stable, but changes according to the demands of the performance—the play before the queen was not the same as the play in the public playhouse, and performances have always taken account of the changing world of contemporary events. Moreover, before a play is a book, when it is only a script and a history of performances, it carries with it no assumption about textual integrity: the audience does not come to theater with a text of the play in their heads, and no expectations are being defeated by new versions. The performers are in control, not the text.

For the Elizabethans, printed texts of plays for the public theater served different interests from those they serve for us. They have always been a way of preserving, however incompletely, the ephemeral experience of performance; but we also consider them extensions of the author, establishing his or her authority over the work. For Shakespeare's age they were rarely that: the playwright in the public theater was an employee of the theatrical company. He wrote what the actors and managers commissioned; they sometimes even provided him with a scenario, and often parceled the work out among a number of writers. Shakespeare is an exception only in the sense that, as an actor and part-owner of his company, he was literally his own boss. The final text belonged to the company, to be revised as the play was made ready for the stage.[13]

Publication was primarily in the interests of the publisher. It was probably also in the interests of the company, though the actors did not believe this—they believed that audiences that could read a play would be less likely to come to see it; and of course, to print a play was to deliver it into the hands of a rival company. Hence the vast proportion of Elizabethan play-texts were never published, and those that were published typically appeared well after their inclusion in the theater repertory. Publication would certainly have been in the interests of the author, but unless the company considered his work unsuitable and refused it, he had no rights to the manuscript whatever: he had been

---

[13] For an excellent discussion of Shakespeare's plays as literary property see James J. Marino, *Owning William Shakespeare* (Philadelphia: University of Pennsylvania Press, 2011).

paid for it, and his interest ended there. Even for published plays, the author's interest ended with the sale of the manuscript: there were no royalties, and insofar as there was any sort of copyright, it belonged to the publisher, not the author. This was beginning to change; and by the early seventeenth century we find playwrights claiming their works, and objecting to the publishers' free hand with them, but nothing resembling copyright belonged to the author until the next century.

Most Elizabethan plays appear in print, therefore, without an author's name attached to them.[14] Even for the most famous and popular plays of the period, the author is often a shadowy figure, for whom we have only a name, and sometimes not even that. If we want a paradigm for the fate of the playwright in Shakespeare's England, we may take the printing history of Marlowe's *Doctor Faustus*, an Elizabethan classic, revived constantly, performed throughout Europe by traveling players, and tremendously popular long after its notorious author's murder in 1593. It was composed sometime around 1590, and appears to be a collaboration, with someone other than Marlowe composing the comic scenes.[15] It was published only in 1604, and numerous times thereafter, but in two very different texts. In three editions from 1604 to 1611 it is credited to "Ch. Marl."; thereafter, in a much revised form, to "C. Mar.," and in the latter case an early owner of the only extant copy of the 1616 edition has expanded the author's name to "Marklin." So the very famous author of this very famous play dissolves. Both the surviving versions of *Doctor Faustus* are clearly at some considerable distance from whatever Marlowe wrote; and the play makes more sense as a cultural artifact than as a key to Marlovian psychobiography.

The presentation of plays in Renaissance texts is worth pausing over. The first quarto of *The Merchant of Venice*, in Figure 2.1, summarizes the play's several plots on the title page. Shakespeare's name comes last; the fact of frequent performance is given precedence. The play in the folio, in contrast, tells nothing but the title—it has become literature. The quarto of *King Lear*, in Figure 2.2, offers even more information on

---

[14] But see again, for important exceptions, Lukas Erne, *Shakespeare as Literary Dramatist* (Cambridge: Cambridge University Press, 2003).

[15] For a summary of the arguments, see Eric Rasmussen, *A Textual Companion to Doctor Faustus* (Manchester: Manchester University Press, 1993), pp. 62–75.

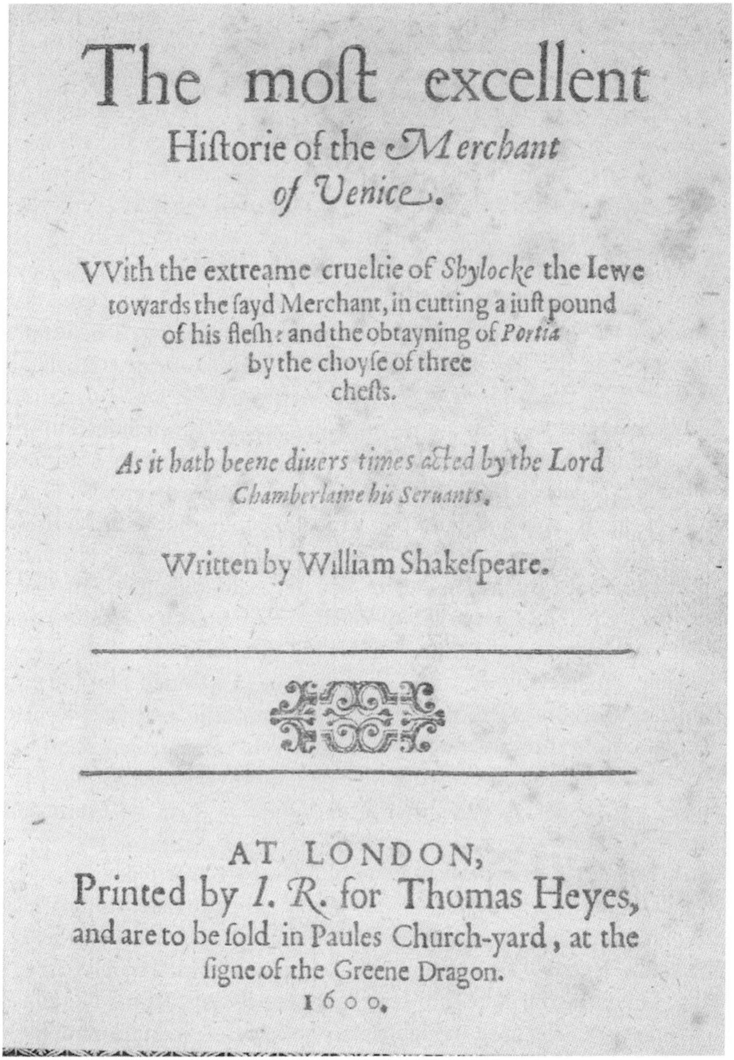

The moſt excellent

Hiſtorie of the *Merchant of Venice*.

VVith the extreame crueltie of *Shylocke* the Iewe
towards the ſayd Merchant, in cutting a iuſt pound
of his fleſh: and the obtayning of *Portia*
by the choyſe of three
cheſts.

*As it hath beene diuers times acted by the Lord
Chamberlaine his Seruants.*

Written by William Shakeſpeare.

AT LONDON,
Printed by *I. R.* for Thomas Heyes,
and are to be ſold in Paules Church-yard, at the
ſigne of the Greene Dragon.
1 6 0 0.

FIGURE 2.1 *The Merchant of Venice*, title page of the quarto, 1600. Folger Shakespeare Library.

M. William Shak-ſpeare:

HIS
True Chronicle Hiſtorie of the life and
death of King L E A R and his three
Daughters.

With the vnfortunate life of Edgar, *ſonne*
and heire to the Earle of Gloſter, and his
ſullen and aſſumed humor of
T O M of Bedlam :

As it was played before the Kings Maieſtie at Whitehall vpon
S. Stephans *night in Chriſtmas Hollidayes.*

By his Maieſties ſeruants playing vſually at the Gloabe
on the Bancke-ſide.

LONDON,
Printed for *Nathaniel Butter*, and are to be ſold at his ſhop in *Pauls*
Church-yard at the ſigne of the Pide Bull neere
Sᵗ. *Auſtins* Gate. 1 6 o 8

FIGURE 2.2 *King Lear*, title page of the quarto, 1608. Folger Shakespeare Library.

its title page. Shakespeare's name is now in very large type: he has now become a selling point. The play is described as a historical account of a king and three daughters who all die; there is a subplot with an unfortunate aristocratic youth who pretends to be mad; we are promised in addition to suffering, a significant amount of clown material; and the fact that it was played before King James is a strong recommendation.

The folio, however, calls the play simply *The Tragedy of King Lear*: it has become not a chronicle history but a tragedy. Once Shakespeare graduates to folio that is all the information provided. Moreover, *The Merchant of Venice* in the folio is divided into acts, and *King Lear* into acts and scenes,[16] whereas none of the plays in quarto have act and scene divisions: their conventions are not those of classical drama, just as movies now, even when they are versions of plays, do not have acts with pauses between them. Shakespeare plays (with the possible exception of plays designed for the Blackfriars, such as *The Tempest*—see below, pp. 79–80 [C3.P25]) are not conceived in acts and scenes; these have been devised by editors for particular editions. Shakespeare quartos also appear without any introductory matter, such as a dedication or commendatory verses, as would have been normal in other sorts of books. More strikingly for dramas, they include no list of dramatis personae and no scene locations. These were only occasionally supplied in play quartos, but a number of the folio plays are provided with them.

For comparison, how do we now present the texts of plays? Why do we begin with the cast of characters? We want all the necessary information in advance, and we want that information to be fixed. The characters have names and titles and relationships that we can master before we experience the play. We sometimes even take flashlights with us to performances so that we can check the names of the characters as they enter—this constitutes essential information for us, and we do not want to allow it to simply materialize from the action and the dialogue. It is, moreover, information that we think of as

---

[16] All four folios are erratic about act and scene divisions; all the plays announce at the opening *Actus Primus. Scæna Prima*, but several then have no further act and scene notations. The folio text of *Hamlet* marks acts and scenes only through Act 2, scene 2. Nicholas Rowe's Shakespeare, 1709, was the first edition to provide acts and scenes throughout.

essential to the *action*: the play is first the characters, and then what they say and do.

This is not, however, how Renaissance plays work. For example, how do we know that the king in *Hamlet* is named Claudius? He is never named in the play; he is never called anything except the king. Claudius is a name used only for a single stage direction in the second quarto and folio texts, for his first entrance ("Enter Claudius King of Denmarke"), and never thereafter. It is not used for the speech headings, where he is simply "King." It is never used at all in dialogue, and there is no cast of characters in any of the early editions. If it were not for that single stage direction, he would have no name in the play.

What then is a character in a Renaissance play? If Claudius is never named in the dialogue or in the speech headings, why *does* he have a name in the play? For whose benefit is he named in that unique stage direction? The answer can only be, for Shakespeare's. But in fact, characters in this drama are no more fixed than texts; Claudius's name hidden in a stage direction is surely relevant to the fact that Polonius in the first quarto is called Corambis, Reynaldo is called Montano, and Voltimand is called Voltimar. The last might be some-body's muddle, but nothing except a change in the script can explain the other two. But what could the point have been? Was there some significance to a Polish allusion in the two years between the publica-tion of Q1 and Q2, and did Corambis become Polonius to capitalize on that? Or did the editing work the other way, and is Corambis covering up a Polish allusion that was unwise in 1603, but had become harmless by 1605? And what about the names Voltimand and Voltimar— Voltimand is unknown elsewhere, but Voltimar sounds like a version of Valdemar, in which case this Danish courtier would be named after a Danish king: is Voltimar/Valdemar therefore the name that was intended? There are, obviously, no answers to questions like these, but they do help to indicate how problematic Shakespearean texts are even on the most basic level of the characters' names.

The printed texts all make a claim to stability that the play seems insistently to deny. In fact, each of the three books makes a different sort of claim. The first quarto title page reads, "The Tragical Historie of Hamlet Prince of Denmarke By William Shakespeare. As it hath beene diverse times acted by his Highnesse servants in the Cittie of London: as also in the two Universities of Cambridge and Oxford, and elsewhere."

This text invokes several kinds of authority: the author's name (still relatively uncommon on the title pages of play texts); the fact that it was a popular play performed by the company that the new king had just taken under his patronage; and the three locations, London, Oxford, and Cambridge, centers respectively of power and learning, implying that the most important and richest and wisest audiences have approved of the play.

If we press on these claims, however, they become shaky. The Globe was not in the city of London but across the river on the south bank; public theaters were explicitly forbidden in London after 1594 (but the title page might therefore be evidence that the first quarto is in fact the text of the ur-*Hamlet*, which we know was in existence in the early 1590s). And theatrical performances by professional companies were explicitly forbidden in the universities too, so the claim about Oxford and Cambridge can at most mean that the King's Men performed in the university towns—though even this is puzzling, not to say dubious, since the Oxford Town Council repeatedly went on record during this period banning public performances of plays within the city limits. Were there exceptions that are not recorded, or did the actors manage to get around the ban somehow (e.g., performing in some gentleman's house), or did they set up their stage somewhere just outside the city limits? Or is the title page's claim simply a fabrication designed to add topographical and academic prestige to a popular play?

There is evidence that the play was an intellectual favorite. Gabriel Harvey noted that it pleased "the wiser sort": "The younger sort takes much delight in Shakespeares Venus, & Adonis: but his Lucrece, & his tragedie of Hamlet, Prince of Denmarke, have it in them to please the wiser sort."[17] The note has been dated to 1600–1 (that is, before the play was in print in any form); the wiser sort were therefore audiences, not readers. But this cannot imply university productions: theater in the universities was maintained as an academic prerogative, part of the educational system; the actors were students and dons, the plays were classic or neoclassic texts. It is clear what kind of imprimatur is being

---

[17] The note is included in a marginale in his copy of Speght's Chaucer (1598). The volume is now in the British Library, Add. MS 42518, folio 422^v. See the detailed discussion by Leo Kirschbaum, "The Date of Shakespeare's 'Hamlet'," *Studies in Philology*, 34.2 (April, 1937), pp. 168–75.

claimed by Q1 for this play, but it is much less clear whether the imprimatur is reliable.

The second quarto, on the other hand, makes a purely textual claim: the play has been "newly imprinted and enlarged to almost as much againe as it was, according to the true and perfect Coppie." This is addressed specifically not to audiences who have enjoyed the play and might want a memento of it, but to purchasers of the text represented by the first quarto. Moreover, no claim is made that the first quarto is defective, only that it is a shortened version—the "true and perfect copy" is twice as long. But this new text cannot have been an acting text of the play. It would take far longer than the two hours that is always cited in the period as the performing time of plays in Elizabethan public theaters—more than twice as long to perform as, say, *Romeo and Juliet*, *Macbeth*, or *The Tempest*. Perhaps the "true and perfect copy" was the copy that preserved all the possible versions of the text, scenes that were played but also those that had been deleted to produce a performing version—as the Beaumont and Fletcher folio says its texts include "all that was acted and all that was not."[18]

The Shakespeare folio claims that its texts are "the true original copies," adding a layer of authenticity to the quarto's "true and perfect copy." In one respect, however, the first quarto text of *Hamlet* is more "complete" than that of the second quarto and folio, the text that has become standard for us: it includes striking stage directions for the ghost's appearance in the queen's bedchamber "*in his night gowne*," and for Ophelia's mad scene, "*Enter Ofelia playing on a lute, and her haire downe*."[19] It also includes an exchange between Horatio and the queen conveying information one would have thought was essential, but which was apparently deleted as the play was revised. After the play scene, which has confirmed Hamlet's suspicions about his uncle's guilt, he has his confrontation with his mother. She has summoned him to berate him for his behavior to the king, but he quickly takes control of the interview, killing the intruding Polonius and setting up the soul-searching glass before the queen. This is so effective that it prompts the ghost to reappear, to recall Hamlet to his "blunted purpose"—he has

[18] *Comedies and Tragedies Written by Francis Beaumont and John Fletcher* (London, 1647), "The Stationer to the Readers," sig. A4^r.

[19] *Hamlet* Q1, sigs. G2^v, G4^v.

been told to leave the queen to heaven; his quarry is Claudius. His continuing focus on his mother is, in this revenge drama, a distraction. Nevertheless, he proceeds to extract a promise from her to stop sleeping with her husband: this is apparently all he wants from her. What he neglects to determine is whether she was complicit in his father's murder, and indeed, this is left unclear throughout the play. But the first quarto includes a conversation between the queen and Horatio in which, late in the play, her innocence is made evident.[20] Even in this text, Hamlet never knows whether his mother is guiltless; but was the scene deleted precisely to leave the question of her complicity an open one, for the audience as well? This bears on the whole question of completeness and of what was considered to be a true and perfect copy.

If we take the folio's "true original copies" to mean the final authorized texts, we have to remember that the texts were authorized not by Shakespeare, but by the company, who were the owners of the texts. The implications of this are strikingly evident in *Macbeth*, which includes demonstrably nonShakespearean passages providing additional material for the witches. The folio text, which is the only text, is therefore a revised version. Why was this considered the right text to include in the folio? Had Shakespeare's original been lost? Or had it simply been superseded, and was the authorized text whatever version the company was performing in the 1620s? What is a true original copy, and what constitutes authenticity?

Comedy and tragedy

Perhaps loose ends are, if not essential to tragedy, at least endemic, especially in revenge plays: is revenge ever satisfyingly complete? Certainly that quintessential Elizabethan revenge play *The Spanish Tragedy* leaves a great deal unaccounted for. *The Spanish Tragedy* is the second part of a two-part play. The first part survives only in a revised version published in 1605 as *The first part of Ieronimo. With the warres of Portugall, and the life and death of Don Andrea.* In Henslowe's diary for 1592–3 the two plays are usually called *Don Horatio* and *Ieronymo* or

---

[20] *Hamlet* Q1, sig. H2^{v}.

The Comedy of Ieronymo—*The Spanish Tragedy* could be thought of as a comedy. Comedy is perhaps being used here as a generic term for drama—the *OED* gives no support for this usage in English, but the German traveler Thomas Platter recording a visit to the Globe in 1599 to see *Julius Caesar* refers to the play (in German) as both a tragedy and a comedy,[21] just as in Italian *commediante* and in French *comédien* are generic terms for actor.

Perhaps, however, the ingenious plotting of Hieronymo and the definitive dispatch of the villains did produce a play that, for the Elizabethans, was as much comic as tragic. In any case, tragedy and comedy are not simply opposites. Even the most unrelenting Shakespearean comedies have their potentially tragic elements: the father condemned to death in *The Comedy of Errors*, the forsaken love and attempted rape in *The Two Gentlemen of Verona*. The darkest tragedy often includes parodic elements—Hamlet making jokes about the ghost in the cellerage; Edgar in *King Lear* deceiving the blind, despairing Gloucester into thinking he has fallen from Dover Cliff (a scene that in performance invariably gets a laugh); Marcus in *Titus Andronicus* describing Lavinia's tragic mutilation through wordplay and an extended series of puns. Very late in the *Symposium* Socrates tells Agathon and Aristophanes, tragic and comic dramatists, that their arts are the same. Presumably Socrates was not recommending that Aristophanes start writing tragedies, but for a dramatist like Ben Jonson, for whom tricks and deception are the essence of both comedy and tragedy, the precept is almost self-evident. And it has often been remarked that *Othello*, the tragedy of a jealous husband, an innocent wife, and a clever, malicious servant, has the structure of comedy.

One kind of resolution of tragic potential is the reversal of the tragedy through a twist that is essentially comic, producing a form of tragicomedy. The resolution of *Measure for Measure* is accomplished not by sending the villain Angelo off to be executed, but by undoing the damage he has done by treating him as he has treated Claudio. This is in effect a parody of his own behavior, just as resolving Mariana's tragic fate by disguising her as Isabella and sending her to bed with the faithless Angelo is a parodic gesture. The resolution of *Much Ado*

---

[21] Chambers, *William Shakespeare*, vol. 2, p. 322.

About Nothing is similarly parodic, making Claudio marry someone who is the double of Hero, whose death he believes he has caused, the mysterious double being Hero impersonating herself. Such plays do not abort the tragic movement, but reverse it: comedy here is the reversal of tragedy. Moreover, in the cases I have cited, the comedy depends on the possibility of tragedy.

Don Horatio and its sequel *Ieronymo* or *The Spanish Tragedy* were presumably written before 1588, since the surviving play makes no allusion to the Armada. In Henslowe's records the plays are occasionally recorded as being played in sequence, but for the most part *Ieronymo* was played alone. Apparently, therefore, the first part was less popular, and by the early 1590s was dropping out of the repertory. But there is a good deal in *The Spanish Tragedy* that assumes knowledge of prior action, in particular, of the love affair between the dead Spanish hero Don Andrea and the Spanish princess Bel-Imperia, which is briefly referred to in the opening speech of Andrea's ghost in *The Spanish Tragedy*. Andrea wants revenge not only for his death at the hands of the Portuguese prince Balthazar, who has been captured by the Spanish and now resides at the Spanish court, but as the play progresses for Balthazar's intention to marry Bel-Imperia, with the approval and encouragement of her villainous brother Lorenzo. The old love affair is discussed again when Bel-Imperia's current lover Horatio, Andrea's best friend, tells Bel-Imperia the circumstances of Andrea's death, and a certain amount of important detail surrounding the love affair is assumed to be known—that the Duke of Castile, father of Bel-Imperia and Lorenzo, was bitterly opposed to the match, and that Bel-Imperia's servant Pedringano was employed in some way by the lovers, and was protected from Castile's wrath by Lorenzo.

The 1605 play *The First Part of Ieronimo*, obviously based on the original play, fills in some but not all of this. Lukas Erne in a seminal article on the two plays says of *The First Part of Ieronimo*, which he refers to as *1 Hieronimo*, that "It represents a post-1600 revision of Kyd's genuine first part—called 'doneoracio' in Henslowe's diary—of which about one-third survives in the text of *1 Hieronimo*."[22] Erne points to a particularly telling moment: in *1 Hieronimo* Bel-Imperia

---

[22] "'Enter the Ghost of Andrea': Recovering Thomas Kyd's Two-Part Play," *English Literary Renaissance* 30.3 (November, 2008), pp. 339–72. The passage quoted is on p. 340.

gives Andrea a scarf to wear in battle. When he is killed by Balthazar, Horatio takes the scarf from his body and swears to wear it himself. Near the beginning of *The Spanish Tragedy*, Horatio recounts Andrea's death and shows Bel-Imperia the scarf, and she recognizes it as the one she gave Andrea.[23] It is difficult to imagine the two scenes in the first play being invented on the basis of this brief allusion in the second. But *1 Hieronimo* also includes new material that is a direct parody of *The Spanish Tragedy*. *1 Ieronimo* appears to have been the old play revised for performance by one of the children's companies; it burlesques the play, and in particular makes fun of the fact that Hieronymo is being played by a child, noting how small he is, that his sword is too big for him, and so forth. Here parody has been incorporated into tragedy—by the time *The Spanish Tragedy* was a perennial success it was also a basis for comedy, and its prologue had become its parody.

What makes for a satisfactory conclusion, and why would the first part of *Hieronymo* have disappeared? Why was it not necessary for the second part? Part 2 of *Tamburlaine* makes no sense without part 1. Part 2 of *Henry IV* is occasionally performed on its own, but with little success—the prior history of Hal and Falstaff is necessary. But perhaps in the case of *The Spanish Tragedy* there is a recognition that Hieronymo really is the interesting figure (he is not very significant in the first part); and also, perhaps having loose ends, having a significant amount of material an audience does not understand in the play, is part of the tragic point. Hence the deliberately baffling play within the play that Hieronymo presents before the king and the court. A note addressed to readers of the published text says, "*Gentlemen, this play of Hieronymo, in sundrie Languages, was thought good to be set downe in English more largely, for the easier understanding to every publique reader.*"[24] Hieronymo has earlier said his play will be performed in Latin, Greek, Italian, and French. Balthazar, one of the performers, objects: "But this will be a meere confusion,/ And hardly shall we all be understoode."[25] Hieronymo, however, both on stage and in the book, stands firm; thus readers are being treated differently from audiences—the book is not the play.

---

[23] 1.4.42.

[24] *The Spanish Tragedy* (1592), sig. K3^{r} (in modern editions 4.4.10sd).

[25] Ibid. sig. K1^{v} (4.1.180).

The macaronic play within the play is designed to be baffling for audiences, then, but clear for readers. Even for readers, however, the conclusion of *The Spanish Tragedy* is confusing: the king demands an explanation for the carnage he has just witnessed, which he gets twice from Hieronymo, first at length and then more briefly (essentially repeating what he has already said); and then the Viceroy tells about the collusion of Bel-Imperia with the murder of the villains—Hieronymo had sworn to keep this secret. The king asks Hieronymo "Why speak'st thou not?" and Hieronymo says he will say nothing, and bites out his tongue. What more, indeed, is there to say? But the play certainly acts as if there is more. Explanations claiming that what the king wants from Hieronymo is more information about the complicity of Bel-Imperia are unconvincing; the secret has already been revealed. Erne deals with the issue by saying the king's demand works in the theater because none of the critics of the several recent productions complained about it, but this is really beside the point; it is one of the things that are rewritten in the revision of 1602, so the Elizabethan actors saw it either as a problem or at least as a complication not worth keeping. In the revision Hieronymo says a good deal more, rehearsing and rejoicing in his revenge.

If the original ending works theatrically, as Erne says, that is because we want something left unsaid: Hieronymo's silence represents his refusal to give satisfaction; this is his final triumph. Even in the revised version the retribution inflicted on both villains and avengers does not at all subsume the revenge—Hieronymo's final invective merely recalls the play's series of outrages; it is designed to keep all wounds open. There is always more to say; the energy of revenge tragedy is never exhausted. Thus in the archetypal myth of Atreus and Thyestes, the demand for retribution extends through the generations. Seneca's *Thyestes*, an essential model for Elizabethan revenge tragedy, concludes with the same sort of exultant celebration of the hero's outrageous vengeance that Hieronymo produces; but we know that *Thyestes* is only a small part of an extended vicious cycle: his son is Aegisthus; in the future lie Agamemnon, Clytemnestra, Orestes, Electra. That family tragedy is concluded in Aeschylus's *Eumenides*, the third drama of his *Oresteia* trilogy, but only by a literal *deus ex machina*, with the god declaring revenge no longer a valid motive, and establishing a system of human justice—revenge can be aborted, but never satisfied.

The inconclusive ending of Hieronymo's drama is a model for the maddening conclusion of *Othello*, when Iago is asked to explain himself—in effect to explain the play—and he replies "What you know you know./ From this time forth I never will speak word." What is left unexplained, for both those on stage and for us, is the motivation for villainy. How much of the play's tragic power is in its loose ends?

Between stage and book

Troilus and Cressida was entered in the Stationers' Register in 1603 by James Roberts, the printer of the quartos of *A Midsummer Night's Dream*, *The Merchant of Venice*, and *Titus Andronicus*, but this publication never took place. The play was first issued in 1609 by a different publisher, in a quarto which exists in two states. The first has a title page that calls the play "The Historie of Troylus and Cresseida" and declares that it was "*acted by the Kings Majesties* servants at the Globe." But during the course of printing this was replaced by a new title page, which removes the information about performance and says instead "The famous historie of Troylus and Cresseid. *Excellently expressing the beginning* of their loves, with the conceited wooing of *Pandarus*, Prince of *Licia*." It is true that Pandarus does woo Cressida on behalf of Troilus, but this is a peculiar summary of the play's action. It is, however, curiously similar to the summary of *The Merchant of Venice* on the title page of the quarto printed by Roberts in 1600 (see Figure 2.1): "The most excellent Historie of the *Merchant of Venice*. With the extreame crueltie of *Shylocke* the Jewe towards the sayd Merchant, in cutting a just pound of his flesh: and the obtayning of *Portia* by the choyse of three chests." This seems to imply that Shylock obtains both his pound of flesh and Portia. As for "Pandarus Prince of Licia," the fact that Pandarus is Lycian is never mentioned in *Troilus and Cressida*, though it can be found in Homer; all this suggests an editor who is not much invested in Shakespeare's dramaturgy, but views the play as part of a long literary continuum.[26]

---

[26] The introductory chapter of Zachary Lesser's *Renaissance Drama and the Politics of Publication* (Cambridge: Cambridge University Press, 2004), pp. 1–4, includes a valuable discussion of issues relating to the publication of *Troilus and Cressida*.

The second state of the quarto also includes a prefatory epistle addressed from "a never writer, to an ever reader" (the "never writer" being someone speaking for the publisher) saying that the play was *"never stal'd with the Stage, never clapper-clawd with the palmes of the vulger."*[27] This may mean that the play was never performed, implicitly accounting for the suppression of the first title page; but it may instead mean that it was performed not at the "vulgar" Globe but at some more elite venue, such as the Inns of Court. The publisher may, of course, have been misinformed; but critical opinion has for the most part taken the view that the play was initially performed at one of the Inns of Court, and sometime later at the Globe, but was not a success at the public playhouse and therefore did not remain in the company's repertory. If that is correct, as Kenneth Muir suggests, "it seems most likely that this epistle was written soon after the private performance of the play and before the public performance," in anticipation of the aborted earlier publication.[28]

The epistle is directed specifically to the reader of plays, for whom the fact that this play was *"never stal'd with the stage"* is a particular virtue. The publisher, that is, changes his tune: he first says you will like the play because it has been performed by the best company at the best theater, and then presents the play as being unsullied by performance. Even so, Shakespeare's comedies in performance constitute a powerful recommendation for this one:

> [They] are so fram'd to the life, that they serve for the most common Commentaries, of all the actions of our lives, shewing such a dexter-itie, and power of witte, that the most displeased with Playes, are pleasd with his Commedies. And all such dull and heavy-witted worldlings, as were never capable of the witte of a Commedie, coming by report of them to his representations, have found that witte there, that they never found in them-selves, and have parted better wittied then they came.[29]

This says both that if you liked *Love's Labour's Lost* and *The Merchant of Venice* you will like this play, and also that even people who

---

[27] *The Famous Historie of Troylus and Cresseid* (1609), sig. ¶2ʳ.

[28] Kenneth Muir, ed., *Troilus and Cressida* (The Oxford Shakespeare, Oxford: Clarendon Press, 1982), p. 193.

[29] *Troylus* (1609), sig. ¶2ʳ.

disapprove of theater admire Shakespeare's plays. But *Troilus and Cressida* is even better than plays on stage *"for not being sullied, with the smoaky breath of the multitude,"* a play for reading. It is, moreover, in the tradition of classical comedy: it is as witty *"as the best Commedy in* Terence *or* Plautus," the delight of the educated and sophisticated. Moreover, you are urged to buy this quarto now; for when Shakespeare is dead and his comedies *"out of sale,"* no longer sold, *"you will scramble for them."*[30] Reading Shakespeare gives you far more enduring access to Shakespeare's wit than ephemeral performances do, just as the only access we have to the wit of Terence and Plautus is the texts of their plays.

There is, then, a balancing act here between the benefits of theater and library, performance and reading, public and private. And yet the underlying assumption is that you would not buy the play, would not want the play—indeed, the publisher would not print the play—if it had not been performed; Shakespeare's success in the public theater both validates his plays and makes them marketable. Something has to be explained away, accounted for, to justify the publication of an unper-formed play. Soon enough, of course, the published texts of plays would be the only basis for the performance of Shakespeare. But even in Shakespeare's lifetime there was an overlap between play texts as a memento of, or the basis for, performance, and as reading matter—and also, of course, for something in between, the "play-reading," a private, unstaged reading aloud, which made the book of the play performative in the same way poetry was in the period.

[30] Ibid., sig. ¶2^{v}.

| 3 |

Some Works

The Jonson and Shakespeare Folios

From plays to works

How does a text become a "work"? Modern bibliographical theorists distinguish the work from the text. As H. R. Woudhuysen
explains in a summary of the argument, the work is "a sort of Platonic
idea" which "may be based on one or more texts."[1] The Ben Jonson first
folio, issued in 1616 and edited by Jonson himself, was titled *The
Workes of Benjamin Jonson.* The first section consisted of plays. This
caused surprise and some disapproval: Jonson was criticized for including his plays in a volume of works.

> *To Mr. Ben Johnson, demanding the reason why he call'd his playes
> works.*
>   Pray tell me *Ben,* where doth the mystery lurke, What others call a
> play, you call a worke.[2]

---

[1] "Editors and Texts, Authorities and Originals," in Lukas Erne and Margaret Jane
Kidnie, eds., *Textual Performances* (Cambridge: Cambridge University Press, 2004), p. 40.
This is obviously not Jonson's point in calling his plays works, though it may be related to
the seventeenth-century debate.
[2] *Wits Recreations* (1640), no. 269, sig. G3^v.

The Idea of the Book and the Creation of Literature. Stephen Orgel, Oxford University Press.
© Stephen Orgel 2023. DOI: 10.1093/oso/9780192871534.003.0003

Plays for the popular stage were not "works." An admirer refuted the critique, not, however, by defending plays, but by making Jonson an exception:

> Thus answer'd by a friend in Mr. Johnsons defence.
> The authors friend thus for the author sayes.
> Bens plays are works, when others works are plaies.[3]

The question of what a "work" is, is related to the question of what a book is. The Latin word for book, *liber*, means both a scroll or codex (the modern form of book, with the pages bound at one edge) and part of a book; and in the latter case, not what we mean by a book. A book for us is a volume of written material, which may be transformed into something not material at all, but a series of textual images legible on an electronic screen (an e-book), or the text read aloud (an audiobook)—that is, the book is both its physical embodiment and its content, but it is the whole work. To the ancients, however, large important works were not books; rather, they were collections of books. Thus, there are twelve books of the *Aeneid*, ten of the *Pharsalia*, twenty-four of the *Iliad* and *Odyssey*, five books of Moses comprising the Torah;[4] and in English, *Troilus and Criseyde* in five books, *The Faerie Queene* in six and a bit of a seventh—perhaps intended to be twelve or thirteen—*Paradise Lost* in ten (following Lucan) or twelve (following Virgil), *Paradise Regain'd* in four, *The Prelude* in thirteen or fourteen, *Paterson* in five or six. Servius in the fourth century, beginning his commentary on the *Aeneid*, says he will discuss *numerus librorum, ordo librorum*, the number and order of the books comprising the epic. By late classical times a typical work was made up of a number of books, reflecting the physical makeup of the work, with each book occupying a separate scroll; and for several centuries after the invention of printing the

---

[3] Ibid., no. 270.

[4] The twenty-four books of the *Iliad* and *Odyssey* were not referred to as books by the Greeks—the first Greek writer to call a section of a work *biblos* appears to have been Diodorus Siculus in the first century BC. See Carolyn Higbie, "Divide and Edit: A Brief History of Book Divisions," *Harvard Studies in Classical Philology* 105 (2010), pp. 16–17. The Torah consists of five books only in English. In Hebrew, each of the five books is a *chumash*, meaning literally a fifth (of the whole Torah, literally the law); *sefer* in the phrase *Sefer Torah*, the book of the Torah, is literally a scroll, though it is now used for a book.

design and production of substantial texts preserved that sense, sometimes even starting the page numbering over.

But what constitutes a "work," a text that we recognize as important literature or philosophy or science, a book that is not merely written matter but something we value and preserve, and therefore produce in large handsome volumes on good paper and sell for a great deal of money; something that is kept, edited, reprinted, not simply read and discarded? Jonson calling his plays works would be analogous to our calling comic books literature—and that that is starting to happen, with the comic book rebranded a graphic novel, as the play was renamed a work—or to publishing the screenplay of a successful movie and declaring it literature. This much more rarely happens, even in the case of famous authors who wrote screenplays, for example, Faulkner, who wrote eight, and Fitzgerald, who wrote three. One would think that their names alone would warrant publication of those scripts, but not only are they not considered literature, they are not considered marketable.

Before 1600, in the decades leading up to Jonson's *Workes*, even when plays were popular enough in the public theaters to be worth publishing, the author's name was generally not felt to contribute to their marketability. *Tamburlaine* and *The Spanish Tragedy*, both hugely successful on stage, were published anonymously; the latter was first credited to "M. Kid" in Thomas Heywood's *Apology for Actors* (1612), when the play had been in theaters for at least twenty-five years (and the identification went unnoticed until the late eighteenth century).[5] In this case, it seems more likely that Kyd's authorship was generally known but not considered of much interest than that only Heywood was aware of it. But *Tamburlaine* was not ascribed to Marlowe until the nineteenth century, and here the question of contemporary knowledge of his authorship is much more uncertain.[6] For comparison, the directors and stars of popular films are celebrated today, but the authors of the screenplays are largely ignored. Shakespeare was well known as a

---

[5] Heywood, *Apology* (1612), E3^{v}. The ascription was first noted in Thomas Hawkins's *The Origin of the English Drama* (1773).

[6] For the history of ascriptions of the authorship of *Tamburlaine* see András Kiséry, "An Author and a Bookshop: Publishing Marlowe's Remains at the Black Bear," *Philological Quarterly* 91.3 (Summer 2012), pp. 361–92.

poet after 1593 with the publication of *Venus and Adonis*, which names him as the author (though not on the title page); but no play is credited to him until *Love's Labour's Lost* in 1598—not *Romeo and Juliet, Richard the Second, Richard the Third, Henry the Fourth*: these were all very popular and successful, both as plays and books, but the author's name was not a selling point. What was considered the selling point in the printed editions of these plays was the name of the acting company, or the fact that it was played publicly "to great applause." A little later, the fact that the play was performed before the queen or king would be prominently featured on the title page; the royal audience was a guarantee of quality.

But soon enough format was a sufficient guarantee of quality. In 1610 Sir Thomas Bodley warned his first librarian Thomas James not to acquire for the Bodleian library any "riffe-raffes" and "baggage books," in which he included almanacs, pamphlets and "Englishe plaies."[7] The library, however, not only acquired the Shakespeare first folio in 1623 but even provided a special binding for its copy.[8] This probably does not indicate any change of heart about plays, but it certainly acknowledges the dignity of the format—a folio was not a "riffe-raffe." In 1664, the library replaced the volume with the second issue of the third folio, which includes seven additional plays that had been credited to Shakespeare in his lifetime: the most desirable edition was not the first edition, but the newest and most comprehensive one, and the library now wanted to be up to date with its Shakespeare plays. (By 1910, when first folios had become seriously valuable, the library bought back its original copy for £3000, the highest price it had ever paid for a book.)[9]

---

[7] W. D. McCray, *Annals of the Bodleian Library, Oxford, A.D. 1598–A.D. 1867* (London: Rivington, 1868), p. 66.

[8] The folio was one of a consignment of ten books bound for the library at the same time. Andrew Honey, the library's Senior Conservator, has recently determined that "the First Folio was covered in a different more expensive high quality dark brown leather." See Peter D. Matthews, "Leather Cover of the Bodleian First Folio," available only online at https://www.academia.edu/30971029/Leather_Cover_of_the_Bodleian_First_Folio (accessed January 15, 2022).

[9] £3000 in 1910 was the equivalent of about $500,000 today, from a twenty-first-century perspective a modest sum for a first folio. The library had to make a public appeal for funds to keep the book in England; the purchaser thus preempted was Henry Clay Folger.

Jonson's *Workes*

Critical attention has from the very beginning focused on Jonson's audacity in issuing his plays in folio and declaring them "works," but equally audacious was the fact that the volume appeared while he was alive, and that he oversaw its publication. Most volumes that publishers declared Works in English were scientific, theological, philosophical, or historical, and their authors were long dead—*Certaine workes of Galens*; *The famous and memorable workes of Josephus*; *The most excellent worckes of chirurgerye of Giovanni da Vigo*; *The workes of Sir Thomas More Knyght*—the last of these included, along with a great deal of political theory and invective, some early poetry. Exclusively literary "works" were for the most part monuments, memorials to great writers of the past—Chaucer, Skelton, John Heywood, George Gascoigne, Sir David Lindsay, all were dignified with volumes of "works" in the sixteenth or early seventeenth century (the Countess of Pembroke's folio collection of her brother Sir Philip Sidney's literary remains in 1598 were not called "works"); and in 1611 Matthew Lownes published a folio of *The Faerie Queene* with "*the Other works of England's Arch-poët, Edm. Spencer.*" But before Jonson, the only English poets whose "works" were published during their lifetimes were the prolific Nicholas Breton, Gascoigne's stepson, in 1577 (at the age of 32), under the title *The Workes of a young wyt*; and Samuel Daniel in 1601, including his play *The Tragedie of Cleopatra*, with a second issue in 1602, and another somewhat different collection in 1607, this time adding two more plays. The fact that Jonson was criticized and Daniel was not probably had largely to do with the fact that Daniel's plays were "closet drama," not intended for the public stage, but even more with the different characters of the two writers: Jonson made enemies, whereas Daniel, even to Jonson, "was a good honest man," though he was "no poet."[10] Daniel's 1601 *Works* was in the Bodleian Library by 1605, and it was Daniel's volume that served as the English model for, and thus also enabled, Jonson's.

---

[10] *Informations to William Drummond of Hawthorndon*, in Jonson, Ben, *The Cambridge Edition of the Works of Ben Jonson*, eds. David Bevington, Martin Butler, and Ian Donaldson, vol. 5, p. 360, line 16.

Although Daniel's *Works* is a handsomely printed folio, it is very clearly a collection of individual pieces. The pagination is not continuous—this is less likely to reflect an adoption of the classical mode than a certain disorganization in the printing house: the volume exhibits curious lacunae. There are no commendatory verses and no table of contents; the only preliminary matter is a dedication to the queen,[11] and the first work in the collection, the six books of the *Civill Warres*, begins abruptly, without even a title, which first appears only at the beginning of Book Five, 134 pages into the work—even the running heads up to Book Five read only "The First Booke," "The Second Booke," etc., with no indication of what work these books are part of. There was doubtless some carelessness in the preparation of the volume, but its haphazard organization also reveals considerable uncertainty about how to present a collection of literary works by a living author some of which had never been printed before. In contrast, Daniel's 1607 *Certaine Small Workes*, though much less lavishly produced, begins with both a table of contents and a long epistle to the reader; and each work has not only its own title page but also a separate dedication. Here too, however, there is much confusion in the organization: the Argument of *The Tragedie of Philotas* is followed not by the play, but by the title page and dedication of *The Tragedie of Cleopatra*. This in turn is followed not by its play, but by the title page of *Musophilus*, with two dedications. Then comes not the poem, but the text of *Philotas*, followed by the long poem *The Letter of Octavia*, and then, finally, the Argument and text of *Cleopatra*. *Musophilus*, which had been announced over a hundred pages earlier, is printed next; and the organization is rational thereafter. The works beginning with the text of *Cleopatra* are paginated continuously by leaves, starting with leaf 1 (though with several errors), but the previous 106 pages are not paginated at all.[12]

---

[11] In the Bodleian copy, a gift from the poet, the dedication to the queen has been replaced with a dedication to the Library, which has been tipped in. For a discussion of the acquisition of the volume by the Library, see John Pitcher, " 'After the Manner of Horace': Samuel Daniel in the Bodleian in 1605," *Papers of the Bibliographical Society of America* 13.2 (June, 2019), pp. 149–86.

[12] There are bibliographical confusions as well: quire A has only seven of its eight leaves. The *ESTC* explains that A8 was intended as a cancel, to replace O7, which has an erroneous catchword. In most surviving copies, however, A8 has been correctly removed,

Clearly Jonson learned from the defects in the production of Daniel's *Works*, and was actively involved in the design and printing of his own huge volume. Daniel's general title page used a standard woodcut cartouche; Jonson's has the complex engraved title specifically designed to his order, and unique to this book. It is not even used in the posthumous second volume, issued in 1640, where it would certainly have been appropriate, nor in the 1692 third folio. Jonson moved all the commendatory poems from the earlier editions of the individual works to the front, including testimonials by George Chapman, Hugh Holland, and three by Francis Beaumont. These are preceded by two poems composed especially for the volume, in Latin by John Selden, and in English by Selden's close associate Edward Heyward. The book thus had a small, carefully curated set of very distinguished testimonials.

Jonson also did a good deal of revising, not only of the texts. As the Cambridge editors explain:

> Jonson's editorial management of his collected writings...idealized his texts by removing evidence of internal development and authorial biography.... Jonson added dedicatory letters to various works, which had the effect of framing strategically the texts which they prefaced. He rewrote several texts in order to convey an impression of premature maturity in himself as young playwright. Instead of reprinting the first play in the collection, *Every Man In His Humour*, as it had appeared in quarto in 1601, Jonson gave to the press the version that he had radically revised some years later. Jonson's dedication to William Camden, calling *Every Man In His Humour* "the first fruits of my studies," thus encouraged the impression that his genius had instantaneously leapt into life in the late 1590s. This impression depends, however, on the 1616 collection beginning with a text that

but O7 remains. See http://estc.bl.uk/F/CP3VDQQ8RVFGPUTEVJISK3Q8PF4GD8X
RGKK7A29YXHYQDXESEQ-01412?func=full-set-set&set_number=069884&set_entry=
000005&format=999 (accessed May 10, 2021). This accounts for the seven-leaf quire A; it also means that quire A was printed after quire O. Sir Walter Greg explains that quire A was originally omitted from the sequence, and when the cancels were printed they were illogically signed A and therefore bound between the prefatory quire and quire B; "clearly leaves 1–4 were intended to replace G3, the title of *Cleopatra*, and leaves 5–7 that of 'Musophilus' (the final blank being discarded)." Greg adds that "In no known copy were the cancels effected." *A Bibliography of the English Printed Drama To the Restoration* (London: The Bibliographical Society/Oxford University Press, 1957), vol. 3, p. 1053. I am indebted to John Mustain for help with this maddening bibliographical puzzle.

was not only preceded by other plays, but must have been rewritten at a later point or points.... Jonson's grouping of the texts into plays, poems, and masques further imposes a narrative onto his career. It implies that he had moved effortlessly out of the playhouse and into the worlds of patronage poetry and crown service, and it carefully locates the poetry in a personal space between the more public arenas of theatre and court.[13]

The revision of works as they were presented in the collection was a revision of the career.

For the dramas in the folio, act and scene divisions are scrupulously indicated, as they also are in the quartos, but though some of the plays are revised to be more literary (as with the added scenes in *Cynthias Revels* and the character sketches in the cast list of *Every Man Out of His Humour*), for *Sejanus* the quarto's scholarly marginalia were removed, and stage directions inserted (*"They passe over the stage," "He turnes to Sejanus clyents"*). The folio's *Sejanus* is thus more theatrical than the quarto's. What is missing throughout the quarto and folio plays, for what the Renaissance recognized as a truly classical presentation, are prefatory arguments; but otherwise, even in quarto Jonson's plays looked distinctly classical. Quartos of English plays for the public theaters normally did not indicate acts and scenes and had little or no paratextual apparatus. It has to be added, however, that the look that was being imitated was not anything authentically classical, but sixteenth-century humanist editions of Roman drama, which provide the plays with arguments and cast lists, and indicate act and scene divisions—Mark Bland suggests that Jonson and his publisher were looking at late sixteenth-century editions of the Roman dramatists, and particularly at a 1583 French edition of Plautus, which Jonson owned.[14]

---

[13] Cambridge Ben Jonson, vol. 1, lxv–lxvi. *The Case Is Altered* was an earlier play than *Every Man In His Humour*, and was not included in the folio, though it was published in quarto by a consortium of booksellers in 1609. It has been assumed that Jonson suppressed the play, as he suppressed his lost early *Richard Crookback*, but Robert Miola in the Cambridge edition explains that "the copyright for *The Case Is Altered* in the years preceding the folio still belonged to the booksellers who published the quarto in 1609.... It is entirely possible that Jonson did not disown *The Case Is Altered* at the time of the folio, but that he did not own it, i.e. he did not have the rights to it for republication." Ibid., p. 6.

[14] Mark Bland, "William Stansby and the Production of *The Workes of Beniamin Jonson,* 1615–16," *The Library* 20 (March, 1998), p. 24. See also Lynn S. Meskill, "Ben

Similarly, the plays in Thomas Newton's collection of English translations of Seneca (1581) are provided with arguments and names of the
speakers; all have act divisions (though not scenes) and several in
addition are prefaced with cast lists. The only plays published in
Greek in England in the sixteenth century, Euripides's *Troades* (1575)
and Aristophanes's *Knights* (1593), have arguments and cast lists, but
no act or scene divisions (as is correct for Greek drama), though the
Knights marks *parabasis, strophe, antistrophe,* etc.[15] The Cambridge
editors characterize Jonson's revisions as being designed "to create a
more visually unified and stylistically classical form,"[16] which is doubtless correct, but Jonson's drama in print had always emulated what the
sixteenth century recognized as classical, with classical meaning specifically Roman.

Even more audacious than the insistence that plays were works was
Jonson's inclusion of his masques and entertainments in the volume.
Many of these underwent far more extensive editing than the plays, to
make clear not only their ethical seriousness but also Jonson's place in
the world of royal and noble patronage. So these "toyes," as Bacon
called them, were weighted down with marginalia citing authorities and
sources, and with commentary describing the productions and specify-
ing the aristocratic performers. Nor did the revisions stop there: sometimes the occasion either did not suit with the seriousness claimed for
the text or subsequently appeared discreditable, and had to be con-
cealed. Thus all Jonson's entertainments commissioned by the City
livery companies were excluded with the exception of that for the
royal entry of 1604, "incorrectly but tellingly retitled as an entertainment 'for the coronation.'"[17] And the masque *Hymenaei,* as it appears
in the folio, suppresses the information that it was written for the

---

Jonson's 1616 Folio: A Revolution in Print," *Études Épistémè* [*sic*] 14 (2008), https://doi.
org/10.4000/episteme.736 (accessed May 12, 2021).

[15] Aristotle implied a three-part structure to the plot (beginning, middle, end); but this
was not interpreted as a dramatic three-act structure until Roman times (the three acts
were protasis, epitasis, catastrophe). The five-act structure of acts and scenes was devel-
oped for Roman drama.

[16] David L. Gants and Tom Lockwood, "The Printing and Publishing of Ben Jonson's
Works," in The Cambridge Ben Jonson, vol. 1, p. clxxi.

[17] The Cambridge Ben Jonson, vol. 1, p. lxvi.

wedding of Frances Howard with the Earl of Essex in 1606: by 1616 the marriage had been dissolved with much notoriety, and the bride and her new husband were in prison charged with complicity in the murder of Sir Thomas Overbury.

The Jonson folio was an immense undertaking, over a thousand pages, with exceptionally generous margins and a handsome layout— only two of the masques, very late in the volume, lapse briefly into double columns (Jonson was by this time no longer constantly on the scene; the printers were probably running out of paper, and perhaps also out of time and patience). The printing took about three years, and involved over 2500 changes in proof.

The Shakespeare folio

The Shakespeare folio has fewer pages, though it comprises more text. It is a great deal less lavish with layout and margins, and though because of an extended interruption it took even longer to print,[18] it certainly represented a better investment: a second edition was warranted after only nine years, whereas there was no call for a new Jonson folio for twenty-four years, and none after that until 1692. It was also, probably inevitably, much less carefully produced, since the author was not involved. The Shakespeare folio is also unlike the Jonson folio in that it is very clearly not Works, and does not claim to be: it is *Mr. William Shakespeares Comedies, Histories, & Tragedies.* Shakespeare in his own time was best known to the reading public as the poet of *Venus and Adonis* and *Lucrece*, but the canonical collection of his writings in the seventeenth century, preserved in the first four folios, included only plays.

The Shakespeare folio was designed to be a very expensive book, but with its double-column text it looks significantly less lavish than the Jonson folio. It was also much less carefully proofread, including about

---

[18] The interruption occurred during the printing of *Richard II*—that is, in the middle of the Histories—and lasted for almost a year, during which the printers produced two other volumes, both of which were expected to sell quickly. The Shakespeare folio was a longer-term investment, and they were in no hurry to finish. See W. W. Greg, *The Shakespeare First Folio* (Oxford: Clarendon Press, 1955), pp. 440–3.

500 press corrections, one-fifth of the Jonson folio's—the latter, of course, included not only corrections but also Jonson's revisions. There was clearly much less editorial oversight than there was with the Jonson volume.[19] The printing of the book appears to have been afflicted with problems similar to those of the 1607 Daniel volume. *Troilus and Cressida* had originally been placed after *Romeo and Juliet*—despite the quarto's characterization of it as "full of the palme comicall" and like "the best commedy in Terence or Plautus," for the folio editors it was a tragedy: certainly it does not end happily. But during the printing of the section of tragedies a problem was encountered with the rights to the play, and it was removed. Assuming that the rights would eventually be obtained, the printers calculated the number of pages the play would require, and continued printing with *Julius Caesar*. By the time the rest of the volume was complete, however, the business of *Troilus* remained unresolved, and its space was filled with a much shorter play, *Timon of Athens* (now generally considered a collaboration with Thomas Middleton), which had almost certainly never been performed. The result was a gap of eleven pages in the numbering between the end of *Timon* and the beginning of *Julius Caesar*.

But after the printing of the preliminaries, which were done last, the rights to *Troilus* were finally negotiated, and it was reinserted at the beginning of the tragedy section—this was as close as possible to its original position, but it meant that *Coriolanus*, which originally began the tragedies, was now preceded by *Troilus and Cressida*, the first three pages of which had already been printed, with the first page unnumbered, but the second and third numbered 79 and 80 (the last page of *Romeo and Juliet* is 77, though to accommodate the new *Troilus* it had to be reprinted and was erroneously numbered 79). Even this was problematic: the original text had been simply a reprint of the 1609 quarto; the restored text was a different one, with many variants from the quarto, and most significantly, with a page-long prologue, which is not in the quarto and was not in the play as it was first being printed in

---

[19] Greg suggests that the most likely proofreader for the volume was the bookkeeper of The King's Men, Edward Knight. *The Shakespeare First Folio*, p. 78. I regret that Ben Higgins, *Shakespeare's Syndicate: The First Folio, Its Publishers, and the Early Modern Book Trade* (Oxford: Oxford University Press, 2022) appeared too late for me to take it into account.

the folio. But since the play originally began on a verso with a blank recto, the new prologue was printed there, in large type with very large margins, to take up the whole page. It was simply headed, however, "The Prologue," with no indication of what it is the prologue to. The three original pages follow, with the remainder unnumbered after 79 and 80; and *Coriolanus* then begins on a page numbered 1. *Troilus and Cressida* is not listed in the volume's table of contents, which would have been printed before the play was finally included.

There are also problematic elements in the design of the huge volume. Jonson's chronological organization had made sense as the author's presentation of his own career. Such an arrangement would probably not have been possible for Shakespeare's editors, requiring more information about the history of the plays' composition than they had; but except in the case of the histories, the generic arrangement is really a grab-bag, with the order of the comedies and tragedies reflecting only the order in which the plays were made ready for the press. And though the histories are organized according to the dates of the reigns involved, even that has its arbitrary element: the sequence covers the century from the reign of Richard II to that of Richard III, but with the much earlier *King John* tacked onto the beginning and the later *Henry VIII* at the end, and with the plays about still earlier British history, *King Lear* and *Cymbeline*, moved into the section of tragedies.

Even the classicizing of the texts by adding acts and scenes was haphazard. The quartos have none. The folio supplies most of the histories with acts, but only occasionally with scenes; and in the second and third parts of *Henry VI* with no act and scene divisions whatever after the opening announcement *Actus Primus. Scæna Prima*. In the tragedies *Hamlet*, as we have seen, has acts and scenes until 2.2, and not thereafter. The Roman plays *Titus Andronicus*, *Julius Caesar*, and *Coriolanus* have acts and no scenes; but *Anthony and Cleopatra* has only the initial *Actus Primus. Scæna Prima*. So do *Romeo and Juliet* and *Timon of Athens,* but *King Lear*, *Othello*, and *Cymbeline* have the full complement. Of the comedies, the first three plays *The Tempest, The Merry Wives of Windsor*, and *Measure for Measure* have both acts and scenes; and thereafter most have acts but no scenes, with the exception of *As You Like It*, *Twelfth Night*, and *The Winter's Tale*, which have both. (Act divisions appear to be original in plays for the private theaters—for example, *The Tempest* at the end of Act 4 has Prospero onstage, and at the beginning of Act 5 has him entering. This might mean that a scene is missing, but it is more likely that it indicates a pause in the action, to be filled, for example, with music.)

Representing the author

The Jonson folio was obviously an important precedent for the Shakespeare folio, even if the precedent was erratically followed. But there is a significant difference between the two books, which is apparent at the outset: the Shakespeare folio has the author's portrait on the title page, but there is no portrait of Jonson in the folio of his works. The volume has only the elaborate engraved title page, clearly designed to Jonson's order, which, as we have seen, is unique to this book—it could not be repurposed, and was not even reused in subsequent editions of Jonson's own work.

The 1616 folio was designed as an epitome of Jonson's career, but as I have indicated, he did not want his portrait in his book. The only surviving portraits of Jonson, whether painted or engraved, all derive from a single prototype by Abraham van Blyenberch (Figure 3.1).

Visually, this is Jonson's immortality, but no allusion to Blyenberch or the portrait survives in Jonson's writings—apparently it simply did not mean much to him. A Blyenberch portrait of Jonson is recorded among the Duke of Buckingham's paintings, and it was probably Buckingham, not Jonson, who commissioned the portrait. Buckingham and Jonson became closely associated in 1621, during the preparations for the masque *The Gipsies Metamorphosed,* written for Buckingham. That would have been a logical time for Buckingham to want a portrait of his poet—Blyenberch left England in 1622.[20] So this is Jonson in his late forties.

The only portraits Jonson memorialized are two lost ones. Of the first, by his friend Sir William Borlase, MP and High Sheriff of Buckinghamshire and not otherwise known as a painter, Jonson says in a poem called "The Poet to the Painter", "You made it a brave piece, but

---

[20] The National Portrait Gallery, which owns the painting, dates it 1617. This seems to me very unlikely.

FIGURE 3.1 Abraham van Blyenberch, portrait of Ben Jonson. © National Portrait Gallery, London.

not like me."[21] The other is the miniature described in the poem "On His Picture Left in Scotland," which was entirely too much like him, depicting his "hundred of grey hairs" and "rocky face" at the age of 47.[22] It is surely not irrelevant that in his prefatory poem to the Shakespeare folio facing its author's portrait on the title page, Jonson admonished the reader to "look / Not on his picture, but his book."

After Jonson's death in 1637, however, his image became essential to his works. In 1640 the version of the Blyenberch portrait engraved by Robert Vaughan (Figure 1.22) faced the title page of the second edition of the folio. He is more stylishly dressed than Blyenberch's Jonson, and is now crowned with laurel. The motto on the cartouche declares him "the most learned of English poets." The engraving had been done many years earlier—it was in existence by 1627—and book collectors by the end of the century began regularly adding it to their copies of the 1616 folio, as if something were missing.

---

[21] *Underwood,* 52.
[22] *Underwood,* 9.

But nothing was missing, and Jonson's resistance to being identified with his picture, rather than his book, was, even during his lifetime, eccentric. The 1613 edition of Florio's Montaigne included a handsome bust of Florio (though not one of Montaigne); Chapman's 1616 Homer showed the translator as semidivine, with his head in the clouds and a hint of a halo; Michael Drayton's 1619 *Poems* had a grimly elegant frontispiece portrait. Shakespeare's editors put the portrait front and center. Jonson's attitude must have seemed highminded but quixotic: author-portraits helped to sell books. So, also in 1640, Vaughan's Jonson faced the title page of the quarto of *An Execration Against Vulcan,* and an appropriately classicized version by William Marshall introduced the duodecimo of his translation of Horace's *Art of Poetry*. The frontispiece of the huge 1692 folio was a much grander revision of the portrait, and more graceful and gracious versions appeared in the eighteenth century depicting a less formidable and more sociable Jonson.

Shakespeare's portrait for the 1623 folio was by Martin Droeshout, a young and inexperienced artist. At Shakespeare's death, in 1616, he was fifteen years old; he was twenty-two when the folio was published, and this image is, so far as we know, his first commissioned work. If the engraving derives from a portrait made from life, the portrait must have been done by someone else and Droeshout must have adapted it many years later. In fact, Droeshout's presence on the title page of this elaborately produced, very expensive book is a puzzle. The portraits included in similar volumes in the period are for the most part provided by a small group of very accomplished artists: Simon van de Passe, Cornelis Boel, William Hole, Robert Vaughan, William Marshall.[23]

---

[23] Indeed, so problematic has the portrait seemed that it has been doubted that Droeshout the Younger can have been responsible for it, or even that he was an engraver. Mary Edmond, "It Was For Gentle Shakespeare Cut," *Shakespeare Quarterly* 42.3 (1991), pp. 339–44, argues energetically that the folio engraver was in fact Droeshout's uncle, Martin Droeshout the elder; but since there is no surviving work by this artist with which to compare the Shakespeare portrait, the claim is speculative at best. Edmond also claims that there is no documentary evidence for the younger Droeshout as an engraver, or indeed, at all after his birth record in 1601. Christian Schuckman, however, in "The Engraver of the First Folio Portrait of William Shakespeare," *Print Quarterly* 8.1 (1991), pp. 40–3—obviously published too late for Edmonds to take it into account—shows that the younger Droeshout emigrated to Spain in the late 1620s, and reproduces a number of engravings done by him there. One of these bears a striking similarity to the Shakespeare

Moreover, the very fact that the portrait is on the title page is puzzling. Normally the author's portrait, especially if it is engraved, will be facing the title page, as a frontispiece—especially if it is engraved, because it is difficult to combine typesetting and engraving on the same page. If the portrait had been a woodcut, there would have been no problem: woodcuts can be printed on the same press with, and at the same time as, type. Engravings, however, require a different printing technique, and the Shakespeare title page therefore would have had to go through two separate processes. The usual way of dealing with this, if one wanted an engraving on the title page, was to engrave the whole page, as was done for the Jonson folio, Drayton's *Poly-Olbion* (1613), King James's *Workes* (1616), Chapman's Homer (1611/1616), and innumerable other large, important, expensive books. The publishers of Shakespeare were making trouble for themselves.

Opposite the title page, where the frontispiece would normally go, is a poem in large type—this, technically, is the frontispiece.[24] The poem is addressed To the Reader, and urges us to ignore the portrait:

> This Figure, that thou here seest put,
> It was for gentle Shakespeare cut;
> Wherein the Graver had a strife
> with Nature, to out-doo the life:
> O, could he but have drawne his wit
> As well in brasse, as he hath hit
> His face, the Print would then surpasse
> All, that was ever writ in brasse.
> But, since he cannot, Reader, looke
> Not on his Picture, but his Booke.

"Looke / Not on his Picture, but his Booke": the poem construes the portrait and the book as alternatives, or even adversaries. The poem is signed only with the initials B. I., and has always been credited to Ben

---

portrait, and leaves little doubt that Martin the younger is the folio's Droeshout. The explanation for his elusiveness is apparently simply that he was Catholic, and found more patrons in Catholic Spain.

[24] For the second issue of the third folio (1664) and the fourth folio (1685) the engraving was moved to its more normative position facing the title page, with the poem beneath it.

Jonson. This is doubtless correct, but it is worth remarking that Jonson's other dedicatory poem in the volume is signed in his characteristic way, Ben: Ionson, and Jonson did not subsequently include the poem anywhere among his works. In effect, he disowned the poem in the course of dismissing Shakespeare's portrait.

Establishing a canon

It has been suggested that for the publisher Edward Blount, the Shakespeare folio was a bad investment, and even that it bankrupted him because by 1630 he had sold his rights in the book to Robert Allott and was out of business, but it is more likely that Blount, who was nearing 70, simply decided to retire—his printer William Jaggard had died in 1623, and Jaggard's son Isaac, who succeeded him, had died in 1627. Allott clearly considered the Shakespeare folio a valuable property, since he had it reprinted very quickly; it was published in 1632. The second folio, moreover, was firmly modeled on the first, basically a page for page reprint, retaining even the dangling Prologue to *Troilus and Cressida*. But not entirely: in addition to a large number of minor editorial adjustments, it corrects mistakes in Holofernes's Latin in *Love's Labour's Lost*. There is doubtless some pedantry on display in this, but one may wonder what the editor thought was being corrected. Are the mistakes Shakespeare's, or those of the scribe who prepared the play for the press, or of the first compositor incorrectly transcribing a correct manuscript? Or are the mistakes perfectly correct, and is the point that Holofernes's Latin is at fault?

Whether the second folio was a good investment for Allott is unclear. No new edition was called for until 1663, more than thirty years later; and even then, a simple reissue of the book turned out to sell poorly. A year later the volume was republished with seven additional plays that had been credited to Shakespeare in his lifetime—more Shakespeare was more desirable Shakespeare (and the Bodleian Library duly replaced its first folio). This in fact is the rarest of the folios, since a good deal of the stock was destroyed in the London fire of 1666. But in a striking piece of cultural pathology, it was the first folio that ultimately became the seriously valuable one, and the basis of the Shakespeare canon.

The first folio is not at all a rare book. It was published in 1623 in an edition of about 750 copies, of which 233 copies survive; 53 of these are considered complete, including all blanks and preliminaries.[25] That is a large survival rate for a book of the period, and suggests that the book was more treasured than read. For comparison, there are many fewer surviving copies of the Gutenberg Bible, an even more iconic book that constitutes the beginning of printing in the Western world. It was published in 1455; there now exist forty-eight copies, twenty of them complete. And Gutenberg Bibles, unlike Shakespeare folios, are really hard to come by—the last complete copy came up for sale in 1978. It is often claimed that only one copy of the Shakespeare first folio remains in private hands, the implication being that they are impossible to buy; but in fact, institutions sell their copies fairly regularly, and one comes up at auction on average every five years. Recent auction prices for the book have ranged from about $6 million to almost $10 million—the last one sold at Christie's in 2020 for $9,978,000. There are of course no comparable recent sale figures for the Gutenberg Bible, but the complete one that sold in 1978 cost $2.2 million, and in 1984 an incomplete copy, just the Old Testament, sold for $5.4 million. Allowing for inflation, that is more than the Shakespeare folio figures, but of the same order of magnitude. A more informative comparison, however, is with the Nuremberg Chronicle, published in 1493, one of the great monuments of early printing, where the survival figures are about the same as those for the Shakespeare folio. That not-very-rare book comes up for sale frequently. At the annual California book fair there are always two or three copies to be had, usually priced between $90,000 and $150,000.

Obviously the Shakespeare folio is a more desirable book—how much more desirable is indicated by another unusual thing about it: that serious collectors have often wanted to own multiple copies. The Folger Library in Washington has the most by far, at eighty-two; Meisei University in Tokyo has twelve; the New York Public Library six, the British Library five, the Huntington Library four. (Interestingly, the

---

[25] According to Eric Rasmussen, "There are 53 known complete copies with all preliminary leaves and all 445 text leaves. An additional 19 copies are complete save for $^{\pi}$A1, and a further 14 copies are complete save that they lack both $^{\pi}$A1 *and* $^{\pi}$A1+1." (Private communication—thank you!)

first purchaser of whom we have a record, Sir Edward Dering, in December 1623, a week or so after publication, bought two copies.) It is true that not all copies of the folio are identical—that is true of most books published before the eighteenth century—but they are certainly all the same book, and if you were spending many millions to establish your cultural sophistication, surely one copy would be enough. (Henry Clay Folger's desire for multiple copies was reasonable, in that he was interested specifically in the text of Shakespeare, and believed, correctly, that only by comparing many copies could a correct text be finally established.) In contrast, the Nuremberg Chronicle is a much more interesting piece of printing, but libraries do not pride themselves on how many copies they own.

The first folio's price remained fairly stable until the middle of the eighteenth century—there was a new edition of Shakespeare every ten years or so in that period, but editors based their texts on the fourth folio. The return to the first folio as the best text came only after 1760, when Samuel Johnson, preparing his great edition, called attention to the many errors in the fourth folio. After that, the first folio was the "right" folio, and its value began to increase. In 1756 a copy sold for a little over £3; by 1790 the going price was £35. By the beginning of the twentieth century a first folio cost between $5000 and $10,000—not, by this time, because scholars needed it to work from, but because millionaires, especially Americans, with cultural aspirations, wanted it in their collections. At the same time, Shakespeare became a subject of study at universities: the first Shakespeare courses were taught at Harvard, beginning in the 1870s. Shakespeare had become the touchstone of English literacy. Michael Dobson, director of the Shakespeare Institute in Stratford-Upon-Avon, sums it up this way: "during the eighteenth century the folio became the holy book of a new secular religion, bardolatry, . . . and by the late nineteenth century, the first folio was a natural destination for the excess profits of Anglophone millionaires, keen to own symbolic capital in the culture in which they have flourished."[26] The astonishing rise in the book's value is part of the history of both American conspicuous consumption and American public

---

[26] "Whatever You Do, Buy," *London Review of Books* 23.22 (November, 2001). Online at https://www.lrb.co.uk/the-paper/v23/n22/michael-dobson/whatever-you-do-buy (accessed February 21, 2022).

benevolence: Dobson writes, "the surviving Folios have migrated over time from private collections in Britain to privately endowed public ones in North America. In 1902, of 158 known copies, 100 were in the UK, 39 in the USA; today, of 228, there are 44 in Britain and 145 in the States.... Between 1893 and 1928 Henry Clay Folger, president of Standard Oil, bought no fewer than 79." The Folger Library is thus the great monument to that migration, but it was designed to be much more: Dobson observes that Folger opened his library "in 1932 on a site in the middle of Washington DC carefully selected to be on the line that joins the Lincoln Memorial, the Washington Monument, the Capitol and the Supreme Court—as if to write bardolatry into the American Constitution itself."[27]

Inventing romance

The new plays added to the second issue of the third folio included six that eventually again disappeared from the canon; but the seventh, *Pericles*, ultimately became a staple of the Shakespeare repertory, the first of the genre of romances. This new Shakespearean category was created by Edward Dowden in 1877:

> There is a romantic element about these plays. In all there is the same romantic incident of lost children recovered by those to whom they are dear—the daughters of Pericles and Leontes, the sons of Cymbeline and Alonso. In all there is a beautiful romantic background of sea or mountain. The dramas have a grave beauty, a sweet serenity, which seem to render the name "comedies" inappropriate; we may smile tenderly, but we never laugh loudly, as we read them. Let us, then, name this group consisting of four plays, Romances.[28]

Strictly speaking, however, *Pericles* is the only play that really fits the category, a play about a knight who travels the world having adventures, always on the edge of tragedy, but never tragic thanks to a series of happy, utterly improbable coincidences, and who is ultimately rescued by magic and miracle. *Pericles* had been one of Shakespeare's most

[27] Ibid.
[28] *Shakespeare* (London: Macmillan 1877), pp. 55–6.

popular plays in his own time, for readers as well as theatergoers: it went through six quarto editions by 1635, and earned a sneer from Jonson as a "mouldy tale."[29] Its absence from the folio may have been a matter of rights, but the folio compilers may have known that it was a collaborative play (as most modern scholars believe), and omitted it as they omitted *The Two Noble Kinsmen*, Shakespeare's acknowledged collaboration with John Fletcher. On the other hand, several plays that we believe were collaborative—the first two parts of *Henry VI*, *Measure for Measure*, *Timon of Athens*, *Henry VIII*, and *Macbeth* (which acknowledges its nonShakespearean material in its text)—are in the folio, and the editors may simply not have had access to a satisfactory text of *Pericles*.

It is worth pausing over the belated inclusion of *Pericles* in the canon, since the play figures so significantly in the construction of the modern Shakespeare. The seven plays added to the folio in 1664 were, in addition to *Pericles, The Yorkshire Tragedy, The Puritan Widow, Locrine, Thomas Lord Cromwell, The London Prodigal*, and *Sir John Oldcastle*. In this, the editors were both selective and haphazard: there were several more plays credited to Shakespeare in his lifetime that they missed, and in at least one case they apparently did not read beyond the title page: *Sir John Oldcastle* declares in a prefatory note that it is not by Shakespeare, and is in fact correcting the version of Oldcastle presented in Shakespeare's Falstaff. Nevertheless, the 1619 quarto of the play published by Thomas Pavier has Shakespeare's name on the title page—the original 1600 quarto does not—and that was enough to make it Shakespeare in 1664.[30]

Over the next century, the seven plays moved in and out of the Shakespeare canon. Nicholas Rowe in 1709 included them in his edition. Pope banished them in 1725, but his publisher included them

---

[29] "No doubt some mouldy tale / Like *Pericles*, and stale / As the shrieve's crust, and nasty as his fish...." *Ode to Himself* (on the failure of *The New Inn*). Ben Jonson, *Poems*, ed. Ian Donaldson (London: Oxford University Press, 1975), p. 355. The shrieve is the sheriff, who collected leftover and frequently stale food for the poor.

[30] Ten plays were issued in quarto by the publisher Thomas Pavier in 1619, with the intention of creating a collected Shakespeare by reprinting the existing quartos. The project was halted by the proprietors of the incipient first folio, though the printer for both was William Jaggard. Several of the Pavier quartos had false earlier dates on their titlepages, to imply that they were not new editions. Two of the ten plays, *The Yorkshire Tragedy* and *Sir John Oldcastle*, were not by Shakespeare.

in the second edition of Pope's Shakespeare three years later—more Shakespeare was more marketable Shakespeare, and purchasers of a complete Shakespeare might be willing to replace it with a more complete Shakespeare. Edmond Malone in 1780 settled the matter for later editors by rejecting all but *Pericles*: there was something in Malone's idea of Shakespeare that did not suit with six of the seven plays (and he would have read beyond the title page of *Sir John Oldcastle*). But *Pericles* was another matter: there was by 1780 something in *Pericles* that the idea of Shakespeare could not do without. What that something was, however, changed a number of times over the next two centuries.

We might assume that what Malone considered necessarily Shakespearean in it was its claims to transcendence, its affinities with *Anthony and Cleopatra* and *The Winter's Tale*—in short, its "lateness"—but those only became part of the play's character a century later: for Malone it was—*self-evidently* (this is worth emphasizing)—an early play, one of Shakespeare's earliest: he dated it 1592.[31] For Malone, *Pericles* was Shakespeare before he became Shakespeare (rather like the current critical status of *Edward III*).

It remained an early play until 1839, when John Payne Collier called attention to a reference to a performance of *Pericles* in 1608 that described the play as new. He also cited George Wilkins's novel *The Painful Adventures of Pericles Prince of Tyre*, published in 1608, which declares itself based on the play, and has significant verbal similarities to it. Subsequently, however, Collier had his own doubts, deciding that *Pericles* was in fact an early play that Shakespeare reworked. This was the line that most critics thereafter took, until late in the century, when Edward Dowden declared it the first of the late plays, and invented the category of romance for them.

For us, *Pericles* is a late play—one would say obviously, except that for so long, to so many careful readers (including Coleridge), it seemed obviously early. Given the date now universally accepted, 1608, we can see it as concluding the period in which Shakespeare composed his

---

[31] See the excellent paper on the early/late question by Lucy Munro: "Young Shakespeare/Late Shakespeare: The Case of *Pericles*," *Actes des congrès de la Société française Shakespeare* [online], 34|2016, http://journals.openedition.org/shakespeare/3668; DOI:10.4000/shakespeare.3668 (accessed April 30, 2019).

greatest and most uncompromising tragedies—it almost seems designed as an antidote to them. It comes two or three years after *King Lear*, a year or two after *Macbeth*, within the same year as *Anthony and Cleopatra* and *Coriolanus*. The plays of the following three years are *Cymbeline*, *The Winter's Tale*, and *The Tempest*. These share with *Pericles* a dramatic reliance on nonrealistic and sometimes magical modes of action, and in them tragedy can be reversed, and find a way through evil and suffering to a happy ending. If the happy endings seem forced, we should remind ourselves that forced and illogical endings are nothing new in Shakespeare: the tragic ending of *King Lear*, the defeat of King Lear and the death of Cordelia, are Shakespeare's revision of the story he found in the chronicles. In all the sources, Lear is restored to his throne and Cordelia rules after him. It is Shakespeare's tragic ending that is forced, and would have been entirely unexpected for the original audiences. And even earlier, there is nothing conclusive about Shakespearean endings: think of *Love's Labour's Lost* and *Twelfth Night*, with their unexpectedly postponed marriages; *Measure for Measure* with Isabella's silence at the Duke's proposal; *All's Well That Ends Well*, which concludes with the ambiguous observation that "All yet seems well."

But for readers before Dowden, *Pericles* was—obviously—Shakespeare learning his craft. Where we cite passages that seem to echo *King Lear* and *The Winter's Tale*, verse of a sort *obviously* not available to the Shakespeare of *The Two Gentlemen of Verona* and *Titus Andronicus*, Malone pointed to the obvious imperfections and awkwardnesses of the first two acts, the use of Gower as a narrator and of dumb shows, elements characteristic of the drama of an earlier era; and as he finally writes, "[t]he wildness and irregularity of the fable, the artless conduct of the piece, and the inequalities of the poetry, may, I think, be all accounted for, by supposing it either his first or one of his earliest essays in dramatick composition."[32]

The elements Malone cites are still obvious to us, though we have found ways of accounting for them that allow the play to remain late. As for the sound of the verse, the first two acts remain a problem, usually dealt with by invoking a collaborator, but occasionally

---

[32] *Supplement to the Edition of Shakspeare's Plays Published in 1778 by Samuel Johnson and George Steevens*, 2 vols. (London, C. Bathurst et al., 1780), vol. 2, p. 186.

explained (like the inclusion of Gower and the dumb shows) as Shakespeare being deliberately archaic. Passages in acts 3 to 5 certainly sound like passages in *The Winter's Tale* (both Malone and Coleridge considered *The Winter's Tale* also to be an early play), but what "sounds like" Shakespeare has varied from age to age. In Shakespeare's own age, Robert Allott's *Englands Parnassus: or the choycest flowers of our moderne poets,* an anthology of modern poetic excerpts published in 1600, ascribes John of Gaunt's dying speech from *Richard II* to Drayton, and several passages by William Warner to Shakespeare. Shakespeare does not sound to us like Drayton or Warner, but in 1600, at least to one reader, he did.

So the sound of Shakespeare is not really the test. *King John* and *The Merry Wives of Windsor* do not sound like each other, but both are Shakespeare. *Titus Andronicus* for a long time sounded so little like Shakespeare that many critics from the eighteenth to the mid-twentieth century worked hard to remove it from the canon. Nevertheless, it remained there, serving for one set of commentators as potent evidence that Shakespeare could write bad plays, and for another that since Shakespeare could not have written so bad a play, the whole notion of the Shakespeare canon was suspect. (Now, however, it has become a good play.) Shakespeare's final history play *Henry VIII* has for the last century been assumed to be a collaboration with John Fletcher, though there is no evidence to support this view except the fact that there are sections of it that do not sound to us like Shakespeare—or do not sound like what we want Shakespeare to sound like. Computer data does find Fletcher's hand in *Henry VIII*—or at least finds it for those who are looking for it—but the cautionary example of *The Elegy for William Petre*, declared by the computer to be by Shakespeare and then, soon after, shown to be by John Ford, should warn those of us who are not computer engineers to remain agnostic: the computer engineers from the beginning declared that the program used to examine the *Elegy* was improperly designed.[33]

---

[33] See Ward E. Y. Elliott and Robert J. Valenza, "Glass Slippers and Seven-League Boots," *Shakespeare Quarterly* 48.2 (Summer, 1997), pp. 177–207, and the continuation of the debate in *Computers and the Humanities* 36.4 (November, 2002), pp. 455–60. A detailed version of the controversy is at https://www1.cmc.edu/pages/faculty/welliott/hardball.htm.

It is undeniable that the first two acts of *Pericles* are radically different in style from the rest of the play. Critics who want to insist that the play is all by Shakespeare, as F. D. Hoeniger in the 1963 Arden 2 edition and, though more cautiously, Doreen DelVecchio and Antony Hammond in the New Cambridge edition do, have to assume that the first two acts have suffered egregiously in transmission, even more egregiously than the last three, which also have serious textual problems—though as Suzanne Gossett points out in the excellent Arden 3 edition, the first two acts are in fact more satisfactorily printed in the first quarto than the rest of the play, which suggests a more satisfactory manuscript.[34] The alternative to ascribing the differences between the two parts of the play to issues of transmission is to see the play as a collaboration, with the stylistic infelicities of the first part the work of the collaborator. Similarities in vocabulary and syntax between the play and Wilkins's *Painful Adventures* at critical points make it arguable that if the play is a collaboration, Wilkins was Shakespeare's collaborator.

Commentators have resisted the suggestion because Wilkins was a writer of little distinction and a thoroughly bad character; and they do not like the idea of Shakespeare collaborating with a hack and a scoundrel; but the idea is not inconsistent with what we know about the business of theater in Shakespeare's time. The fact that Shakespeare's only acknowledged collaborator is the important and successful John Fletcher may certainly imply that Shakespeare did not stoop to collaborating with hacks; but it may equally mean only that we do not know much about Shakespeare's collaborations (to say nothing of his feelings about them), since the folio does not name them, and the one play we know he wrote with Fletcher, the superb *The Two Noble Kinsmen*, was not included in the folio. (I see no reason to assume that Shakespeare had anything to do with the ghostly *Cardenio*.)[35] And

---

[34] *Pericles*, ed. Suzanne Gossett, Arden 3 (London: Bloomsbury, 2004), p. 16.

[35] The Master of the Revels records a payment in July 1613 to The King's Men for performing a play at court called *Cardenio*. Or at least, we think that was what the play was called: the record actually gives the title as "Cardenna," and says nothing about it being by Shakespeare. The connection of this lost play with Shakespeare derives from a record made forty years later: the publisher Humphrey Moseley, who was undertaking to codify and publish the works of the major English playwrights, registered his intention to publish a play called "The History of Cardennio, by Mr Fletcher, and Shakespeare."

of course it is also quite possible that Shakespeare thought better of Wilkins than we do.

Wilkins was not a prolific writer; he was by profession an innkeeper—more accurately, a brothel-keeper—though when his son was born in 1605 he listed himself in the church register as "George Wilkens, Poett." Doubts have been expressed about whether this can be the same George Wilkins, but we know of no other writer by that name. He collaborated with William Rowley and John Day in a play called *The Travails of the Three English Brothers* (1607), and in the same year his own play *The Miseries of Inforst Mariage* was performed by the King's Men. The New Cambridge editors find this surprising and declare the play "bad," but surely the King's Men would not have agreed; and in any case, it was sufficiently popular for its published version to go through four contemporary editions (that is more than all but a very few Shakespeare plays). Wilkins was also an occasional pamphleteer, and appears to have collaborated with Dekker and Heywood, perfectly respectable talents.

This is a small literary career, but not a contemptible one. I see nothing inconceivable in the idea that Wilkins, having provided the

---

Moseley never did publish the play; but it is surely relevant that he registered at the same time *The Merry Devil of Edmonton* by Shakespeare—this is a play that had been published anonymously in 1608 and in five editions thereafter, and had never been ascribed to Shakespeare. Mosely also registered two other "Shakespeare" plays, *Henry the First* and *Henry the Second*, said to be collaborations with a minor playwright named Robert Davenport—Davenport was writing plays in the 1620s, well after Shakespeare's death. Moseley also did not publish those, and they have, like *Cardenio,* disappeared. Nine years later, in 1660, he registered three more plays by "Shakespeare": *The History of King Stephen, Duke Humphrey, A Tragedy,* and *Iphis and Iantha, or a Marriage Without a Man, a Comedy.* Nothing more is known of them; and as for the ascription of any of these plays to Shakespeare, obviously no reliance can be placed on Moseley. But why have we been looking so assiduously for *Cardenio* and ignoring *Henry the First, King Stephen,* and all those others? The only answer probably is that for several centuries we have really wanted a connection between Shakespeare and Cervantes. In 1728 Lewis Theobald published a play called *The Double Falsehood,* based, he said, on a manuscript he had acquired of a Shakespeare play with a plot from *Don Quixote*—Theobald said he had three manuscripts of the play; he does not say the play was called *Cardenio.* The plot of *The Double Falsehood* is indeed adapted from the Cardenio episode in *Don Quixote,* but the character who should be named Cardenio, and who would therefore give the play its name, is named Julio. There is no evidence beyond Theobald's word that the manuscripts existed—he offered to allow people to examine them, but did not in fact do so—and all three have disappeared.

King's Men with a notably successful play, should have tried his hand at another, and produced the first two acts of *Pericles*. It is true that these do not sound much like *The Miseries of Inforst Mariage*, but neither does the rest of *Pericles* sound like *King John* or *The Merry Wives of Windsor*; and in any case, the play in the early scenes is trying to sound like Gower. Shakespeare, I suggest, liking the plot and finding Wilkins's first two acts enough to go on with, touched them up and finished the play—I assume that at this point Shakespeare took control. Critics who want to rescue "late Shakespeare" from the coarseness of the play's brothel scenes assume that Wilkins wrote them, and therefore that he contributed more to the play than the first two acts, but I do not see anything unShakespearean in the brothel scenes. The textual problems remain, of course, but they are similar to those of the 1608 quarto of *King Lear*. Much of the textual difficulty seems to me to reflect the nature of the manuscript copy the printers would have had to work with—as with *King Lear*, a draft with many revisions, and difficult to read. We cannot rectify the text; we must work with what we have. It undeniably presents insurmountable difficulties for a modern editor, but it is worth reminding ourselves that in Shakespeare's age it was in most respects a satisfactory reading text, satisfactory enough to be reprinted substantially unchanged five times in twenty-five years.

Moreover—this is worth emphasizing—it was a satisfactory *performing* text. In 1610 a group of players in Yorkshire were arrested and charged with sedition: they had given performances of *King Lear*, *Pericles*, and a lost play about Saint George that the authorities claimed were (or perhaps had had introduced into them) Roman Catholic propaganda—the members of the troupe were Catholic. In their defense the actors replied that their performing texts of *King Lear* and *Pericles* were the printed quartos. Since these had been duly licensed for publication, they could not be considered seditious. (This was not held to be a sufficient defense—the court took the position that the licensing of plays was a different matter from the licensing of books: plays are social events that involve crowds, which are much more dangerous than individual readers.) What is significant for our purposes, however, is that these actors found in the first quarto of *Pericles* the basis for an adequate performing script. Much of the difficulty editors have had with *Pericles* has to do with its failure to read like the edited texts of the folio. But its unedited look has much in common with the first quartos of *Hamlet* and *Romeo and Juliet*, and its often baffling textual problems are similar, as I have said, to those of the first quarto of *King Lear*, which, for all its confusions, seems to derive ultimately from Shakespeare's original draft of the play. We can emend that archeology out of *Pericles* and turn it into a normative reading text only by rewriting it.

Still, the issue of collaboration remains a vexed one. The two parts of *Pericles* are quite as unlike as the serious and comic scenes of *Doctor Faustus*, which is assumed to be a collaboration; but it is also clear that the text we have of *Doctor Faustus*, first published in 1604, is a highly compromised one, very far from Marlowe's and his collaborator's original, which would have been produced at least twelve years earlier. By 1604, moreover, Marlowe was long dead. This is not at all the kind of narrative we have for *Pericles*, with Shakespeare writing in 1608 and the play published in the next year, when Shakespeare was very much alive. Why were the two parts left so strangely discordant?

One line of argument, adopted by the New Cambridge editors, is that the question of authorship does not matter: what matters is simply that it is an excellent play. This sounds like a way of moving beyond the authorship issue; but in fact it is really simply an extension of it, since the whole point of the argument is to justify including the play in a complete Shakespeare. There are many excellent Elizabethan and Jacobean plays not by Shakespeare that languish in scholarly editions with few readers. The only reason *Pericles* is widely read today is that Shakespeare's name is attached to it. The authorship question is the only question; the play's excellence is relevant only in so far as it enables us to claim that Shakespeare wrote it.

But once we have settled on the date, 1608, the play becomes "late," and "late Shakespeare" for us implies a calm and wise playwright, Shakespeare after all that turbulent drama arriving at acceptance and reconciliation. If *Pericles* is to be the gateway to Shakespearean romance, there are still things we need to rescue the play from. The brothel scenes have been a major stumbling block, and constitute the principal argument for Wilkins's continuing involvement in the play's composition after the first two acts. Certainly as the text reads, Lysimachus behaves badly, though it is not clear how reprehensible he would have been found in 1608—for comparison, in Sidney's *Arcadia*, the pastoral romance of the noble hero Mucidorus and the virtuous heroine Pamela includes an attempted rape, but Mucidorus continues to be a hero. Modern editors and directors of *Pericles*, however, import material from Wilkins's *Painful Adventures* and rearrange and delete sections to make Lysimachus less debauched and Marina more vulnerable and thereby more persuasive, which is to say, more "feminine." This could be seen as making the play "late," though I would call it an attempt to make the play more acceptably modern.

But in fact the play is very much of its time: Marina in the brothel is not only articulate but also fully in command, both of her situation and of Lysimachus—a very Shakespearean woman, if we think of Portia, Rosalind, Lady Macbeth, Cleopatra, Paulina. What is characteristic of both Shakespeare and his age, however, is the way Marina is disposed of, married off to Lysimachus and given no say in the matter, not one word, even of assent. This is especially striking since her mother Thaisa, earlier in the play, is so forceful about choosing her own husband: the play clearly represents this as a possible option for women. Why is it not an option for Marina? Why, indeed, would Marina want to marry Lysimachus the smarmy brothel-creeper? What has become of the Shakespeare of *As You Like It*—or shall we say that at this point the author of *The Miseries of Inforst Mariage* has reappeared, and that the ending predicts an unhappy future for Marina? But the concluding disposition of Marina was probably seen as a perfectly conventional, and therefore acceptable, ending, just as the perfunctory marriage of the thrillingly articulate Paulina to Camillo at the end of *The Winter's Tale*, without a word of assent from Paulina, is offered by that play as part of a satisfactory conclusion.

In devising the drama of Shakespeare's career, *Pericles* gave Malone a beginning and Dowden an ending. We have completely bought into Dowden's idea of romance as an authentically Shakespearean genre— the less anachronistic category of tragicomedy has had little attraction for us, though many of Shakespeare's comedies and all the works we think of as "problem plays" would fit comfortably into it. It is not a classical genre, though it is certainly a Renaissance one, and Italian theorists had justified it through an energetic critical debate. Jonson the classicist not only accommodated tragicomedy to his dramatic art but also elevated it to the top of the triumphal arch in his folio frontispiece.

Modern conceptions of genre are different from those of the Renaissance. Our categories are exclusive and definitive; theirs tended to be inclusive and analytic. For the Renaissance critic, to find a new category for a play was not to abandon the old ones. J. C. Scaliger calls the *Oresteia* both a tragedy and a comedy, just as the quarto of *Troilus and Cressida* compares the play to those of Plautus and Terence, while for the folio editors it was a tragedy. In their historical context, these claims do not contradict each other. We have adopted the category of romance because we believe that certain kinds of seriousness are inappropriate to comedy, and because it gives us a way of accounting for the late plays' commitment to nonrealistic modes. We have thereby shed light on the relation of four late plays to each other, but we have also thereby obscured their relation to the rest of Shakespearean drama.[36]

In fact, the "sweet serenity" that for Dowden characterized his four romances omitted a great deal. The villains at the end of *The Tempest* are firmly unrepent; *Cymbeline* concludes with some (not all) of the evil characters safely dead, but also with a king who acknowledges the radical fallibility of his judgment; there are losses at the end of *The Winter's Tale* that the unveiling of Hermione and the finding of Perdita cannot restore—the dead son and heir Mammilius, the lost husband and faithful servant Antigonus. Shakespearean comedy is often tragicomedy: *The Merchant of Venice, Much Ado About Nothing, Measure for Measure.* Even the sunny comedy of *As You Like It* opens with banishment and family conflicts, and John Fletcher's sequel to *The Taming of the Shrew, The Tamer Tamed,* has Kate dead within two years of her dubiously happy marriage. Much of *Anthony and Cleopatra* is comic. Shakespeare turned the story of *King Lear* into a tragedy, violating both history and the play's own expectations; and we have already observed that the tragedy of *Othello* has the structure of a comedy.

---

[36] For a fuller discussion of the genre issues, see my essay "Shakespeare and the Kinds of Drama," in Stephen Orgel, *The Authentic Shakespeare* (New York: Routledge, 2002), pp. 143–58; and my introduction to *The Tempest* in the Oxford Shakespeare (Oxford: Clarendon Press, 1987), pp. 4–5.

| 4 |

Poetry and Drama

Why is drama in verse? Aristotle defined *mimesis* as an imitation of an action; the action as drama represents it, however, is very much reordered and refined, as poetry is, with none of the hesitations, interruptions, and sheer messiness of action in the real world. Moreover, one of the essential elements of Greek drama was melody, so from the beginning drama was both performative (rather than literary) and related to ritual. Greek tragedy dramatized the nation's mythology, and thus was both historical and religious; but the comedies of Aristophanes too are in complex poetic meters: drama was a form of poetry; and Aristotle's treatise is therefore *The Poetics* ($Περὶ$ $ποιητικῆς$), not something like *The Theatrics* or *The Histrionics*. And although Roman drama was more clearly conceived as entertainment and literature, it took its form from the Greek tradition. In its depiction of everyday life it too speaks verse—slaves and workmen are metrically indistinguishable from the gentry.

English dramatic texts, both sacred and secular, were from the beginning in verse—even Henry Medwall's *Fulgens and Lucres*, the earliest English secular drama, with its debates and orations, which was based, moreover, on a prose source, is entirely in verse. Dialogues in the period (for example, Erasmus's *Colloquies*) were characteristically in prose; but they were not designed for performance, and did not need to be memorized. Medwall was doubtless following the classical dramatic tradition, but it is doubtful that the authors of mystery plays,

The Idea of the Book and the Creation of Literature. Stephen Orgel, Oxford University Press.
© Stephen Orgel 2023. DOI: 10.1093/oso/9780192871534.003.0004

also in verse, were looking at Plautus, Terence, and Seneca, and they certainly were not looking at Euripides and Aristophanes: drama was simply a form of verse. The surprise, then, is that when Jane Lady Lumley translated Euripides's *Iphigenia in Aulis* around 1550, she did it in prose. The translation was not simply a linguistic exercise, but shows both additions and significant interpretation. Possibly she was treating the play, with its disputes and philosophizing, as a form of dialogue, and therefore did not translate the choruses, which would logically have been in verse; but also, she was, for a moment, and privately, reimagining the genre of tragedy.

The use of prose in English drama was largely an Elizabethan innovation. John Lyly could not have known Lady Lumley's *Iphigenia*, and the only English model for his five prose comedies appears to be George Gascoigne's *Supposes*, translated from Ariosto's *I Suppositi*— *I Suppositi* was a prose comedy that was subsequently redone in verse.[1] According to Louise George Clubb, however, "the verse *Suppositi* was an outlier that had no, or very few, imitators."[2] To put it into verse was not, then, a way of "regularizing" it: quite the contrary; it was an attempt to change its genre entirely, to create a new genre of comedy—the Italian *commedia erudita*, unlike tragedy or pastoral, was invariably in prose. Clubb writes "The language was a Boccaccian-inflected modern prose, more or less Tuscan, depending on the playwright's origins, with socially different levels of style and room for slang and some dialect."[3] These plays would certainly have been known in England, and the fact that their language derives from Boccaccio is surely relevant to the fact that Lyly's dramatic language is that devised for his novel *Euphues*. Continental sources for English prose drama appearing in England or in English include Machiavelli's *Mandragora* (*c.*1518), published in London in Italian by John Wolfe in 1588, and the Spanish *Comedia de Calisto y Melibea* or *Celestina* of Fernando de Rojas (1499), which is in prose, though the English adaptation published by John Rastell (*c.*1525) is in

[1] Andy Kesson gives an excellent account of Lyly's originality, success, and importance in *John Lyly and Early Modern Authorship* (Revels Plays Companion Library, Manchester: Manchester University Press, 2014).

[2] Private communication—thank you!

[3] Louise George Clubb, "Commedia Erudita: Birth and Transfiguration," in Michele Marrapodi, ed., *The Routledge Research Companion to Anglo-Italian Renaissance Literature and Culture* (Abingdon: Routledge, 2019), p. 117.

verse. Another significant model was Thomas Hoby's translation of the erudite dialogues of Castiglione, *The Courtyer of Count Baldessar Castilio* (1561), declared on its title page to be "very necessary and profitable for yonge gentilmen and gentilwomen abiding in court, palaice, or place."

I am concerned here with the intersection of poetry and drama, and more specifically, with three dramatists who were also poets, and how their two modes interact—the ultimate question I want to consider is how Shakespeare's career would appear to us if his poems had been, from the beginning, thought of as an essential part of his works, if the first folio had been works instead of plays. The two contrasting examples are obvious ones, Marlowe and Jonson, two of the three greatest dramatists of Elizabethan/Jacobean England, who were also two of the greatest poets; and we have, on the whole, no trouble putting these two literary careers together. Jonson's poetry in its satiric mode is closely related to his drama, and Marlowe's passionate classicism and imaginative transgressiveness make the plays and the poetry often seem to comment on each other.

There is, however, a crucial difference between these two careers. Jonson's canon was assembled and curated by the poet himself; the image presented in the works is largely his own creation. But the Marlowe canon consisted during his lifetime only of whatever circulated in manuscript—it is of course impossible to know how much of the work that comprised—and there was no attempt at a collected works until the nineteenth century. In 1594, the year after his death, three plays were published with his name on the title pages: *The Massacre at Paris*, *Edward II*, and *Dido Queen of Carthage*, the last "written by Christopher Marlowe and Thomas Nash." *Edward II* was reissued in 1598, 1612, and 1622. The very popular *Tamburlaine* was published three times in the 1590s, but anonymously, and was not ascribed to Marlowe until the nineteenth century—it took a forged entry in Henslowe's diary, the work of the notorious John Payne Collier, for the attribution to become definitive, a fact that is curiously appropriate to Marlowe's subversive career.[4] *Hero and Leander*, which had presumably circulated in manuscript, was finally published twice in

---

[4] For the history of the attribution of authorship to *Tamburlaine* see András Kiséry, "An Author and a Bookshop: Publishing Marlowe's Remains at the Black Bear," *Philological Quarterly* 91.3 (Summer, 2012), p. 364.

1598 in two different forms, the version as Marlowe left it and a much longer version completed by George Chapman. The latter text was reissued eight more times before 1637. Marlowe's translation of Ovid's *Amores* appeared in a partial version in 1599 paired with a collection of epigrams by John Davies, and then in a complete version, still accompanied by Davies' epigrams, in 1603, 1630, and 1640. The translation of the first book of Lucan's *Pharsalia* appeared in 1600, and was not reissued. His best-known poem "The passionate Shepheard to his love" appeared in the anthology *Englands Helicon* in 1600 credited to "Chr. Marlow," along with "The Nimphs reply to the Shepheard" and "Another of the same nature, made since" both credited to "Ignoto." The first of these was attributed to Sir Walter Ralegh in Isaac Walton's *Compleat Angler*, 1653; there were in addition a number of other contemporary imitations and responses. Marlowe's most famous play *Doctor Faustus* was not published until 1604, attributed to "Ch. Marl.", in what is clearly a very compromised version (the "A text"); this was reissued twice, in 1609 and 1611. In 1616 a revised version (the "B text") with additional material appeared, now ascribed to "Ch. Mar.", which was reissued in 1619, 1620, 1624, and 1631—this became the standard text. *The Jew of Malta* by "Christopher Marlo" was published once, in 1633. The play *Lust's Dominion* appeared in 1657 with Marlowe's name on its title page—the play is now ascribed to Thomas Dekker in collaboration with at least two others. The first attempt at a collected works did not appear until 1826, published by William Pickering; this was prompted by Charles Lamb's enthusiastic praise of Marlowe in his *Specimens of English Dramatic Poets* (1808). Pickering's Marlowe included *Tamburlaine* but also *Lust's Dominion*, as well as Davies's *Epigrams*, on the assumption that the 1599 volume's title *Epigrammes and elegies by J. D. and C. M.* implies that both works are collaborative, and thus that at least some of the epigrams are therefore by Marlowe.

Shakespeare in *As You Like It*, quoting a famous line from *Hero and Leander*, offers a curiously bland summary of Marlowe's career: "Dead shepherd, now I feel thy saw of might / Whoever loved that loved not at first sight" (3.5.82–3). This mildly erotic pastoral couplet seems oddly out of touch with the complex and lurid life that even the earliest biographies produced for Marlowe—certainly for Shakespeare's age there was more to Marlowe's poetry than mildly erotic pastoral. In

Hero and Leander, Leander's rhetorical stratagems and Hero's sacrilege at the very least complicate the drama of innocent first love, and the frankly homoerotic description of Leander's beauty attains a complex political life in *Edward II*. The worldly cynicism of the Ovid translations is dramatized in the erotic and social worlds of *Dido Queen of Carthage* and *The Jew of Malta*, just as Leander's irresistible beauty is translated into the military and political contexts of *Tamburlaine*. And the overarching aspiration of all the work is summed up in the blasphemous parable of *Doctor Faustus*.

One cannot create a similarly neat synthesis for the relation of Jonson's poetry to his drama. Indeed, there are many places where the assumptions of the poetry seem positively at odds with those of drama—the celebratory mode that figures so strongly in his poetry is evident in *Cynthias Revels*, a bid for court patronage that disappeared from the repertoire almost immediately, but is otherwise for the most part present in the plays only ironically, in the effusions of Sir Epicure Mammon, for example, or in Volpone's praise of his gold or Mosca's ode of love to himself. And the ethical heroism that fills Jonson's poetry is largely absent from the plays—there are few enough good people among his characters, such as Asper in *Every Man Out of His Humour*, but they tend to be either marginal, like Peregrine in *Volpone*, ineffectual, like Bonario and Celia, or not significantly better than the bad people, like Lovewit in *The Alchemist*.

Shakespeare is another matter. As we have seen, for readers Shakespeare was a poet until 1598, when his name first started to appear on the title pages of his plays; and even after that, during his lifetime the two major narrative poems were far more widely read than any of the drama. Nor is Shakespeare the poet easily accommodated to Shakespeare the playwright: *Venus and Adonis* and *Lucrece* seem not to relate in any clear way either to the collection of sonnets or to the infinite variety of the drama.

By 1640 the narrative poems had lost their popularity, and have since been at best marginal to the Shakespeare canon. The sonnets, on the other hand, which were the least known of his nondramatic poems until the nineteenth century, had by the twentieth century become essential to the construction of the canonical Shakespeare. Both their preservation at the outskirts of the canon and their subsequent transformation into keys to Shakespeare's psyche involved a good deal of revision and emendation, first in John Benson's heterosexualized versions and subsequently in those of the eighteenth-century editor Edmond Malone, who did more to define what we mean by Shakespeare than anyone since the editors of the first folio.[5] Malone's versions of the most problematic of these poems vary significantly from the original texts, but they have essentially replaced the originals in the modern Shakespeare, which is also accompanied by a good deal of elucidation and interpretation.

To ask how Shakespeare would appear to us had his poems been included in the folio is not to privilege poetry over plays, text over performance—on the contrary, *Love's Labour's Lost* and *Romeo and Juliet* at certain crucial dramatic moments include sonnets, and *As You Like It* has some fun with Orlando's love poems pinned on trees. If the poems had been part of the folio we might take the fact that lyrics appear in plays more seriously—at the very least, we would look at them differently. Poems were intended to be recited, not just read; lyrics are in fact just as dramatic as dialogue is; there is a significant element of performance in the poems. Why do the courtiers of Navarre write sonnets to the ladies of France; why do Romeo and Juliet recite sonnets to each other? Surely Shakespeare's sonnets are relevant to this question.

The sonnets are especially enlightening when they are read against *Hamlet*. Consider two of Hamlet's extended soliloquies from 2.2 and 3.1: just as in the sonnets, questions, exclamations and conjunctions of alternative possibilities are key structuring features. The sonnets are full of questions—Music to hear, why hear'st thou music sadly? Shall I compare thee to a summer's day? What is thy substance, whereof art thou made? But the questions that resonate most intriguingly with Hamlet's character are those that function as preparations for rationalization, and that are really rhetorical questions, functioning primarily as exclamations, like Hamlet's "Ah what a rogue and peasant slave am I! / Is it not monstrous . . . ?" Sonnet 119 begins with such a series:

[5] For an excellent survey of the editorial history of the sonnets in relation to sexuality, see Bruce Smith, "Shakespeare's Sonnets and the History of Sexuality: A Reception History," in Jean Howard and Richard Dutton, eds., *The Blackwell Companions to Shakespeare: The Poems, Problem Comedies, Late Plays* (Oxford: Blackwell, 2003), pp. 4–26. For Malone's influence on Shakespeare studies generally see Margreta de Grazia, *Shakespeare Verbatim* (Oxford: Oxford University Press, 1991).

> What potions have I drunk of siren tears
> Distilled from limbecks foul as hell within,
> Applying fears to hopes, and hopes to fears,
> Still losing when I saw myself to win!
> What wretched errors hath my heart committed,
> Whilst it hath thought itself so blessèd never!
>
> (1–6)

But instead of setting up any solutions, the rhetorical questions simply clear the space for the rationalization that follows: "O benefit of ill, now I find true / That better is by evil still made better" (9–10). These lines, in light of the suffering expressed in the beginning, appear a piece of sophistry designed to make good of the ill. In other sonnets, the recognition expressed by the question also seems to seek no solution; it functions as a rhetoric to express conclusions already decided, as in the opening of sonnet 97: "How like a winter hath my absence been / From thee, the pleasure of the fleeting year! / What freezings have I felt, what dark days seen! / What old December's bareness everywhere!" (1–4). As the modern punctuation recognizes, in all these cases the questions are not really questions; their exclamatory mode avoids probing the only painful solution, as if that is already known: break off the love affair. Instead of acting as mimetic moments of indecision, they act more like deferrals of action and decision. They are escapes: the articulation of the recognition, the formalization of painful truth into question or complaint, allows the speaker to keep the truths at bay or in question.

A similar mechanism is at work in the sonnets' many chains of alternatives, usually hinging on an important "or." The opening of sonnet 148 is a good example.

> O me, what eyes hath love put in my head,
> Which have no correspondence with true sight;
> Or, if they have, where is my judgment fled,
> That censures falsely what they see aright?
>
> (1–4)

This seems to explore possibilities, but the vacillations around the word "or" also work to defer any resolution. And when it seems in the conclusions of these sonnets that one alternative is chosen or one answer given, the conclusion, on closer inspection, is almost never a simple one. The endings of sonnets 130 and 117 offer examples. "My mistress' eyes are nothing like the sun / ... And yet by heaven I think my love as fair ..." The "think" suggests a lack of certainty; similarly, in sonnet 117:

> Accuse me thus, that I have scanted all
> Wherein I should your great deserts repay ...
> Bring me within the level of your frown,
> But shoot not at me in your wakened hate:
>> Since my appeal says I did strive to prove
>> The constancy and virtue of your love.
>
> (1–2, 11–14)

The couplet's "strive" puts into question the "constancy and virtue of your love" with which the speaker seems to conclude the poem rather too neatly—I did strive, but did I succeed? Is there not a plaintive undertone—at least I tried?

The soliloquies in *Hamlet* share many of these tensions and uncertainties. Like the sonnets, they hinge on questions, recognitions, and alternatives. One central question in the "rogue and peasant slave" soliloquy of 2.2 is the self-accusatory "Am I a coward?" (l. 506), while the hinge in 3.1 is the question of whether "To be, or not to be." In this great drama of indecision, the soliloquies are the ultimate expressions of that indecision, moments that represent the ambivalent workings of the mind. But in the context of the complex staging of questions and alternatives in the sonnets, these soliloquies seem more rhetorical than mimetic. In 2.2, like the sudden turn in many of the sonnets, the line, "Fie upon't, foh!—About, my brain" (522), seems to show Hamlet turning from accusing himself over his cowardice to resolving on action. The result of this turn is the plan to test his uncle's guilt by staging the play. "If a [he] do blench / I know my course" (532–3), seeming to dispel the question of cowardice in resolute action. But as in the sonnets' false resolutions, this conclusion is not simple or direct at all. Why does Hamlet require confirmation of his uncle's guilt when a few moments before he was certain that he had been "prompted to my revenge by heaven and hell" (519) and that he should have already "fatted all the region kites / With this slave's offal" (514–15)? In light of this earlier certainty, the conclusion of the soliloquy is a retreat into another deferral of the required action, the revenge on Claudius. So "Am I a coward?" becomes the real question being avoided.

Similarly evasive is the "To be or not to be" soliloquy of 3.1. At the beginning of the speech, Hamlet lays out the available actions: to bear suffering in the mind or to take action against his troubles which are conceived as the sea, seeming to slide from the suggestion of revenge to suicide by drowning. But, like the rhetorical questions of the sonnets, these alternatives are empty. No genuine grappling occurs here, no true representation of indecision. The soliloquy is already stacked in favor of the deferral of the decision. From "Ay, there's the rub" (64) through his series of posed questions, the speech leads inexorably to the conclusion that we "lose the name of action" (87). This conclusion is no conclusion at all as it takes no stance on the alternatives presented at the beginning of the speech. These soliloquies do not show indecision but its deferral; the questions posed and the alternatives considered outline the formal trappings of self-debate but without substantial engagement with the alternatives. This is especially clear in the "rogue and peasant slave" soliloquy, where the "decision" Hamlet comes to has already been decided earlier in the scene when Hamlet tells the players that he has written "a speech of some dozen or sixteen lines" for them to insert in the play they are to perform, so the apparent racking of the brain in the soliloquy is a staged one—but for whose benefit other than for Hamlet himself; or perhaps more accurately, for Shakespeare himself? There is a real resonance between the staged questions and alternatives of the sonnets and the complex mediations of the soliloquies.[6]

The drama of poetry

Jonson declared his epigrams "the ripest of my studies." These followed the plays in his folio collection—the plays, scripts for the popular theatre, were anomalies in a volume of Works, but epigrams were properly classical. The Shakespeare folio is evidence enough that by 1623 Jonson had made his point about the plays. Still, Jonson considered his epigrams his most mature works, and Jonson is for literary history as much a poet as a playwright. The court entertainments were another anomaly in a volume of works, but they were essential to

---

[6] Martin Dodsworth provides a detailed and brilliant analysis of these issues in *Hamlet Closely Observed* (London: Athlone Press, 1985).

Jonson's sense of himself. His involvement in the world of aristocratic patronage and connoisseurship, amply revealed in the masques and poetry, is an essential element in our sense of his career. Had Shakespeare's poems been, from the outset, part of the canon, we might at the very least take seriously his involvement in that same social world of patronage, erudite readers, and aristocratic admirers. Certainly the dedications to his two long narrative poems and the care with which they were prepared for and seen through the press make clear that his ambitions extended beyond the stage.

The poems were not included in the first folio probably, as I have suggested, for simple, practical reasons. The volume was put together by The King's Men, the acting company of which Shakespeare had been a principal shareholder, playwright, and performer, as a memorial to their most admired colleague. What they owned the rights to, and what chiefly concerned them, was the plays. The book was thus inevitably as much a monument to The King's Men as to its principal dramatist. Moreover, the narrative poems were still selling well in 1623, and to have acquired the rights to reprint them would have been difficult, if not impossible. As for the sonnets, who knows? Shakespeare was apparently not involved in the publication of the 1609 quarto, the only edition in Shakespeare's lifetime, which seems to have generated little interest—so little, in fact, that John Benson's edition, published in 1640, could assert that, "by reason of their Infancie in his death," they were essentially unknown. This explanation presumably means that the sonnets appeared too close to Shakespeare's death to be noticed, a claim that is both false and illogical.

The editorial history of Shakespeare's poems is an index to how complex and conflicted our sense of Shakespeare the poet has been. The first quartos of *Venus and Adonis* (1593) and *Lucrece* (1594) are well printed, elegant little books. They addressed an audience of readers who knew the classics, both Latin and English; they recall, in both their physical presentation and versification, recent editions of Ovid, Spenser, and Sidney. Both poems include fulsome dedications to the Earl of Southampton, a glamorous young aristocrat (he was nineteen when *Venus and Adonis* appeared) who was, moreover, the ward of William Cecil, Lord Burghley, Queen Elizabeth's chief minister. Ambitious Elizabethan poets got on in the world in this way, by finding a generous aristocratic patron, whose taste, praised in a lavish dedication, in turn constituted a marketable endorsement. That it initially worked for Shakespeare is indicated by the fact that the *Lucrece* dedication is significantly warmer than that for *Venus and Adonis*; the fact that there are no further dedications to Southampton implies that it ultimately failed to pay off. For though Southampton was liberally endowed with taste and charm, when at the age of twenty-one he became financially independent, he was also heavily in debt. Artistic patronage does not live by taste alone.

The aura of aristocratic patronage was not, however, the only attraction of Shakespeare's first published poetry. *Venus and Adonis* was witty, inventive, and stylish; it was also daring, erotically explicit, even amoral. Though it seems to us sexually more comic than pornographic, its immense popularity was cited in Shakespeare's own time as an index to the decline of morals among the young, or the literate classes, or—in an extraordinary example—the Roman Catholic church. Thomas Robinson, a lapsed friar, in a pamphlet published in 1622 called *The Anatomy of the English Nunnery at Lisbon* described the comfortable life of a father confessor to the nuns there: "Then after supper it is usuall for him to read a little of *Venus* and *Adonis*, the jests of *George Peele*, or some such scurrilous book: for there are few idle Pamphlets printed in *England* which he hath not in the house."[7] *Lucrece* is less obviously licentious, but for all its moralizing, it lingers provocatively over the way Tarquin's rising lust is heightened by the chaste Lucrece's fears and pleas, a clear appeal to the Renaissance erotic and sadistic imagination. Though it was far less popular than *Venus and Adonis*, there were five editions in Shakespeare's lifetime and four more seventeenth-century editions after his death. Moreover, the elements we find tiresome in these two poems, their formality, dilation, extensive description, and digression—in short, the sheer undramatic quality of these narratives by our greatest dramatist—would have been a good part of what contemporary readers admired: these qualities were what put Shakespeare as a narrative poet in the league of Spenser and Marlowe. At the same time, their focus on the political implications of rape on the one hand and the sexual power of women on the other have a striking relevance to our own social and political history, and

---

[7] [Thomas Robinson,] *The Anatomy of the English Nunnery at Lisbon in Portugall* (1622), 17.

thus through the sexual politics of these poems they have taken on a new and complex critical life.

The sonnets are editorially and bibliographically another matter entirely. They were, to begin with, not a book. At least some of them circulated initially in manuscript: the miscellaneous writer Francis Meres in 1598 praises Shakespeare's "sugred Sonnets among his private friends."[8] There is no reason to doubt that the sonnets were being read in manuscript in the 1590s, but the only independent evidence for it is the inclusion of versions of two of them in print in a collection called *The Passionate Pilgrim* in 1599. Other than these, none of the sonnets are quoted or appear in commonplace books until after their publication in the 1609 quarto, and even then, very few are cited.[9] We must conclude that they simply were not popular.

The two sonnets in *The Passionate Pilgrim* appear along with three poems excerpted from *Love's Labour's Lost*, and the entire volume, consisting of twenty poems, is credited on its title page to Shakespeare: Shakespeare in 1599 was marketable as a poet. And while it is difficult to imagine Meres's "sugred" applying to sonnets like "They that have power to hurt and will do none" or "Th'expense of spirit in a waste of shame," the adjective certainly describes many of the poems written to the beloved young man. There was nothing secretive about the mode of publication Meres describes; manuscript circulation was a normal mode of transmission for much lyric poetry in the period. Even such monuments of Elizabethan verse as Sidney's *Astrophil and Stella* and Donne's *Songs and Sonnets* were initially conceived as coterie literature, and presumed a relatively small readership of uniform tastes: the poet was writing for an audience he knew. Donne refused to allow his lyric poetry to be published in his lifetime; he wrote to his friend Sir Henry Goodyer in 1609 that he sought for himself "a graver course, then of a Poet, into which (that I may also keep my dignity) I would not seem to relapse"[10]—publication would be identifying himself as a professional

---

[8] *Palladis Tamia, Wits Treasury* (1598), fols. Oo1^v–Oo2^r.

[9] Versions of ten sonnets have been found in nineteen manuscripts compiled up to the end of the 1630s. See Gary Taylor, "Some Manuscripts of Shakespeare's Sonnets," *Bulletin of the John Rylands Library* 68.1 (1985), p. 215. Sonnet 2 was by far the most popular, appearing in thirteen manuscript versions, all after 1620.

[10] John Donne, *Letters to Severall Persons of Honour* (1651), p. 103. See Ted-Larry Pebworth, "John Donne, Coterie Poetry, and the Text as Performance," *Studies in English*

poet, and that would be a step downward. Nevertheless, at his death there were 187 poems among his papers, which were subsequently published by his son—not thinking of himself as a poet did not keep Donne from writing poetry, though John Donne, Junior, honored his father's wishes to the extent of identifying the author of the poems simply by the initials J. D.[11] The Shakespeare of the "sugred sonnets" was clearly not unwilling to "relapse" into a poet (perhaps he was even eager to do so), and he was very much the Shakespeare of the social world implied by the dedications to *Venus and Adonis* and *Lucrece*. As for those tougher nuts the obscure courtly allegory *The Phoenix and the Turtle*[12] and the Spenserian lament *A Lovers Complaint*, they have seemed bafflingly unlike the Shakespeare of the plays, and it is only in the past few decades that *A Lovers Complaint* has been accepted as Shakespeare's at all; but if we view them in the context of Shakespeare's other poetry, they will appear consistent with its literary ideals and intellectual milieu.

How the sonnets got into print is unclear, but there is no reason to believe that the 1609 quarto was surreptitious. The publisher Thomas Thorpe had printed play quartos, including Ben Jonson's *Volpone* and *Sejanus*, and Shakespeare certainly might have given him a manuscript of sonnets to publish. The manuscript was not, however, prepared with the sort of care evident in the texts of *Venus and Adonis* and *Lucrece*, and it seems more likely that Thorpe had some other source than the author for his copy, which also would not necessarily have been in Shakespeare's hand. Whether Shakespeare approved of the publication or not is unknowable, but the issue would not have been a significant one: intellectual property is largely a modern concept, and the rights to the poems would have belonged to whoever owned the manuscript.

Literature, 1500–1900 9.1 (Winter, 1989), pp. 61–75. For manuscript circulation in the period see Arthur Marotti, *Manuscript, Print, and the English Renaissance Lyric* (Ithaca, NY: Cornell University Press, 1995), and Harold Love, *Scribal Publication in Seventeenth-Century England* (Oxford: Clarendon Press, 1993).

[11] *Poems by J.D. With Elegies on the Authors Death* (1633). Donne was identified by initials through five more editions, and was finally named on the title page of the edition of 1669.

[12] The poem was one of several appended to Robert Chester's long poem *Loves Martyr or, Rosalins Complaint* (1601). It is untitled, though the volume's title page announces the subject of the several additional poems to be "the Phoenix and Turtle."

In contrast to the earlier dedications to Southampton, obviously seeking patronage, the sonnets volume is dedicated not by the poet but by the publisher to an unknown and unidentifiable Mr. W. H., "the only begetter of these ensuing sonnets," whatever that means—if it means the beloved young man, it also means that Thorpe cannot name him, or even that he does not know who he is: the W. H. could stand for "Whoever He may be," or just "Who He?" The two names most frequently suggested, Henry Wroithesly Earl of Southampton, the dedicatee of the two early narrative poems with his initials reversed, and William Herbert Earl of Pembroke, the patron of Shakespeare's theatrical company and dedicatee of the first folio, are both impossible: referring to an earl as "Mr." was actionable. Though there are occasional muddles in the book, Thorpe's copy must have been clear enough, because the text is on the whole a satisfactory one. Its editorial problems are undeniable, but they are not, for the most part, the fault of the printer.

Why, given the continuing success of *Venus and Adonis* and *Lucrece*, the sonnets were not popular in 1609 is difficult to say, but it should make us take with a grain of salt the claim that Shakespeare's name on a title page was enough to guarantee a publisher's profit. The tantalizing evidence of emotional turmoil and illicit sex that makes them irresistible to us apparently was not a big selling point for Shakespeare's contemporaries: it was in Sidney's sonnets (which strike us as relentlessly literary) that early readers found the satisfactions of autobiography and erotic revelation. The usual explanation for the Shakespeare sonnets' neglect is that the vogue for sonnets was past; but in 1609 the vogue for Shakespeare certainly was not. Shakespeare's sonnets in print remained what they had had been in manuscript: coterie literature, experimental and daring both linguistically and erotically, difficult and seriously playful. The fact that their attractiveness to that coterie audience did continue is clear from the fact that a number of these sonnets reappear in commonplace books of the period; the fact that the number is very small indicates that the audience remained small even after publication. There was no second edition until 1640, twenty-four years after Shakespeare's death.

That edition, moreover, involved wholesale revision. The publisher John Benson, capitalizing on the undiminished sales of *Venus and Adonis*, produced a volume of what looked to be not old-fashioned sonnets but new Shakespeare love poems. The transformation involved both format and erotics: many of the sonnets are run together, making them twenty-eight line poems, and all are given titles, such as "Self-Flattery of her Beauty," "Upon the receipt of a Table Book from his Mistress," "An Entreaty for Her Acceptance," so that most of the love poems addressed to the young man are now addressed to a woman. To accomplish this, it was necessary only to change three masculine pronouns within the poems to feminine ones and supply a few gendered titles, but since the sonnets to the young man form a fairly consistent narrative, that was sufficient to change the story. Benson's motive was probably not any nervousness about Shakespeare's sexuality, but simply to bring the poems up to date, and transform the book from an Elizabethan sonnet sequence to a volume of Cavalier love lyrics. Shakespeare himself was thereby revised into what for the new age constituted a properly romantic and acceptably manly subject.

The folio editors' decision to limit their grand memorial volume to the work of Shakespeare the dramatist meant that not many years after his death, even for the reading public, Shakespeare the poet had become definitively Shakespeare the playwright, and there was eventually little market for the poems. Benson's volume, despite its title *Poems: Written by Wil. Shake-speare. Gent.*, included a good deal of nonShakespearean material, such as Marlowe's famous "Passionate Shepheard to His Love" with a couple of replies, a collection of Ovidian imitations by Thomas Heywood, and "An Addition of Some Excellent Poems...By other Gentlemen." Sales were not sufficient to warrant a second edition.

The poems were first included in a comprehensive Shakespeare in Nicholas Rowe's six-volume edition of 1709, published by Jacob Tonson; but they were an afterthought, issued as a seventh volume edited by Charles Gildon in 1710. Even this was hardly an edition, since it simply reproduced the text of Benson's 1640 *Poems*, with all its revisions and even some of its nonShakespearean verse; but it did make of Tonson's Shakespeare the first that could be claimed to be in any sense Complete Works. In 1709 Bernard Lintot had included the text of the 1609 sonnets in an edition of Shakespeare poems, probably simply as a way of getting around Tonson's copyright, but the book did not sell well and was not reissued. The poems, still in Benson's versions, appeared again in Pope's Shakespeare of 1725, but then disappeared from Theobald's and Hanmer's editions of 1733 and 1744, even though both claimed to represent *The Works of Shakespeare*. And though Edmond Malone in 1780 abandoned Benson's 1640 revisions and returned, more or less, to the original texts, this did not earn the poems a place in the canon. George Steevens, appalled by the Shakespeare revealed in Malone's versions of the sonnets—a Shakespeare in love with a young man, a Shakespeare full of lust and committing adultery with a promiscuous married woman—declared that "the strongest act of Parliament that could be framed, would fail to compel readers into their service,"[13] and refused them a place in his Shakespeare of 1790. The original sonnets still represented something that the idea of Shakespeare could not tolerate. Though the poems appeared occasionally in the nineteenth century among the Complete Works, it was not until well into the twentieth century that their inclusion became routine; and indeed, Benson's 1640 volume, with its adjusted versions of Shakespeare's sexuality, was still being reprinted in the mid-nineteenth century.[14] But since the sonnets are the closest we are able to get to Shakespeare in an autobiographical mode, they eventually became essential documents in his afterlife. Needless to say, the changing version of the inner Shakespeare that the biographical and critical tradition has produced over the centuries has not always coincided with the afterlife constructed out of the plays, hence Steevens's indignant exclusion of the sonnets from his complete Shakespeare.

It is Shakespeare's drama that we chiefly prize—the narrative poems are formal and even undramatic precisely because of their "poetic" qualities, the rigid stanzas and the rhetorical elaboration; and though we find a real narrative movement by reading through the sonnets as a volume (treating it, in effect, as a kind of narrative, or at least as a series of dramatic moments), the sequence as a whole is difficult and obscure, and operates on a level of abstraction that seems at odds with the imaginative specificity of the plays. Of course by the time one reaches the end of the sequence the speaker, the poet, has acquired much of the quality of a dramatic character: the sonnets, for all their abstruseness,

---

[13] Steevens's comment appears in *The Advertisement to the Plays of William Shakespeare* (1793). See Colin Burrow, ed., *Shakespeare: The Complete Sonnets and Poems* (Oxford: Oxford University Press, 2002), p. 138.

[14] For a fuller discussion, see my essay "The Desire and Pursuit of the Whole," in Stephen Orgel, *The Invention of Shakespeare* (Philadelphia: The University of Pennsylvania Press, 2022).

are intensely realized emotionally. If we only know Jonson's characters from the outside, we only know the figures in the sonnets from the inside.

The character of the poet

Our three poet-playwrights are very different kinds of people. Marlowe has a double, triple, or even quadruple life—the poor boy whose intelligence gains him a superb education, genuinely scholarly, an excellent classicist, seemingly on the verge of a brilliant literary career, but also self-destructive, on the fringes of society, even an underworld figure, living a dangerous life as a government spy, apparently involved in counterfeiting, certainly sexually transgressive, considered danger-ous enough to warrant indictments, and possibly even murdered on the orders of his sometime employers high up in the government. *Doctor Faustus* and *Hero and Leander* seem appropriate expressions of this sort of life—perhaps too perfect, as if the life has been partly con-structed out of the writings, rather as if we decided on the basis of *Macbeth* that Shakespeare knew too much about the psychology of murder not to be at least implicated in it, if not actually guilty of it himself.

Jonson is another poor boy made good through intelligence and education, but he wants to fit in; his lusts seem more normative, in the sense that they are more attuned to his materialistic, early capitalist society. The lust is for money, food, beautiful things, the good life, most of all patronage, which is the key to all those other things. But he wants more than this: he wants to be admired, to be a social and ethical arbiter, to dictate, to teach, and especially not to be subservient to the people who patronize him. All of this sometimes comes out as haran-guing or pontificating, or complaining because he is not taken seriously as a social critic and ethical guide—the patrons move on to someone else, audiences do not appreciate being told what they should and should not like. Jonson was what we would call a control freak; just the opposite of Shakespeare, who let his plays do the talking, and gave audiences something to identify with even in his villains. In his way Shakespeare was as eager for patronage as Jonson, but, at least in the sonnets, he could acknowledge the humiliation involved in a way that

Jonson never could. But of course Shakespeare's most reliable patron was the theater audience, the most untrustworthy of patrons for Jonson.

Of the three, Shakespeare is the most complete outsider, entering the London world via the theater, as both playwright and actor, and during the plague years of 1592 and 1593, when the theaters were closed, turning to poetry to produce his two long narrative poems. These were popular with readers—which means successful for the publisher and booksellers—but failed to produce a reliable patron; and when the theaters reopened Shakespeare settled in to make theater his career, eventually becoming a shareholder in the very successful acting company of which he was a member, in effect becoming his own boss. Might the sonnets suggest that there was some sense of disappointment in this? The speaker of the sonnets acknowledges himself to be, as a playwright, dependent on the "public means which public manners breeds" (Sonnet 111), and he compares himself to "an unperfect actor on the stage" (Sonnet 23), but he speaks as a frustrated poet, admiring a glamorous, ultimately unresponsive patron. There is of course no way of knowing how much autobiography is in this, but the relation of poet to patron as it is imagined in the sonnets cannot be irrelevant.

Poetry as drama

What then is the relation of poetry to drama—what do the two have to do with each other? One could say that plays were in verse simply because they had always been in verse.

There are a small number of early exceptions: Lady Lumley's *Iphigenia*, Gascoigne's *Supposes*, Lyly's comedies; and a little later *The Merry Wives of Windsor*, *Epicene*, *Bartholomew Fair*, and individual scenes in plays that are for the most part in verse; but these soon enough ceased to be exceptions. Drama was continually being reimagined, and some drama was eventually, fitfully, reimagined as prose. Even after the major reinvention of drama during the Commonwealth and after the Restoration, however, heroic drama still spoke verse. Prose was the language of comedy.

But how significant is the difference between poetry and prose—is poetry simply prose put into meter and sometimes rhyme? Sidney both affirmed and denied it:

the greatest part of Poets have apparelled their poeticall inventions in that numbrous kinde of writing which is called verse: indeed but apparelled, verse being an ornament and no cause to Poetry.... It is not riming and versing that maketh a Poet, no more then a long gowne maketh an Advocate, who, though he pleaded in armor, should be an Advocate and no Souldier. But it is that fayning notable images of vertues, vices, or what els, with that delightfull teaching, which must be the right describing note to know a Poet by: although indeed the Senate of Poets hath chosen verse as their fittest rayment, meaning, as in matter they passed all in all, so in maner to goe beyond them: not speaking (table talke fashion or like men in a dreame) words as they chanceably fall from the mouth, but peyzing [weighing] each sillable of each worde by just proportion according to the dignitie of the subject.[15]

The pleasure poetry gives was a problem for this Calvinist. When Sidney praises poetry for "that delightfull teaching, which must be the right describing note to know a Poet by," the delight is what makes it poetry, but it is delivered by the teaching, and could be seriously problematic. Gavin Alexander perceptively observes that "always in Sidney a literary-theoretical model of poetic delight aiding poetic teaching is undermined by representations of delight being pursued for its own sake."[16] For Horace in the *Ars Poetica*, poets wish *either* to instruct *or* to delight, "*aut prodesse volunt aut delectare*,"[17] but the critics of Sidney's age were above all moralists, and therefore poetry to justify itself had to do both; the pleasure enabled the instruction, and the pleasure was a danger. The essence of Sidney's defence of poetry is, in fact, that it is didactic—if it only gives pleasure it is indefensible. The poet's language itself is special, not "table talke" but "peyzing [weighing] each sillable of each worde by just proportion"; this, not verse, is what makes it poetry. Nevertheless "the greatest part of Poets" use "that numbrous kinde of writing which is called verse." Sidney acknowledges the point, but fails to engage with it: if verse is "an ornament and no cause to Poetry," why do most poets—including Sidney himself—write

[15] *An Apology for Poetry*, in *Elizabethan Critical Essays*, ed. G. Gregory Smith (Oxford: Oxford University Press, 1904), vol. 1, pp. 159–60.

[16] "Sir Philip Sidney's *Arcadia*," in Andrew Hadfield, ed., *The Oxford Handbook of English Prose 1500–1640* (Oxford, 2013), p. 233.

[17] *Ars Poetica* line 333.

in verse, and even in rhymed verse? The insistence that rhyme and meter are merely ornamental dismisses poetry's most obvious pleasures, and makes the poet indistinguishable from the philosopher.

Sidney wants poets to be philosophers, not mere versifiers. According to William Drummond, Jonson was of two minds about the matter: he agreed, and then apparently thought better of it. He said that "he wrote all his [poems] first in prose, for so his master Camden had learned him" and that "verses stood by sense without either colours [rhetorical ornaments] or accent [meter]," but then Drummond adds "which yet other times he denied."[18]

Plays are nominally about people talking to each other and acting on each other. But in the plays of Shakespeare's age, and for generations before and several generations after, those people talked to each other in verse—normally, unproblematically: drama was a verse medium, verse was the normal language of drama, and it was plays in prose that were unusual. One way to account for this is to say that the characters in drama are not people, and this is one of the ways that characters differ from people: they do not talk like people. But that also means that they do not think like people, do not have psychologies motivating them—their motivations are a function of the plot of the play (this is particularly clear in plays like *Volpone* and *The Alchemist*, where the characters are entirely static, and the whole play depends on plot). Why do characters talk in verse? Clearly not because the playwright is interested in any realistic portrayal of our world; nevertheless the very fact that they do speak in verse makes them more memorable for us than all the people around us who speak our language—Hamlet, Falstaff, Lady Macbeth, King Lear, are much more alive for us than most of the people we deal with. A famous psychoanalytic study takes as its subject Hamlet and Oedipus, making the characters independent of their authors. This is a modern phenomenon: for Samuel Johnson, *Hamlet* was seriously implausible. It was Coleridge who made *Hamlet* Shakespeare's deepest expression of himself; even so, the psychoanalyst's subject is not Shakespeare, but Hamlet. For us, poetry in drama "realizes" something, renders it more vivid than events in the everyday world.

[18] lines 293–5, Cambridge Ben Jonson, vol. 5, p. 378.

In plays that are in verse, however, some characters speak prose—the Porter in *Macbeth*, Juliet's nurse, Pandarus and Thersites, Autolycus— and we say that their prose makes those characters more like people, in effect, more real. Common people in plays generally speak prose, aristocrats speak verse. Does this only reflect how little we know about aristocrats? Did the aristocrats in Shakespeare's and Marlowe's audience see the poetical characters as reflecting themselves? There are hardly any aristocrats in Jonson's drama, but in *Volpone* and *The Alchemist*, everybody speaks verse all the time. Perhaps this reflects not on the characters, but on the world of the play and the kind of control the playwright is exercising over it; and perhaps the fact that the poetical plays are the ones we admire most says something about the psychology of audiences, about the way we want to see our world represented.

| 5 |

How To Be a Poet

Becoming a poet

None of the major poetic figures of the 1580s and 1590s—
Shakespeare, Marlowe, Sidney, Spenser, the young Donne—was
a professional poet. Sidney was an aristocrat and independently
wealthy; Shakespeare was an actor and part owner of the theatrical
company he performed in and wrote for; Marlowe was a number of
things including playwright and spy—the latter probably paid better
than the former; Spenser was a private secretary and then a civil servant
in Ireland; Donne at the very beginning of his poetic career was a
private secretary until he did himself out of a job by marrying the
boss's ward without permission. The major professional poets are
marginal figures in the history of English poetry as we have constructed
it: Thomas Churchyard, Thomas Tusser, Nicholas Breton, George
Gascoigne (Gascoigne started as a professional soldier). Poetry was,
for the figures we consider the major poets, a means to some other end:
for Sidney the end was social and personal (in fact, biographers have a
good deal of trouble dealing with Sidney's imaginative writing—the
most recent biography, by Alan Stewart, which is excellent on the
political and diplomatic material, scarcely even mentions *Astrophil
and Stella* and *Arcadia*); for Spenser it was a way of getting a better
job, getting out of Ireland and installed at court, not necessarily as a
poet; for Marlowe…who knows? It was one of a number of things he

The Idea of the Book and the Creation of Literature. Stephen Orgel, Oxford University Press.
© Stephen Orgel 2023. DOI: 10.1093/oso/9780192871534.003.0005

did, maybe simply as part of his education, maybe to bring himself to the attention of important and powerful men who would be impressed with his wit and intelligence and dubious moral principles, and would employ him to do something other than write poetry. Was this, in fact, one of the things that attracted the attention of Burghley, Elizabeth's chief minister, and Walsingham, the head of the Elizabethan secret service? That he was intelligent and willing, and could adopt any number of alternative personae? It is also to the point that for Donne, Marlowe, and (for ten very productive years) Spenser, nothing was printed. Manuscript circulation, like poetry, was an extension of the personal and social life.

For Shakespeare, one would say that writing narrative poems was a logical extension of writing plays, except that the poems look so little like the plays. This is less true of Marlowe; but the long narrative poems of both poets have the look of an attempt to craft a quite different kind of career. Marlowe's *Hero and Leander* was unpublished at the time of his death, though it was licensed for publication four months later, so a manuscript was among his papers. It may have been in circulation, though there is no evidence that this was the case—it is cited frequently after it was published in 1598, but beyond the Stationer's Register entry there is no reference to the poem before that. The Shakespeare poems, on the other hand, appear as carefully printed little books from the first. Unlike Marlowe (and Donne, and for much of his career Spenser), Shakespeare published his poetry. It seems clear that Shakespeare turned to poetry because plague had closed the theaters throughout much of 1592–4; but this of course does not account for the character of the two poems he published, or for the way he went about it.

As we have observed, they were prefaced by lavish dedications to the young Earl of Southampton. Park Honan describes Southampton at this period:

> Just before he turned twenty-one the young Cambridge graduate had the appeal of an androgynous icon and a potentially great patron. Sir Philip Sidney's death in 1586 had left room for a new inspirer, a symbol of high attainment in art and war. Southampton was manly enough to hope to fight in battle, but attractive enough to elicit delicate verses. Noting his attendance with the queen at Oxford, John Sanford in a Latin poem claimed that no one present was more comely, "though his mouth yet blooms with tender down"

(*Apollinis et musarum euktika eidyllia*, 1592). In the same year a poem of fifteen pages in Latin entitled *Narcissus*, by his guardian's secretary John Clapham, was dedicated to the young earl. A group of writers loyal to Essex and Southampton formed around them.[1]

The poems themselves imply that Shakespeare was seeking not only cash from Southampton but also an entry into the world of aristocratic patrons and erudite readers. At the very least, this would have produced for him a less unstable audience than the public theater spectators, with more clearly calculable tastes; at best it would have earned him a place in some noble household, with an annuity, which was the most desirable sort of patronal endowment. That was the kind of poet Shakespeare was trying to be. He was a little too early for Southampton, who at the age of nineteen was still the ward of Burghley, whom he was shortly to offend deeply by refusing to marry Burghley's granddaughter. The consequences of this were considerable, both for the young man and for English poetry. Honan writes, "In resisting his guardian, the earl incurred more than Burghley's mere displeasure, since the law held that if a ward would not marry at his lord's request, on coming of age he must pay him what anyone would have given for the marriage. Southampton thus faced paying an enormous fine, said to be £5000, on turning twenty-one in October 1594."[2]

Nevertheless, Southampton was already reputed to be a potential patron for aspiring poets—Thomas Nashe in 1594, the year Southampton came into his majority, praised him in precisely those terms: "A dere lover and cherisher you are, as well of the lovers of Poets, as of Poets themselves."[3] By 1598 John Florio, making him one of the dedicatees of *A Worlde of Wordes*, writes that "I have lived some yeeres" in his "paie and patronage"[4]—Florio was teaching Southampton Italian, and therefore was offering his patron access to more than English poetry. Other writers courted him, apparently less successfully: in 1597 Southampton was the dedicatee of *Clitophon and Leucippe*, a translation from Achilles Tatius ("Resting thus in hope of your

---

[1] *DNB* under Wriothesley, Henry, third earl of Southampton.
[2] Ibid.
[3] The dedication to *The Unfortunate Traveller. Or the Life of Jack Wilton* (1594), sig. A2ᵛ.
[4] *A Worlde of Wordes* (1598), sig. a3ᵛ.

Honours curtesie, I cease"[5]); in 1603 Samuel Daniel dedicated a panegyric welcoming James I to him, and in 1604 another romance, *The Historie of Lysimachus and Varrona*, was cautiously dedicated to him ("fearing to grow offensive through tediousnes, I commit this simple work to your Lordships patronage"[6]). But, as Honan continues:

> Ironically, Southampton had little but enthusiasm to offer any poet. He hardly had funds to spare; he lived on a fixed allowance and faced paying a gigantic fine to Burghley, plus another vast sum to get his estates out of wardship. After he turned twenty-one in 1594, his need for money became desperate. In November of that year, he leased out part of Southampton House, and a few years later had to sell off five of his manors.[7]

Shakespeare's most immediate model in the search for a patron in 1593 was a poet who has essentially disappeared from literary history, Abraham Fraunce, who was attached to the household of the Countess of Pembroke, Sidney's sister, and in 1591 and 1592 published a group of pastorals and a long mythological poem with commentary called *The Countess of Pembroke's Yvychurch* dedicated to and including a role for the Countess. Fraunce grew up in Shropshire and was educated first at Shrewsbury School, then at St. John's College, Cambridge, after which he studied law at Gray's Inn. He may have known Philip Sidney at Shrewsbury (Sidney was several years older), and Sidney became his patron while he was at Cambridge. Upon Sidney's death Sidney's sister Mary Herbert, Countess of Pembroke, continued to sponsor him. After taking his law degree he returned to Shrewsbury, where he worked as a barrister in the Welsh prerogative court. The Pembrokes' patronage extended to his professional career: the earl recommended him for the position of Queen's Solicitor in the Welsh court (the recommendation was unsuccessful). And though Fraunce was not dependent for his income on his writing, it clearly constituted an important vocation for him, as it did for Sidney, the soldier-politician, who was also a poet, essayist, and novelist.

[5] [William Burton,] *The Most Delectable and Pleasaunt History of Clitophon and Leucippe...newly translated into English by W. B.* (1597), sig. a3[v].

[6] [John Hind], *The Most Excellent Historie of Lysimachus and Varrona* (1604), sig. a3[v].

[7] *DNB* under Wriothesley.

Meres names Fraunce, along with Sidney and Spenser, as the best poets for pastoral. *The Countess of Pembroke's Yvychurch* is a large three-part compendium. The pastorals in the first two parts include translations of Tasso's Italian play *Aminta*, Thomas Watson's Latin epic *Amyntas*, and Virgil's second eclogue, all into properly classical quantitative hexameters (i.e., with the scansion determined by the length of syllables, as in Greek and Latin verse, rather than by stress, as in English). *Amyntas*, the heart of the volume, is a vast elegiac pastoral in which the shepherd Amyntas mourns the death of his beloved Phyllis over twelve days, at the rate of one hundred lines per day. The third part of the collection consists of a retelling of stories from Ovid interspersed with an extensive mythographic commentary, including the Venus and Adonis story.

Domesticating quantitative verse

For modern readers, Fraunce's hexameters in the aggregate are admittedly numbing; but contemporary critics cited him with admiration, and the translation of *Amyntas* was popular enough to go through five editions between 1587 and 1596—Shakespeare's *Venus and Adonis* was eventually more popular, but for contemporary readers Fraunce's success is notable, the more so since the work is in quantitative meter. The patronage doubtless had something to do with its success: Sidney's sister shared her brother's tastes, and some of his popularity evidently accrued to her. English quantitative verse represents a huge investment of time and intelligence, and a just evaluation must view it in its own cultural context. The best book on the subject, and still a richly rewarding survey, is Derek Attridge's *Well-Weighed Syllables: Elizabethan Verse in Classical Metres* (1974), but even Attridge begins his study apologetically, by declaring the verse "patently weak" and "by present standards, unquestionably bad."[8] Still, devising a system of quantitative poetry in English was a project that major poets and critics took seriously, and condescending to the past is not a useful way of understanding it. Fraunce's work was not, in the 1590s, unquestionably bad.

---

[8] Derek Attridge, *Well-Weighed Syllables: Elizabethan Verse in Classical Metres* (Cambridge: Cambridge University Press, 1974), pp. 2, 3.

Sidney wrote a good deal of quantitative verse, and Spenser and Gabriel Harvey discussed it and exchanged examples. The larger assumption behind Roger Ascham's and Harvey's proposals for the reform of English poetry was that the "barbarous" England of the time could be rectified by the application of classical rules.[9] A return to the classics held out the promise of culture and civility—not only in poetry, of course, but poetry seemed a particularly clear example. Nobody thought the transformation would be easy; a hectoring and bullying tone is common throughout the discussion. But a good deal of energy in the Elizabethan age went into the devising of strategies for becoming the new ancients, strategies of translation and adaptation, and the invention of appropriately classical-sounding models for vernacular verse, the domestication of the classic.

The most successful and admired classical translations of the latter half of the sixteenth century were Arthur Golding's Ovid and Thomas Phaer and Thomas Twine's Virgil; both are in fourteener couplets, and both went through many editions by the end of the century. The fourteener couplet was essentially a ballad measure, and it is frequently derided by modern critics as doggerel, but it was sophisticated enough in 1598 to be the verse adopted by Chapman for his translation of the *Iliad*. All these translators were serious classicists, and something about English fourteeners sounded appropriate to them. It is tempting to conclude that for Elizabethans who wanted to classicize English verse, popular poetry was at fault precisely because it was popular. Attridge observes that "the regular iambic thump of most of the English verse written in the fifteen-sixties and seventies must have made Latin lines, with their lack of immediately apprehensible rhythm, seem particularly alien."[10] Was the new system a way of rendering poetry no longer immediately attractive, and thereby elite? The application of quantitative rules to English verse was a fairly late strategy; and though the new order was never widely adopted, for a few decades in the sixteenth century the effort did not seem quixotic. Fraunce's hexameters are in fact, even by modern standards, often supple and mellifluous:

---

[9] See, for a fuller discussion, my *Wit's Treasury* (Philadelphia: University of Pennsylvania Press, 2021), pp. 46–56.

[10] Attridge, p. 53.

> If that I mourne in woods, these woods seeme al to be mournyng,
> And broade-brauncht oake trees their upright topps to be bowing.
> Yf that I sigh or sob, this pine-tree straight by the shaking,
> This pearles [peerless] pine-tree for company seem's to be pyning,
> As though himself felt th'enduring pangs of *Amyntas*.[11]

Attridge (somewhat grudgingly) finds Fraunce the most successful of the English quantitative poets: "The movement produced little verse as good as this—which is, of course, more a censure of the movement than a commendation of Fraunce."[12] Adept poets managed to have it both ways, producing quantitative poetry that also reads beautifully as accentual free verse:

> Constant *Penelope*, sends to thee carelesse *Ulisses*,
> write not againe, but come sweet mate thy selfe to revive mee.
> *Troy* wee doe much envie, wee desolate lost Ladies of *Greece*:
> Not *Priamus*, nor yet all *Troy* can us recompence make.
> Oh, that hee had when hee first tooke shipping to Lacedemon,
> that adulter I meane, had beene o'rewhelmed with waters:
> Then had I not lien now all alone, thus quivering for cold,
> nor used this complaint, nor have thought the day to bee so long.[13]

This is a song text set by William Byrd, the opening of Penelope's epistle to Ulysses, the first of Ovid's *Heroides*, translated by an anonymous poet into quantitative measures. This example is unique in Byrd's vast oeuvre: even when Byrd set Latin quantitative poems, he did not set them quantitatively. But Byrd understood the scansion perfectly, setting long syllables to half notes and short syllables to quarter notes. The music even corrects three errors in the metrics. The poem is ascribed to Thomas Watson, because he was acquainted with Byrd and wrote at least one (nonquantitative) song text for him. But the attribution is surely incorrect: Watson was a thoroughly proficient classicist, who wrote much more Latin poetry than English. He would not have made mistakes in composing hexameters. Byrd was more expert than his poet here, and his amendment of the scansion is a

---

[11] *The Countess of Pembrokes Yvychurch* (1591), Second Part, sig. H4ᵛ.
[12] Attridge, 194.
[13] William Byrd, *Psalmes, Sonets, & songs of sadnes and pietie* (1588), sig. E3ʳ.

tiny indication of how actively involved in the issue of poetic quantity English culture actually was at this time.[14]

The quantitative rules in English allowed for considerable latitude: given the lack of standardization of spelling, many syllables could be rendered long or short by varying the orthography. Moreover, since it was rarely clear in what sense an English syllable could be called long or short, the rules were always a work in progress, and different poets applied them differently, but for the most part, English syllables were simply declared long if they were stressed. The surviving ancient accounts of prosodic quantity were for the most part concerned with music, and the verse they considered was Greek.[15] Though the rules of Latin verse were based on the Greek system, it was only imperfectly applicable to Latin, and far less applicable to English—hence the consistent confusion of syllabic length with stress.

The recent critic Sharon Schuman writes, "The whole system of classical Latin prosody must have been tremendously attractive to the English versifiers, flexible as it was (allowing them to escape the confinements of jog-trot doggerel), yet based on simple, consistent rules of vowel quantity and position."[16] Clearly there is some tendentiousness here (the escape from "jog-trot doggerel" was an escape from the prosody of Golding's Ovid and Chapman's *Iliad*) and the "simple, consistent rules of vowel quantity" were not so simple and consistent that they precluded continual debates precisely about vowel quantity, about what constituted a short or long syllable in English. But it must be true that the system itself was attractive merely because it was a system, setting up rules for composition and evaluation, and because these were derived from classical precedent.

The crucial element in classicizing English poetry, however, was the abandonment of rhyme, and it was this that eventually produced the greatest resistance. Samuel Daniel, defending traditional English poetry

---

[14] For a full discussion, see Stephen Orgel, "Measuring Verse, Measuring Value in English Renaissance Poetry," in Martin McLaughlin, Ingrid D. Rowland, and Elisabetta Tarantino, eds., *Authority, Innovation and Early Modern Epistemology* (Leeds: Legenda, 2015), pp. 97–103.

[15] For a summary of ancient texts on poetic quantity, see Ronald A. Zirin, *The Phonological Basis of Latin Prosody* (The Hague: Mouton, 1970), pp. 42–54.

[16] Sharon Schuman, "Sixteenth-Century English Quantitative Verse: Its Ends, Means, and Products," *Modern Philology* 74.4 (May, 1977), pp. 335–49, p. 339.

against the strictures of Thomas Campion, considers the quantitative system essentially an irrelevance:

> For we are tolde how that our measures goe wrong, all Ryming is grosse, vulgare, barbarous.... We could well have allowed of his numbers had he not disgraced our Ryme; which both Custome and Nature doth most powerfully defend: Custome that is before all Law, Nature that is aboue all Arte.[17]

"We could well have allowed of his numbers had he not disgraced our Ryme": the metrical system is not worth arguing about; rhyme is the issue. Rhyme was the crucial badge of barbarism, the essential departure from the classical ideal. Thus, Francis Meres, having compared Chaucer with Homer and declared him "the god of English poets," nevertheless singles out *Piers Plowman* as the one truly Homeric English poem: "As *Homer* was the first that adorned the Greek tongue with true quantity, so *Piers Plowman* was the first that observed the true quantitie of our verse without the curiositie of Rime."[18] That the poem is claimed to observe "true quantity" indicates how vague the sense of quantity in English could be. It is certainly arguable that Phaer's and Golding's fourteeners achieve a kind of prosodic "quantity," a supple and varied verse rhythm that is obviously not alien either to the English language or to the ballad measure within which they are working. The claim that the verse of *Piers Plowman* respects quantity is surely incorrect, but to Meres in 1598, the absence of rhyme was the key element.

By 1619 Jonson could tell Drummond that "Abraham Fraunce in his English hexameters was a fool"[19]—a fool to write English hexameters; clearly they were still being read in 1619. As for rhyme, according to Drummond Jonson "detesteth" all rhymes other than couplets, which he considered "the bravest sort of verses," and "cross-rhymes [alternating rhymes, abab, etc.] and stanzas...were all forced."[20] Jonson himself wrote both cross-rhymed and stanzaic poetry: it was quantitative verse that this classicist never wrote. Nevertheless, in *The English Grammar*

[17] *A Defence of Ryme* (?1603), in Smith vol. 2, pp. 357–9.
[18] Francis Meres, *Palladis Tamia: Wits Treasury* [...] (1598), fol. 279^{r-v}.
[19] *Informations*, Cambridge Ben Jonson, vol 5, p. 362 (line 37).
[20] Ibid., 359, lines 3–7.

(published posthumously in 1641) he declared his support for adapting the quantitative system to English verse, but for what one might call patriotic rather than poetic reasons:

> Not that I would have the vulgar and practised way of making abolished and abdicated, (being both sweet and delightful, and much taking the ear) but to the end our tongue may be made equal to those of the renowned countries, Italy and Greece, touching this particular.[21]

The project could never be more than approximate, since English offered no real equivalents to classical syllabification, and in any case, the prosody was not controlled by pronunciation, and often conflicted with it.

Thomas Campion confronts the problem directly:

> Above all the accent of our words is diligently to be observ'd, for chiefly by the accent in any language the true value of the sillables is to be measured. Neither can I remember any impediment except position that can alter the accent of any sillable in our English verse. For though we accent the second [syllable] of Trumpington short, yet is it naturally long, and so of necessity must be held of every composer. Wherefore the first rule that is to be observed is the nature of the accent, which we must ever follow.[22]

This passage argues that accentuation in English is always to be observed, but not in the case of the long-by-position rule (a vowel followed by two consonants is long), which in fact determines a large percentage of the cases in English (for example the -ing ending of participles, which are long by position, but invariably short and unaccented in speech). In these cases, as in the case of "Trumpington," poetry and English are two different languages. What can "yet is it naturally long" mean—are the rules of Latin scansion rules of nature? The most serious problem in Campion's system, however, is that accent or stress is conflated with quantity—the assumption is that stressed syllables are always long, which is certainly not the case. By the

---

[21] Cambridge Ben Jonson, vol. 7, pp. 358–9.
[22] In Smith, vol. 2, pp. 351–2.

sixteenth century this contradiction was inherent in the whole project of adapting a quantitative verse system to English.

Spenser too worries the issue of stress and quantity, using as his example the word *carpenter*, "the middle sillable, being used shorte in speech, when it shall be read long in Verse." He continues, "For why, a Gods name, may not we, as else the Greekes, have the kingdome of oure owne Language, and measure our Accentes by the sounde, reserving the Quantitie to the Verse?"[23] The language is ours; we may do as we like, but "reserving the Quantitie to the Verse" means that English in verse is not English as it is spoken (where the word would have to be pronounced, impossibly, with two long syllables, which for Spenser means two stressed syllables, *càrpènter*). Quantity in verse is a purely visual matter, to be read and not pronounced aloud. Poetry is a different language. The point is emphasized by the pedagogical handbooks' insistence that Latin verse, on which the system of English quantity was based, be read as prose, with no attempt to sound out the quantities.

As Attridge points out, quantitative metrics were problematic even in postclassical Latin: "by the fifth century A.D. a change had taken place in the pronunciation of Latin" so that "the quantities on which Latin verse was based ceased to be a property of the spoken language and had to be learned for the purpose of scanning and writing poetry in classical metres."[24] An English schoolboy learning Latin prosody would have assumed "that 'long' meant 'stressed' and 'short' meant 'unstressed', since this would be the obvious difference between the two kinds of syllable, and he would know of nothing which might contradict this assumption."[25]

Furthermore, the pronunciation of Latin itself varied widely throughout Europe, and there were violent arguments about it in England. Latin orations, verse, academic drama, and indeed, conversation sounded different depending on the location, even if the locations were Oxford and Cambridge.[26] The common claim that Latin was a universal language throughout Renaissance Europe does

---

[23] In Smith, vol. 1, pp. 98–9.   [24] Attridge, p. 21.   [25] Ibid. p. 47.
[26] In 1542 Stephen Gardiner, Chancellor of Cambridge University, issued an edict forbidding the new pronunciation of Latin and Greek based on Erasmus's theories about authentic classical usage, which was being adopted by the scholarly community.

not take enough into account. Joseph Scaliger found English speakers' pronunciation of Latin so incomprehensible that he assumed they were speaking English to him;[27] similarly, Erasmus reports that a Frenchman addressing a speech in Latin to the Emperor Maximilian was thought to be speaking French, the accent of a German following him was ridiculed, and the Danish visitor "sounded like a Scotsman."[28] Philip Sidney, employing Latin on his diplomatic missions, was told by Hubert Languet that his Latin sounded provincial; by the same token, the French pronunciation Languet used was considered by Erasmus to be egregiously bad.[29] These were obviously not problems with the written language; but spoken and written Latin were only imperfectly related, and spoken Latin was not invariably comprehensible.

Attridge remarks that it is only recently that the spoken language has taken precedence over the written language and writing has been considered a transcription of speech. "The present-day linguist's assumption that the written language is merely a representation of, and therefore secondary to, the spoken language would have puzzled an Elizabethan grammarian, not so much because he felt that the reverse was true, but because he did not make any clear distinction." He quotes the eighteenth-century grammarian James Harris: "oral speech is the effect of reading, reading the effect of writing, and writing the effect of grammar."[30] But even more clearly in English than in Latin, by the sixteenth century spelling had not kept pace with pronunciation, and the written language had long ceased to be an adequate guide to speech. When Hamlet urges the visiting actors to "Speak the speech…as I pronounced it to you" (3.2.1–2) he is concerned with principles of declamation, but he also testifies to the disjunction between the written text and the way it is spoken.[31]

---

[27] Attridge, p. 23.

[28] W. Sidney Allen, *Vox Latina: A Guide to the Pronunciation of Classical Latin* (Cambridge: Cambridge University Press, 1965), p. 107.

[29] *De Recta Latini Graeque Sermonis Pronuntiatione Dialogus* (*The Right Way of Speaking Latin and Greek*), trans. Maurice Pope, *Collected Works of Erasmus*, ed. J. K. Sowards (Toronto: University of Toronto Press, 1985), vol. 26, p. 409.

[30] Attridge, p. 54.

[31] Jonathan Goldberg interestingly complicates the relation between speech and writing in the important essay "Hamlet's Hand," *Shakespeare Quarterly* 39.3 (Autumn, 1988), pp. 307–27.

Classical Shakespeare

Shakespeare never wrote quantitative hexameters, not even for the pedantic poets in *Love's Labour's Lost*, where they would certainly have been appropriate—perhaps his small Latin and less Greek did not extend so far, or perhaps there was simply no way of adapting them to the spoken language of the stage. But much of his early work reflects the classicizing movement of the age, especially *The Comedy of Errors*, *Titus Andronicus*, *The Taming of the Shrew* (the last based on an English version of an Italian comedy that in turn was based on Plautus and Terence). He turned from plays to poetry in 1592–3, writing *Venus and Adonis* and *Lucrece* while the theaters were closed because of plague. These works were addressed to an audience of readers who knew the classics, both Latin and English; they recall, in both their physical presentation and versification, recent editions of Ovid, Spenser, and Sidney.

Venus and Adonis was an early contribution to the new tradition of the Elizabethan erotic narrative poem on classical themes, inaugurated by Thomas Lodge's *Scillaes Metamorphosis*, published in 1589—Shakespeare even uses Lodge's stanza form.[32] Marlowe's *Hero and Leander* must have been composed around the same time—it was entered in the Stationers' Register shortly after Marlowe's death in 1593, and finally published in 1598. Shakespeare may or may not have known Marlowe's poem; it seems likely that the manuscript circulated, though there is no evidence that it did (Shakespeare quotes it in *As You Like It* in 1599, a year after it was published; aside from the Stationers' Register entry, there are no citations of it before 1598). Indeed, any influence may have worked the other way: Marlowe may have known Shakespeare's poem. The reference to Venus and Adonis in *Hero and Leander* suggests Shakespeare's version of the story, not Ovid's:

> *Venus* in her naked glory strove
> To please the carelesse and disdainfull eies,
> Of proud *Adonis* that before her lies.
>
> (1.12–14)

---

[32] The term "epyllion" (little epic), widely used in the nineteenth and early twentieth centuries to refer to these works, has generally been abandoned as anachronistic—there is apparently only one classical instance of the term to refer to a short epic, in Athenaeus. There are classical examples, but they are too various to be grouped together into a single genre.

The genre quickly became a popular one: Thomas Heywood's *Oenone and Paris* appeared in 1594, as did Shakespeare's *Lucrece*, and both Thomas Edwards's *Cephalus and Procris* and Michael Drayton's *Endymion and Phoebe* in 1595, though *Cephalus and Procris* had been entered for publication in 1593.

The Venus and Adonis story conveyed and illustrated a number of often contradictory meanings. Shakespeare's version is subversive of both the original story and the mythographic tradition. At the same time, its overt and teasing eroticism led to its immense popularity in an outwardly puritanical culture. Arthur Golding in his translation of Ovid glosses the story simply and moralistically:

> The tenth booke cheefly dooth containe one kynd of argument
> Reproving most prodigious lusts...
> ...Adonis death dooth shew that manhood strives
> Against forewarning though men see the perill of their lives.[33]

In the Venus and Adonis episode, it is Venus who is guilty of "prodigious lusts"; Adonis is charged only with incautious behavior. Two decades later Fraunce delves farther into the commentaries and finds the story neither ominous nor cautionary:

> Now, for Venus her love to Adonis, and lamentation for his death: by Adonis is meant the sunne, by Venus, the upper hemisphere of the earth (as by Proserpine the lower) by the boare, winter: by the death of Adonis, the absence of the sunne for the sixe wintrie moneths; all which time, the earth lamenteth: Adonis is wounded in those parts, which are the instruments of propagation: for, in winter the son [*sic*] seemeth impotent, and the earth barren: neither that being able to get, nor this to beare either fruite or flowres: and therefore Venus sits, lamentably hanging downe her head, leaning on her left hand, her garments all over her face.... Adonis was turnd to a fading flowre; bewty decayeth, and lust leaveth the lustfull, if they leave not it. Equicola, expoundeth it thus: Adonis was borne of Myrrha; Myrrhe provoketh lust: Adonis was kilde by a boare, that is, he was spent and weakened by old age: Venus lamenteth, lust decayeth.[34]

---

[33] *The xv. Bookes of P. Ovidius Naso, Entituled, Metamorphosis* (1567), sig. A4ʳ.
[34] *The Third Parte of the Countess of Pembrokes Yvychurch* (1592), sig. M4ᵛ.

In the basic narrative source, Ovid's *Metamorphoses*, the Venus and Adonis story is one of the songs Orpheus sings after the death of Euridice and his failure to bring her back from the underworld—these are the songs that make all nature fall in love with him and exemplify the power of poetry. Adonis is the end of a family saga, a series of love stories most of which are linked genealogically. Golding's claim that the subject is "prodigious lusts" is correct; Orpheus begins, "I sing of boys beloved by gods and girls stricken with forbidden passions (*inconcessis ignibus*) paying the penalty for lust,"[35] though the lesson is less a warning against lust than an acknowledgment of how much a part of nature it is. The family saga begins with Pygmalion, a virtuous sculptor living in a wicked town, who despaired of finding a chaste wife and created an ivory statue of an ideal woman. He prayed to Venus, who answered his prayer and brought the sculpture to life. Their daughter Paphos founded the island city named for her and specially favored by Venus. Her son Cinyras had a daughter named Myrrha, who conceived a violent incestuous passion for her father. She contrived to sleep with him muffled, so that he did not know her; but when he discovered her identity he threatened to kill her, and she fled. Heavily pregnant, and full of a sense of the enormity of her sin, she prayed for release, and was transformed into the myrrh tree, and as a tree she gave birth to Adonis, her son and brother.

The child grew to be surpassingly beautiful, so that even Venus fell in love with him, and thus, Ovid says, avenged the lust the goddess had inspired in his mother. Venus was so deeply in love that she "avoids even the heavens; Adonis is preferred to heaven."[36] When she was summoned to Olympus and had to leave him, she cautioned him against hunting dangerous animals, explaining, through the story of Hippomenes and Atalanta, whom she had turned to beasts, that wild animals hate her—the story accounts for the impending tragedy, but is also a reminder of her power and authority, and a warning against treating her favors casually. Nevertheless, Adonis was a courageous hunter, and pursued a boar and was gored by it in the groin—Ovid's word is "*inguine*," the genitals. As he died, Venus returned, and desperate with grief, transformed him into an anemone. In Ovid's account

---

[35] *Metamorphoses* Book 10, lines 152–4.   [36] Ibid., line 532.

Adonis is the innocent victim of other people's crimes in the distant past. He is, indeed, merely a pawn in nature's huge game of revenge on Venus. Ovid's moral is that the world is violent and passionate, and though there are explanations for what happens in it, they are explanations that depend on being able to take a much longer view than any of the participants can ever have. Only the readers of poetry can have it.

In Ovid, the love of Venus and Adonis is powerfully reciprocal. Adonis goes hunting not to escape from Venus, but because it is what active young men do. And though in Ovid's account lust has consequences, not in Golding's moralistic sense—the passion can no more be resisted than the consequences can be avoided; both are part of nature. Thus Abraham Fraunce is in one respect more true to Ovid than Golding: Fraunce cites the commentators who find allegories of nature in the stories, but not rules for behavior. Spenser in *The Faerie Queene* also sees the story not as a morality, but as an allegory of creativity in nature: in the Garden of Adonis in Book 3, Venus has undone the tragedy by rescuing Adonis from the boar, whom she has "emprisoned for ay," and the two spend eternity endlessly making love (Book 3, canto 6, stanzas 46–9). The love is endlessly productive, not frustrating or tragic. Their conjunction represents the best aspects of nature, its prolific creativity, and it is purely a good thing. In contrast to the sexual explicitness of Shakespeare's poem, however, the love in Spenser is oddly inert: most of the time Adonis is asleep, and Venus "takes her pleasure" while he is unconscious. For once in Spenser, there are no problems about sex, and no issues of marriage or chastity. The myth is an allegory of Aristotelian physiology: the male provides the species with form, the female with substance—how this is accomplished while the male is asleep is not explained. In the narrative, the love eventuates in the birth of perfect womanhood, a pair of chaste twins, Belphoebe and Amoret; the former mirrors the virginal chastity of Queen Elizabeth, the latter the chastity of married love, the two ways in which women can be virtuous.

Spenser has some trouble maintaining both these figures as positive ideals because women are so completely conceived within his poetry as the objects of male desire, as not having any independent will or action outside the context of that desire—in order to create an independent woman who is not a witch, the heroic Britomart, Spenser conceives her as a knight, essentially a transvestite, a woman who performs as a man.

Even the seductive witch figures, of whom there are many in *The Faerie Queene*, do nothing except desire and be desirable, and their own desire is enabled by the fact that they themselves *are* desirable (thus men are, tautologically, attracted to them because they are attractive). If women were not beautiful, there would be no problem: the witch is a wicked witch, but her power derives from her desirability—she is what men want—so there is a good deal of slippage over the question of where the wickedness is located. Even though Spenser is always representing his chaste women as staunchly defending their virtue, the virtue is also always in danger; the beauty which is the outward face of virtue is also responsible for the male desire which threatens it, and which constantly pursues it. So the threat of rape, not the promise of marriage, is assumed to be the consequence of beauty and virtue. Feminine beauty is held responsible for the masculine violence that is directed against it—both the beautiful witch (the bad example) and the goddess Venus (the good example) are the active figures in their love affairs. This view of womanhood both idealizes women and turns them into sexual objects, but it also paradoxically makes them responsible for whatever happens sexually.

Shakespeare's version of the story is explicit about Venus's responsibility for the destructive lust; but the passion is entirely one-sided, and all the beauty in *Venus and Adonis* belongs to the asexual youth, recalling (or perhaps anticipating) the epicene youth of the early sonnets, the master-mistress of Shakespeare's passion, but equally unavailable for sex. Shakespeare's Adonis is also quite as passive as Spenser's, but in Shakespeare there is no way for Venus to "take her pleasure." His sexual coldness, moreover, is clearly provoked by Venus's behavior: she attempts to get him aroused by shaming and haranguing him. Adonis ascribes his lack of libido to his youth, but the poem presents Venus as powerfully unattractive, and Adonis finally declares her not the goddess of love, but of "sweating lust." Certainly she is represented as singularly inept at making love—she simply throws herself on top of Adonis; instead of attempts at foreplay, she coaxes and berates him. But at the conclusion, accounting for the tragedy, Venus describes the lethal boar "nuzzling...in his soft groin," imagining an intimate caress of a sort she herself never tried with him. Indeed, she recognizes the boar as a version of herself:

> Had I been toothed like him, I must confess,
> With kissing him I should have killed him first...
> (1117–18)

And love as it is presented in the poem becomes the model for all future love:

> Sorrow on love hereafter shall attend...
> It shall be fickle, false, and full of fraud;
> Bud, and be blasted in a breathing while....
> (1136, 1141–2)

Shakespeare in one sense turns the erotic tradition around, making Venus a rapist, but in another sense he follows the sexual objectification of women to its logical conclusion—Venus is defined by her libido, and in "fickle, false, and full of fraud" Venus is describing herself. In Shakespeare's version of the story, love is violent, amoral, destructive, but also comic: the poem is not at all in awe of its classical material. Its Venus is a parody of the classical goddess of love, not the ideal, perfect and overwhelmingly desirable epitome of womanhood, but a desperate and sexually voracious creature pursuing an idealistic youth who is repelled by her. Her arguments are perfectly standard:

> Make use of time, let not advantage slip;
> Beauty within itself should not be wasted...
> Torches are made to light, jewels to wear,
> Dainties to taste, fresh beauty for the use,
> Herbs for their smell....
> (lines 129–30, 163–5)

They are the arguments conventionally used by men to woo women; they are Leander's arguments to Hero. But Venus's rational arguments do not at all reflect her feelings, "trembling in her passion.../ Being so enraged" (27, 29): lust, violence, and selfishness lie just beneath the reasonable arguments from nature. The moment when Adonis characterizes the goddess of love as "sweating lust" links the poem's titillating comedy with Golding's heavy moralizing, and though Adonis is certainly correct, it is not clear how seriously we are intended to take him: even in the sixteenth century young men were not expected to refuse free sex with no consequences.

Venus's lust anticipates Tarquin's in Shakespeare's poem of the next year. Tarquin is equally possessed, and equally ruthless, but obviously a good deal more dangerous, and not at all comic. He is armed and threatens both murder and something worse, the destruction of Lucrece's reputation.

> "Lucrece," quoth he, "this night I must enjoy thee.
> If thou deny, then force must work my way,
> For in thy bed I purpose to destroy thee;
> That done, some worthless slave of thine I'll slay
> To kill thine honor with thy life's decay;
>> And in thy dead arms do I mean to place him,
>> Swearing I slew him, seeing thee embrace him."
>>> (512–18)

His passion, moreover, has as much to do with male bonding as with physical attraction. The source of his "keen appetite" is Collatine's praise of his wife's chaste beauty:

> Haply the name of "chaste" unhapp'ly set
> This bateless edge on his keen appetite,
> When Collatine unwisely did not let
> To praise the clear unmatchèd red and white
> Which triumphed in that sky of his delight...
>> (8–12)

> ... why is Collatine the publisher
>> Of that rich jewel he should keep unknown
>> From thievish ears, because it is his own?
>>> (33–35)

Tarquin uses threats and physical force rather than harangues, but as with Venus and Adonis, the more ashamed and withdrawn the quarry grows, the more excited the rapist becomes. Tarquin makes Lucrece responsible for the rape:

> ... I come to scale
>> Thy never-conquered fort: the fault is thine,
>> For those thine eyes betray thee unto mine.
> Thus I forestall thee, if thou mean to chide:
> Thy beauty hath ensnared thee to this night...
>> (481–5)

The rape takes place in a single line—"O, that prone lust should stain so pure a bed!" (684)—and subsequently Lucrece too blames herself:

> Make me not object to the telltale day:
> The light will show charactered in my brow
> The story of sweet chastity's decay,
> The impious breach of holy wedlock vow;
> Yea, the illiterate that know not how
> > To cipher what is writ in learnèd books
> > Will quote my loathsome trespass in my looks.
> > > (806–12)

"The impious breach of holy wedlock vow" should be an accusation against Tarquin, but by the end of the stanza, the breach is hers, "My loathsome trespass"; and later, apostrophizing her husband Collatine, she declares herself "guilty of thy honor's wrack" (841).

For Elizabethans, the outrage committed by Tarquin is more than sexual, and the issue of Lucrece's lack of consent is not the principal one. Marriage conferred legal possession; Collatine's rights in Lucrece were property rights, and Tarquin is therefore damaging the husband's property.[37] Moreover, in Renaissance physiology as it descended from Aristotle and Galen, semen was a form of blood, and Lucrece's blood was corrupted by Tarquin's[38]—this is made explicit at the end of the poem, when the pure red of Lucrece's blood is mingled with the black blood introduced by the rape:

> Some of her blood still pure and red remained,
> And some looked black, and that false Tarquin stained.
> > (1742–3)

The question of Lucrece's compliance is irrelevant. St. Augustine insisted that Lucrece was wrong to commit suicide because she did not accede to the rape.[39] The claim was unsupported by the science of the age, and only became plausible more than a thousand years later.

---

[37] For an excellent statement of the legal issues involved, see Catherine Belsey, "Tarquin Dispossessed: Expropriation and Consent in 'The Rape of Lucrece,'" *Shakespeare Quarterly* 52.3 (Autumn, 2001), pp. 315–35.

[38] See John W. Crawford, "Revisiting Shakespeare's Lucrece: A Social Reason for Her Suicide," *CEA Critic* 59.3 (spring/summer, 1997), pp. 65–9.

[39] The detailed argument is in *The City of God* 1.18 and 19; trans. Marcus Dods (Edinburgh: T. and T. Clark, 1871), pp. 28–30.

After Tarquin's departure, Lucrece spends the long interlude before morning listening to Philomel, the nightingale, herself a victim of rape. She then writes a message to Collatine summoning him home, and as she waits for his return, looks at a painting of the destruction of Troy. She focusses initially on the figure of Hecuba, in whom she sees a model of herself:

> In her the painter had anatomized
> Time's ruin, beauty's wrack, and grim care's reign,
> (1450–1)

but then at greater length on Sinon, the traitor responsible for the admission of the Trojan Horse into Troy, and thus a figure for both Tarquin and her husband, "the publisher / Of that rich jewel he should keep unknown." In this ekphrasis, the viewer is no longer Lucrece, but the reader ("There might you see . . . ," l. 1380). The subject is the fall of Troy, rather than some Ovidian story such as the rape of Philomel, because the implications of the act are public and political, affecting the commonwealth as a whole.

Lucrece is provided with an argument, which does not entirely accord with the poem—from the outset there are various ways of reading and interpreting the material. The poem has an obvious analogue in *Titus Andronicus*, which was new in 1594: rape is the one intolerable political act that justifies revolution. In terms of political history, this is quite striking: rapes are, traditionally, the foundational acts of empire: Jupiter abducts Europa from Asia and carries her off to found Europe; Romulus populates Rome by having his soldiers rape the Sabine women; Dido has her followers carry off the women of Cyprus to be the breeding stock for her new Carthaginian empire. But in *Lucrece* the rape is the trigger for republican resistance: this is the one act not permissible to royalty. It is significant, moreover, that the rape is committed on a wife; this is a critical violation of property and privacy, an instance where human dignity—the dignity not of the wife but of the husband—means more than aristocratic prerogative.

As we have seen, in a marginal note in his copy of Speght's Chaucer, published in 1598 and which he acquired in that year, Gabriel Harvey links *Lucrece* with *Hamlet* as two works of Shakespeare's pleasing "the wiser sort":

> The younger sort takes much delight in Shakespeares Venus, & Adonis: but his Lucrece, & his tragedie of Hamlet, Prince of Denmarke, have it in them, to please the wiser sort.[40]

The note must have been written around 1600–1, well before any version of the play was in print. The wiser sort were theatergoers as well as readers.

Shakespeare's sonnets

The Shakespeare of what Francis Meres calls the "sugared sonnets" is very much the Shakespeare of the social and cultural world implied by the dedications to *Venus and Adonis* and *Lucrece*; but, as Meres's reference to an audience of "private friends" suggests, precisely because the sonnets circulated only in manuscript, their poet is far more deeply embedded in that world than Shakespeare the narrative poet is. The subtext of *Venus and Adonis* and *Lucrece* may be the search for a noble patron, but the sonnets imply a literary circle of taste and wit in which Shakespeare moves with ease. Patronage is still an issue in these poems, with the poet promising to immortalize the name of the aristocratic youth who is addressed, and another poet competing for his attention; but the patronage relationship is no longer simply a matter of dedications. It is here the subject of the poems, and is increasingly intense, intimate, fraught, and even at times explicitly erotic. That sense of intimacy would have been shared, too, by the "private friends," and the social world in which the sonnets circulated was correspondingly complex and sophisticated.

To return to the question of how Shakespeare would appear to us had his poems been included in the folio—had the folio been a volume of Complete Works, rather than Complete Plays—for one thing, as we have seen, Shakespeare's ambitions to move up into the gentry, to be part of the world of aristocratic patronage, would be part of our sense of him, entirely consistent with his revival of his father's application for a coat of arms, the certification that he was a gentleman. The original application had been rejected; the new application was approved in

---

[40] See above, Chapter 2, p. 38.

1596, and the shield with the spear and the motto *Non sanz droict* (not without right) was granted. The motto was in old French perhaps to suggest an ancient Norman ancestry, or perhaps merely to associate the spear of the family name with the chivalric tradition. But the sonnets also give us a Shakespeare we are not entirely comfortable with, less because, quite unexpectedly, a substantial number are love poems to a man, than because they are so relentlessly self-lacerating. For every buoyant sonnet there are three despairing ones; the personality that comes through is not one we associate with the world's greatest playwright. Hence the resistance to Malone's restoration of the 1609 text— as we have seen, the editor George Steevens in 1793 refused them a place in his Shakespeare edition, asserting that "the strongest act of Parliament that could be framed, would fail to compel readers into their service." Everyone remembers that Wordsworth said of the sonnets that "with this key / Shakespeare unlocked his heart," but he also declared them "abominably harsh, obscure, and worthless."[41]

There is, of course, no way of knowing which of the sonnets were circulating among Shakespeare's "private friends" in 1598, but Colin Burrow's summary of the dates proposed by stylometric analysis places only 104–26 after 1598. None of the poems seem to have been composed after 1604. The earliest poems appear to be 127–54, all those chronicling the love for the Dark Lady. Some of this is counterintuitive—there is nothing in the early plays that sounds remotely like sonnet 129, "Th'expense of spirit in a waste of shame...," though of course when the volume was put together for its publication in 1609 later poems could have been added to an earlier collection.

We customarily refer to the sonnets as a sequence, a narrative, or a series of related narratives: a narcissistic young man is urged to marry and produce heirs; the poet is captivated by a beautiful, aristocratic youth—perhaps the same young man, perhaps not—who reciprocates his love for a time, but then treats him with coldness, prefers another writer, has an affair with the poet's mistress; the poet falls in love with a beautiful, dark, married woman—perhaps the mistress of the previous narrative, perhaps not—who betrays him with his dearest friend— perhaps the friend of the previous narrative, perhaps not. But the

---

[41] Both are cited by Burrow, pp. 103, 138.

texture is relentlessly unspecific. Even the repeated claim that the poems will immortalize the beloved's name frustrates us by concealing that name. None of this would matter if we did not want to read the sonnets autobiographically. Attempts to do so began only in the late eighteenth century, and no remotely satisfactory identification of the beloved youth, the rival poet, or the Dark Lady has ever been proposed. Though the sonnets must be, in some respect, autobiographical, we simply know too little about Shakespeare's personal life, and more important, about the imaginative relation between his life and his art, to treat these poems as biographical evidence.

How, then, should we read this book? To begin with, by abandoning any assumption that the implied narrative corresponds with a sequence of events in Shakespeare's life, or that the process of composition bears any relation to the order of the poems in the quarto. The poems range from the style of the earliest Shakespeare to that of the great middle period work. But the groupings, as we have seen, do not move from early to late—some of the poems that are stylistically earliest are in the final group of sonnets, 127–54. Some of the poems were obviously written to be read together: the first seventeen urge a young man to marry and have children; a group of sonnets allude to a sexual betrayal; several poems meditate on a journey that takes him from the friend. Some groups have larger structures of concern—the ambiguous power of poetry; the far less ambiguous power of mutability. But for the most part, the collection seems to have been arranged in its present order long after most of the individual poems were written, and into groups that are associated by theme, imagery, or on occasion by an underlying narrative only glancingly alluded to. Thus the sonnets to the beautiful young man may not have been written together, or to only one young man; just as the mistress and friend in the earlier part of the sequence may not be those of the Dark Lady section. Whatever continuous narratives we derive from the volume are a function of its ultimate arrangement, not of its composition.

There are, however, several anomalies in the arrangement. Sonnet 126, "O thou my lovely boy...," consists of twelve lines of couplets followed by a pair of empty parentheses, a notional couplet to bring the poem up to fourteen lines. This serves as a conclusion to the poems to the beloved young man; and whoever put the collection together must have sensed that some transition was necessary from the abject homoeroticism of sonnet 125, "No, let me be obsequious in thy heart, / And take thou my oblation, poor but free," to the cynical womanizing of sonnet 127, "In the old age black was not counted fair...." The change of tone represented by 126 is indeed radical: this is not the lovely boy for whom the poet "bore the canopy"; this youth is not being urged to marry, or to love the poet, or even to allow the poet to love him. This boy is Nature's minion, and Nature is as fickle as the young man has been. The poet offers no immortalizing verse, but only the most detached of warnings, not even to make use of time, but only to fear it as the consequence of an uncaring Nature:

> Yet fear her, O thou minion of her pleasure:
> She may detain, but not still keep, her treasure....
>
> (9–10)

In the drama of the sequence, the admonition is a little smug, even perhaps a little vengeful: desirable as you are, you're just like the rest of us. Couplets at this point have served to interrupt or reverse or turn off 125 sonnets. Sonnet 126 seems to ask: will six more couplets do it? And the concluding empty parentheses say: will just one more, will seven?

But the transition merely moves the poet from desiring an unresponsive young man to desiring a faithless, adulterous woman. Though the sonnets were clearly written at different periods over many years, their arrangement into individual groups must have been Shakespeare's; but their organization into a published volume is a different matter. If the placement of 126 makes sense, what about Sonnet 145, a lighthearted epigram on Anne Hathaway's name, another anomaly, the only tetrameter sonnet, bizarrely placed between "Two loves have I of comfort and despair" (neither one, clearly, Shakespeare's wife) and "Poor soul, the center of my sinful earth," which has nothing to do with women or love at all? 145 alone of all the poems in the sequence certifies the poet as Shakespeare—awkwardly, for critics who want to argue that the speaker of the sonnets is not to be construed as the author, that the love for the young man no more implies that Shakespeare was gay than *Macbeth* implies that he was a murderer. But given the relentless anonymity of the young man, the Dark Lady, the rival poet, why would a compiler want to identify Shakespeare at this point, especially through a punning sonnet about his wife? Sonnet 135,

"Whoever hath her wish, thou hast thy Will, / And Will to boot, and Will in over-plus," merely teases us with autobiography—the author is named Will; but so is the speaker, and the friend, and the lady's husband: much wit but not much information there. What about the final two sonnets, lighthearted epigrams modelled on the Greek Anthology? They seem, to say the least, out of place: did Shakespeare really have anything to do with concluding his emotionally fraught sequence with them? How do you end this cycle of desire, frustration, abjection?

Collections of sonnets are traditionally love poems that both express the love, and are therefore addressed to the beloved, and chronicle it, recount its course, declare it to the world; but most of all sonnets declare the claims of the author to be a great poet, and are therefore addressed to anybody and everybody. Sonnet 18, "Shall I compare thee to a summer's day...," is the most famous of the sonnets: this is one of many of the love poems to the young man that can be seen to have a gendered subject only because of their placement in the sequence. It regularly appears in modern anthologies with no indication that the addressee is not a woman; but it is clear that the subject is male from the sonnet that follows it, 19, lines 9–12: "Oh carve not with thy hours my love's fair brow / ... Him in thy course untainted do allow / For beauty's pattern to succeeding men." There are often elements in the poems themselves indicating that the beloved is male, but to recognize them depends on a knowledge of the book as a whole. The Shakespeare of the sonnets does not talk about women in this way:

> Shall I compare thee to a summer's day?
> Thou art more lovely and more temperate.

The lovely and temperate are, throughout the volume, masculine attributes; women are far more unreliable. As for the poem's confident declaration of the immortalizing power of verse, in the sequence it is preceded by a sonnet that asks "Who will believe my verse in time to come / If it were filled with your most high deserts?", and goes on to compare the poem to a tomb "That hides your life and shows not half your parts." It is followed by "Devouring Time, blunt thou the lion's paws," which vainly pleads for an ageless—and unambiguously male—beloved.

That, then, is the context within the volume of sonnets. Even out of context, however, 18 is a very unorthodox love poem, to which the gender of the beloved is ultimately irrelevant:

> But thy eternal summer shall not fade,
> Nor lose possession of that fair thou ow'st,
> Nor shall Death boast thou wander'st in his shade,
> As in immortal lines to time thou grow'st.
> So long as men can breathe or eyes can see,
> So long lives this, and this gives life to thee.

The beloved is unchanging and eternal only because the poem is claimed to be. The object of love and celebration is the poet's own craft—the beloved is the poem.

Shakespeare writes his sonnets with a full sense of how conventional the form is, and how much ironic baggage the form itself carries with it; so the interplay between the conventional and the language of real feeling is especially striking—this is one of the organizing principles of the sequence, a continual movement back and forth between the witty and ironic and real cries from the heart, poems that acknowledge that frustrated love is real and very painful. The first twelve of the sonnets to the young man are not love poems; they are admiration or adulation poems. They use a peculiar strategy in persuading the young man to marry: they tell him how wonderful he is, not how wonderful the woman he ought to be marrying is, or how wonderful women in general are. In fact, women are curiously absent from most of these marriage sonnets, and when they are present, they are quite marginal. Marrying is all about producing heirs (sons, not daughters), not about falling in love, and not even about sex. The business of wooing and making love and producing babies has to do with planting gardens, plucking roses, ploughing fields, or with spending money, distilling perfume (5 and 6), playing music, stamping seals in wax. There is nobody in these opening sonnets except the beautiful young - man—and then, suddenly, in 13, the poet appears, openly declaring his love:

> O that you were yourself; but, love, you are
> No longer yours than you yourself here live.
> (1–2)

By sonnet 18 the poet has made himself indispensable—from 13 on, the poems are explicitly love poems. If we read the sonnets in sequence, there is a clear emotional narrative.

These poems say, I can make you immortal, but they also say, I write these poems to get your attention, and also to get the world's attention, to tell everybody both that I love you and that I am a great poet. I am your immortality; but you are also my immortality, the essential, frustrating, faithless, heartbreaking subject that is essential to great poetry, that declares that what is great about poetry is that it fails: fails to make you love me, fails to preserve your name; but thereby preserves my name.

The rhetoric of patronage, and of male friendship generally, was precisely the language of love, and it rendered all such relationships literally ambiguous. Such language does not necessarily imply a sexual relationship; but it is important to add that, by the same token, nothing in the language precludes it either—King James *was* accused of making his favorites his lovers. The language of love in the age implies everything but tells nothing. It is to the point that Shakespeare's Sonnet 20 ends by denying that the poet is sleeping with the young man.[42] Nothing can be taken for granted.

The most famous of these sonnets have been relentlessly sentimentalized—their accessibility to such treatment doubtless explains their celebrity. Often, however, poems that begin with the grandest declarations of love proceed to an account of the passion that is anything but ideal. Thus 116 begins:

> Let me not to the marriage of true minds
> Admit impediments. Love is not love
> That alters when it alteration finds,
> Or bends with the remover to remove.
> O no, it is an ever-fixèd mark...
>
> (1–5)

This poem is often read at weddings. But by the third line the marriage of true minds includes "alteration", and one of the partners is a "remover." By the second quatrain, the "ever-fixèd mark" is definitively

---

[42] Or perhaps not. For an alternative reading, see my *Impersonations* (Cambridge: Cambridge University Press, 1996), pp. 56–7.

alone, by the end of the third quatrain, it is alone "even to the edge of doom." The couplet emphasizes the poet's isolation:

> If this be error, and upon me proved,
> I never writ, nor no man ever loved.

Whether the final line is taken to mean "no man ever loved" or "I never loved any man," surely the most striking thing about it, as about the poem as a whole, is the briefness imagined for any reciprocal love. The poet in this marriage has remained faithful to a lover who has left him at the altar.

The lover's gender in this case is unspecified, though since the poem comes among the sonnets to the young man, the gender is presumably male. When the beloved is a woman, the tone changes radically; the final section, from 127 to 154, includes poems that are the most erotically intense in the volume, but are also characteristically frustrated, sarcastic, and disillusioned. The difference between the poems to the youth and those to the woman has often been viewed in Platonic or Petrarchan terms, with the contrast between spiritual and sensual love being dramatized through the idealized male lover and the passionate and deceitful mistress; but this reading ignores how much sexuality is involved in the love for the young man, "the master-mistress of my passion," and how much deception and betrayal the idealized love struggles to accept and accommodate. Sonnet 42, dealing with the realization that the friend and the poet's mistress are sleeping together, ends:

> But here's the joy: my friend and I are one.
> Sweet flatt'ry! Then she loves but me alone!
>
> (13–14)

The witty speciousness of the reasoning depends on the coordinates that increasingly define the love these poems address: the friend and he are one; the mistress is the other. It is the loss of the friend that chiefly matters, because it is a loss of self. The touch is light in this poem, but the tone is one that can scarcely be maintained—Sonnet 40 has a much more precarious sense of balance about the betrayal by the friend:

> Lascivious grace, in whom all ill well shows,
> Kill me with spites; yet we must not be foes.
>
> (13–14)

This is almost wistful, a testimony to the ultimate powerlessness of the poetry which has been so hyperbolically praised. The mistress and the friend are finally both the other. Shakespeare keeps finding excuses for the young man's behavior, "in whom all ill well shows," whereas there are none for the woman's; but in both cases the poet is in the grip of a profoundly unsettling and disorienting passion that can only partly and intermittently be contained by the power of his mind and his verse.

| 6 |

What Is a Book?

From manuscript to book

When poems for circulation among private friends are reconceived as books they are transformed. The texts, as they are changed from handwriting to type, go from something private and personal to something public and processed, normalized and regularized, and the poems' audience is extended both socially and temporally. When the scripts of plays become books their texts are no longer addressed solely to the actors engaged in preparing a performance, and thence to their audience, but have become works for the study, and to return them to the stage involves a good deal of reprocessing.

Before the nineteenth century, however, the text was not fixed by publication in the way it is for us. We consider the book the end of the creative process, the acknowledgment that the work is finished; but that is a very modern notion, and even now largely inaccurate. Throughout literary history—and for the most part even today—works have changed from edition to edition; and it has always been true that publication removes the text from the control of the author, except in those very rare cases where the author is someone important, prestigious, and likely to be lucrative enough to make demands—both King James and Ben Jonson remained in control of the text of their *Workes*; so in the twentieth century did Stephen King and Harold Bloom. For Virginia Woolf to do so, she had to become her own publisher, and even then

The Idea of the Book and the Creation of Literature. Stephen Orgel, Oxford University Press.
© Stephen Orgel 2023. DOI: 10.1093/oso/9780192871534.003.0006

the texts of her novels differed in the American editions from those in the British editions.

Printing only fixes the text until the work is set in type again, and not merely because formats and typography change, but because revision is often not the work of the author, and not at all the work of the author after the author's death. Every iteration of a text has a new editor with new ideas about what the text really says, or ought to say, and how it should be presented. Is the play we know as *Gorboduc* really called that, or is it *Ferrex and Porrex*? It depends which edition you consult. Shakespeare's last play in its own time was called *All Is True*; in the folio it has become *The Life of King Henry the Eight*, and for us it is simply *Henry VIII*. The text of the 1669 edition of Donne's *Songs and Sonnets* varies considerably from that of previous editions, but whether because new manuscripts had been found or because the poems were being tastefully updated is impossible to say. *Paradise Lost* was first published in 1667 as a ten-book poem in a modest, unadorned quarto volume and then reissued in 1674 as a twelve-book poem in an even more modest octavo. In 1688 it was transformed into a giant folio, with full-page illustrations for every book, and in 1695 this iteration became part of an even larger folio of *Poetical Works of Mr. John Milton*. Each of these editions reimagined the poem and its readership.

Such transformations are obviously not limited to the early modern era, but are part of a continuous process as the nature of literacy itself changes: from tablet to scroll to codex, papyrus to parchment to paper, manuscript to printed book to electronic text. As with technology, so with format: the Renaissance schoolboy's Ovid in a printed octavo with widely spaced lineation inviting annotation was more accessible than the medieval schoolboy's Ovid in a closely written vellum scribal folio, which, however, lasted longer and was more resistant to damage. And for Victorian readers, experiencing Dickens or George Eliot novels in monthly installments was different from experiencing them as hefty three-volume octavos or in portable paper-bound Tauchnitz editions (and different still if read aloud to a family group or silently alone). Jane Austen's works solicit quite different audiences in their discreet early nineteenth-century editions and in modern massmarket paperbacks with dramatic and sometimes even lurid cover art (and an Israeli company advertises *Pride and Prejudice* tights, in hot pink, with an exchange between Elizabeth and Jane Bennett printed on them—"printed tights," it explains, "are a hot fashion trend that adds a touch of style and glamour to any dress,"[1] though it is not explained what Jane Austen has to do with it, and the quoted conversation is about whether Mr. Bingley's sisters are really desirable neighbors, not obviously relevant to hot tights).

What is a book? Books are not simply the subjects they encode. Literature, philosophy, the sciences, theology, exist throughout human history, and as long as they have audiences (not necessarily readers; for millennia they were listeners, and "audiences" are literally "hearers") their life is continuous. For people interested in literature, what form the *Aeneid* is delivered in is largely immaterial, whether recited or published, whether in a manuscript or print, scroll or codex or innumerable editions, even whether in Latin or in translation: the *Aeneid* is the *Aeneid*. But books are not abstract: they are material objects; they have a history, and for any work involving the past, that history is an essential element—the form in which George Herbert's readers read his poetry is an essential element of what they read; and as we have seen, it is immediately apparent that the Herbert we read is something different.

Even blank books are books, though there is a presumption that the pages will eventually be filled. The compiling of commonplace books, collections of useful, thoughtful, notable observations, was part of the work of reading: the commonplace, which for us is a thing not worth saying, to the Renaissance signified a universal truth. In 1572 the printer John Day at the suggestion of John Foxe issued a large folio volume, over 1200 pages, of blank paper imprinted only with ruled headers on the rectos, and entitled *Pandectae locorum communium* [Collections of commonplaces]. *Pandectae* is a Greek word, literally "all-containing," used in late Latin for a collection of laws, and subsequently for any compendium or encyclopedia. The headlines in Day's volume provide topics for the commonplaces (e.g., *Adolescentia, eiusque decorum, indecorum, vitia, virtutes, pericula* [Adolescence, and its manners, bad manners, vices, virtues, dangers]; *Mensurae. Pondera* [Measures. Weights]; *Somnus. Somnia, eorumque interpretationes* [Sleep. Dreams and their interpretations]). The book was essentially a

---

[1] https://www.coline.co.il/shop/tights/text-tights-tights/jane-austen-pride-and-prejudice-tights/, accessed September 27, 2021.

reissue of one published in Basel in 1557. Day's volume has a title page using the elaborate cartouche originally designed for William Cunningham's *Cosmographical Glasse* (1559) declaring its seriousness, a preface explaining how to turn the hundreds of blank pages into a commonplace book, and four pages of an index to the running titles. The book was not a success, and by 1574 Day was recycling the large number of unsold sheets by cutting off the headlines.[2] Nevertheless the blank book still seemed like a good idea, and Hugh Singleton published an even larger edition of the empty *Pandectae* in 1585, which sold equally poorly. John Locke prepared a much more modest exhortation in octavo, sensibly including only a few blank pages, entitled *A New Method of Making Common-Place-Books* (1706).

Blank books are books simply because they consist of pages. Even scrolls, unless they are very short (and are therefore rolls, or *rotuli*), consist of pages glued or stitched together. But the pages are also "leaves"—the sylvan metaphor dates from Roman times; collections of poetry were "*sylvae*," literally forests, related to the assumption that the earliest poetry was pastoral, the songs shepherds composed while tending their sheep in the woods. Sylvan wood was also raw material, and hence the basis for any kind of writing, just as a codex is literally a block of wood; hence Bacon's natural history, a collection of scientific observations, is *Sylva Sylvarum*, "wood of woods," or "wood from the woods." The metaphor was widespread in the Renaissance in neoLatin poetry, but also in English, for example, in Jonson's collections "The Forest," "The Underwoods," "Timber," and Dryden's poetical miscellany of classical translations *Sylvae*. In a tamer form suitable for children it survived in *A Child's Garden of Verses*.

A book may also be its contents, in which case the book need not have pages—electronic books and audiobooks are still books (perhaps, however, this is a form of cultural anachronism, analogous to our saying that we still "dial" a phone number, though telephones have not had dials for many decades, or as we refer to the "horsepower" of automobile motors). The contents, too, need not be written: a graphic novel is a book; so is an atlas, a collection of maps; so is a sketchbook.

---

[2] A few surviving copies of Day's editions of the *Psalms* of 1574, 1575, and 1580, and of Thomas Cranmer's *An aunswere unto . . . Stephen Gardiner* (1580) include pages in which the headlines are intact.

But even the printed book was throughout its early history assumed not to be in its final form. Owen Feltham, in his book of essays *Resolves* (1623), says in the preface that he has provided no printed marginalia, but has left the margins of the book blank for the "Comments of the man that reades" (sig. A2^r). And of course the contents may also be irrelevant to the book's value: many books are acquired for their bindings, for their decorative quality as objects.[3]

Reading and writing

Reading and writing are separate skills, and were taught separately—young women were often taught to read but not to write. Writing, moreover, was not simply a matter of knowing how to form letters and spell. It was a craft: one had to learn to prepare the quill and keep it sharp, and make or procure the ink, and manage it without blotting or smearing. We return to Roger Stoddard's observation that authors do not write books, they produce texts, not always by writing, that get turned into books, by scribes, editors, printers. Until relatively recently most writers had scribes or secretaries (Cicero's scribe was the slave Tiro, inventor of a system of stenography; Bacon's commonplace book was compiled by his secretary; most of Montaigne's essays were dictated); and the transition from that to formal manuscript or printed book often had nothing whatever to do with the author. In an extreme example, the philosopher of Plato's dialogues is Socrates. Socrates was a real person, but who knows how much of Socrates is really in Plato—who is the philosopher in Plato's dialogues, Socrates or Plato? Is Plato transcribing Socrates's dialogues, or is Plato's Socrates in fact a literary persona? We may wish to say that he is both, but that is more an evasion than an answer. In what seems a simpler case, the author of the work we now know as Ranulph Higden's *Polychronicon* is identified in its earliest printed edition, published by William Caxton, only as "Ranulph monk of Chestre," and when Caxton concludes the book with the words "fynnyshed per Caxton," how much credit is he claiming, and for what? This is, however, only apparently a simpler case:

---

[3] See David Pearson, *Books as History* (London: British Library, 2008), for an extensive discussion of the book beyond the text.

there are many earlier manuscripts of the *Polychronicon* to compare with Caxton's text, all differing in some degree from it and from each other, but we have no way of knowing how much they preserve of Higden's original; we are no closer to Higden in them than in Caxton. The relation between the book and the author is rarely a direct and unmediated one, and working backward from the book to the author is similarly indirect and uncertain.

If it is the author we are concerned with, however, that is what we must do: the end product is often all we have; and even when we have an intermediate stage—a scribal manuscript, say—it is no more than that: an intermediate stage. We have not reached the author, but are only a step or two closer to the author. It is a rare case where we have a holograph copy; and a working draft such as Herbert's of *Easter-wings*, where we can see the author in the process of composition, is rarer still.

What do you have to do to turn something into a book? If it is a written narrative you may only have to provide a title and indicate the author—depending on how you came into possession of the narrative, you may or may not know either of these pieces of information; so you might have to invent them, or leave them intriguingly mysterious: "The Tortures of Passion," by A Lady. The narrative may not be a manuscript; it might be something you have made up, or it might have been told to you, and then you have to supply even more—diction, punctuation, format. Suppose it is a collection of letters of an interesting or important person and you want to publish them: you will then need to supply a good deal of additional information. Who was the person, why was he or she important, to whom were the letters written; and you will have to explain various allusions and determine a chronology, creating what we call an edition. An edition is also an attempt to establish a definitive text of anything, with varying amounts of explanatory material; but the "definitive" Donne or Pope or Dickens will be definitive at most for a generation or two, as what we want out of literature and what requires (and constitutes) an explanation changes. But really, almost anything written can be turned into a book: think of all the documents, broadsheets, polemics, street songs from past ages, valuable to us as cultural and social history, though totally disposable in their own time, and requiring a great deal of context to make sense to us.

Robert Darnton describes the "life cycle" of books:

> It could be described as a communications circuit that runs from the author to the publisher (if the bookseller does not assume that role), the printer, the shipper, the bookseller, and the reader. The reader completes the circuit, because he influences the author both before and after the act of composition. Authors are readers themselves. By reading and associating with other readers and writers, they form notions of genre and style and a general sense of the literary enterprise, which affects their texts, whether they are composing Shakespearean sonnets or directions for assembling radio kits. A writer may respond in his writing to criticisms of his previous work or anticipate reactions that his text will elicit. He addresses implicit readers and hears from explicit reviewers. So the circuit runs full cycle. It transmits messages, transforming them en route, as they pass from thought to writing to printed characters and back to thought again. Book history concerns each phase of this process and the process as a whole, in all its variations over space and time and in all its relations with other systems, economic, social, political, and cultural, in the surrounding environment.[4]

This "communications circuit" does not, of course, begin with the invention of printing, and should not be described as limited to it. There was a version of it as soon as written material started to be created and marketed; it was not determined by the technology involved. Scribal publication involved editors and other intermediaries just as publication with type did, and the idiosyncracies of scribes need to be taken into account just as those of press editors and typographers do. But the idea that the production of the book should be seen as a circuit, with the end partly determining the beginning, that the text is partly determined by the reader, that "a writer may respond in his writing to criticisms of his previous work or anticipate reactions that his text will elicit" is worth emphasizing. It is especially true in societies that practice press censorship, in which all books are written at the very least in anticipation of the censor.

---

[4] Robert Darnton, "What is the History of Books?" *Daedalus* 111.3 (1982), p. 67.

Great books

What do books look like? The majestic *Liber Cronicarum* (Nuremberg Chronicle) and the exquisite *Hypnerotomachia Poliphili* (the Love-battle-dream of Poliphilus, or in its 1592 Elizabethan translation, *The Strife of Love in a Dreame*) are two of the most famous books ever produced—how did these become the acme of the book at the end of the fifteenth century, less than forty years after printing was invented? Look back at the page of the Gutenberg Bible in Figure 1.3. Any aids to reading—titles, running heads, decorative initials to indicate new sections, page numbers—had to be added by hand.

The text of the Nuremberg Chronicle, in Figure 6.1, is in a significantly clearer type, and is divided into sections, though not into paragraphs, and the lines are still too long and close together for comfortable reading; the text still presents a daunting mass of black. But the woodcuts are integrated throughout this vast work, so that visually the page is always interesting: the book's attractions do not reside only, or even primarily, in its text.

For us, the *Hypnerotomachia Poliphili* is significantly more legible, partly because of the roman type (which would not have been more legible to sixteenth-century readers in northern Europe and Britain) but even more because of the design of the page, with significant margins and generous leading between the lines (Figure 6.2). Roman type had first been designed by German printers in the 1460s. It was based on a Carolingian manuscript hand, but was thought to be ancient Roman;[5] in that sense it was a classicizing move, an appropriate medium of presentation for the sources of humanist learning. By the 1470s, it had become the standard Italian type face, domesticated most significantly by Nicholas Jenson, a French goldsmith and engraver trained as a printer in Mainz, who came to Venice in 1468, established his press in 1470, and thereafter was a prolific publisher of humanist and Christian classics in the roman type he had designed. Jenson died around 1480. By the end of the century Venice was producing the finest books in Italy, most notably by the Aldine press.

---

[5] See Daniel Wakelin, "Humanism and Printing," in Vincent Gillespie and Susan Powell, eds., *A Companion to the Early Printed Book in Britain, 1476–1558* (Cambridge: D. S. Brewer, 2014), p. 241.

FIGURE 6.1 A page of the *Liber Cronicarum* (Nuremberg Chronicle), 1493.

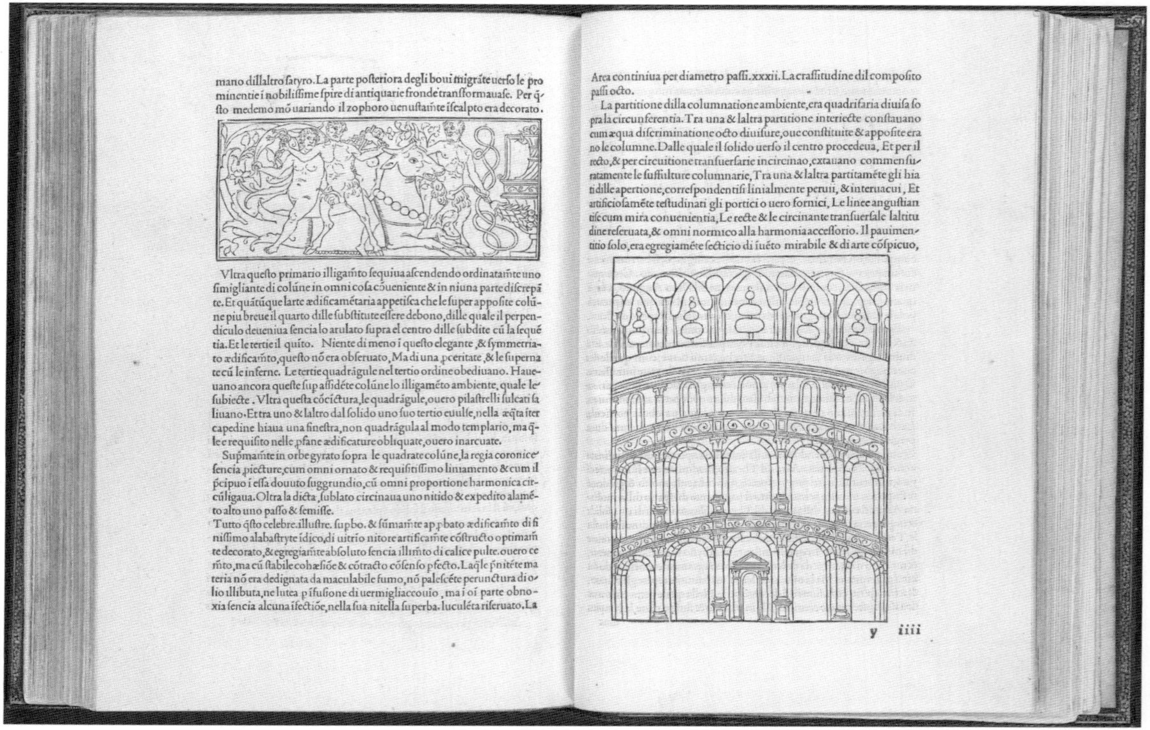

mano dillaltro satyro. La parte posteriora degli boui migrãte uerso le prominentie ĩ nobilissime spire di antiquarie fronde transformauase. Per q̃sto medemo mõ uariando il zophoro uenustamẽte ĩscalpto era decorato.

Vltra questo primario illigamẽto sequiua ascendendo ordinatamẽte uno simigliante di colũne in omni cosa cõueniente & in niuna parte discrepãte. Et quãtũque larte ædificamẽtaria appetisca che le super apposite colũne piu breue il quarto dille substitute essere debono, dille quale il perpendiculo deueniua sencia lo arulato supra el centro dille subdite cũ la sequẽtia. Et le tertie il quĩto. Niente di meno ĩ questo elegante, & symmetriato ædificamẽto, questo nõ era obseruato, Ma di una ꝑceritate, & le superna te cũ le inferne. Le tertie quadrãgule nel tertio ordine obediuano. Haueuano ancora queste sup assidẽte colũne lo illigamẽto ambiente, quale le subiecte. Vltra questa cõcĩctura, le quadrãgule, ouero pilastrelli sulcati saliuano. Et tra uno & laltro dal solido uno suo tertio euulse, nella æq̃ta ĩtercapedine hiaua una finestra, non quadrãgula al modo templario, ma q̃le e requisito nelle ꝓfane ædificature obliquate, ouero inarcuate.

Supmamẽte in orbe gyrato sopra le quadrate colũne, la regia coronice sencia ꝓiecture, cum omni ornato & requisitissimo liniamento & cum il ꝑcipuo ĩ essa douuto suggrundio, cũ omni proportione harmonica circũligaua. Oltra la dicta, sublato circinaua uno nitido & expedito alamẽto alto uno passo & semisse.

Tutto q̃sto celebre. illustre. supbo. & sũmamẽte apꝓbato ædificamẽto di finissimo alabastryte ĩdico, di uitrio nitore artificamẽte cõstructo optimamẽte decorato, & egregiamẽte absoluto sencia illimẽto di calice pulte. ouero cemẽto, ma cũ stabile cohæsiõe & cõtracto cõsenso ꝑfecto. La q̃le ꝑnitẽte materia nõ era dedignata da maculabile fumo, nõ palescẽte peruncture di olio illibuta, ne lutea ꝑ ĩfusione di uermigliaccouio, ma ĩ oĩ parte obnoxia sencia alcuna ĩfectiõe, nella sua nitella superba. luculẽta riseruato. La

Area continiua per diametro passi. xxxii. La crassitudine dil composito passi octo.

La partitione dilla columnatione ambiente, era quadrifaria diuisa sopra la circunferentia. Tra una & laltra partitione interiecte constauano cum æqua discriminatione octo diuisure, oue constituite & apposite erano le columne. Dalle quale il solido uerso il centro procedeua, Et per il recto, & per circuitione transuersarie incircinao, extauano commensuratamente le suffulture columnarie, Tra una & laltra partitamẽte gli hiati dille apertione, correspondentisi linialmente peruii, & interuacui, Et artificiosamẽte testudinati gli portici o uero fornici, Le linee angustiantise cum mira conuenientia, Le recte & le circinante transuersale laltitudine reseruata, & omni normico alla harmonia accessorio. Il pauimentitio solo, era egregiamẽte secticio di ĩuẽto mirabile & di arte cõspicuo,

y iiii

FIGURE 6.2 Two pages of the *Hypnerotomachia Poliphili*, 1499.

Aldus Manutius was a quintessential Renaissance humanist. He spoke Greek at home, and founded his press in Venice in 1494 initially to produce correct texts of Greek and Latin works. The first work printed entirely in Greek in Italy was the *Batrachomyomachia*, the Battle of the Frogs and Mice, published in Brescia in 1474—this text was still considered part of the Homeric corpus, as it had been since Roman times. The first Greek *Iliad* and *Odyssey* published in Europe were printed in Florence in 1488. A few other works in Greek had been published in Italy, but the market was small and the number of available typesetters was of course miniscule. Aldus, however, was determined to restore the ancient texts. He commissioned a new Greek type, with the letters and accents separate, to be correctly arranged by the typesetters, and sought out the most accurate manuscripts in libraries throughout Europe—Venice itself was home to a large number. Between 1495 and 1498 his press issued a great five-volume Aristotle, and an Aristophanes in 1498.

The *Hypnerotomachia Poliphili* was designed to be a modern classic. It is a long and abstruse dream vision probably written in the 1460s by a Dominican friar named Francesco Colonna—this was the first contemporary work printed by Aldus and the first in the vernacular; but its Italian was so convoluted and so heavily Latinate that it was readable only by the most scholarly aficionados—one could hardly call it a vernacular. Its language has often been compared to that of *Finnegans Wake*. For this work Aldus commissioned his elegant new roman typeface and woodcut illustrations that are among the finest produced in fifteenth-century Italy, and printed the book in 1499 in a superbly designed folio on beautiful paper with large margins. Unlike the *Liber Cronicarum*, it is designed to be eminently legible. But not, of course, eminently readable; and by 1508 most of the edition remained unsold. The book was intended as a literary landmark, a beacon of the new classicism, but has remained at the margins of literature, admired but unread, coveted by bibliophiles purely as an art object.

One aspect of the work was not marginal: the integration of text and picture was discreet and elegant, and set a standard for book illustration still evident in modern book design—the illustrations of the *Liber Cronicarum* look bombastic in comparison. In the *Hypnerotomachia*, however, their function is ambiguous. They realize things described in the text but they elucidate nothing, and if they have any value at all in the plot, it is only to give some sense of visual context to an otherwise impenetrable narrative—rather as if Matisse had illustrated *Finnegans Wake* instead of *Ulysses*.[6] The illustrations and typography have almost from the beginning constituted the primary attraction of this book.

Written matter

What needs to be written down, and for whom, and how should it be presented? The earliest surviving writing was on clay tablets, recording imports, exports, and possessions. A little later, inscriptions carved on the more enduring stone memorialized important events and powerful rulers. Initially, then, not literature, which was oral; poetry was recited and memorized, stories and histories told and retold. But among the thousands of clay tablets surviving from the burning of the storehouse of the seventh-century BC Assyrian king Ashurbanipal are twelve tablets preserving the earliest known epic poetry, the Gilgamesh story, composed in the Akkadian language in the second millennium BC, and recorded in Cuneiform script. We would not recognize these tablets as fragments of a book, but by any definition that is what they are—or more precisely, what they became. They were not identified until the mid-nineteenth century, and first translated in the 1870s. That reprocessing was what allowed them to be seen as a book. Between us and this ancient epic, then, are the archeologist, decipherer, transcriber, and translator.

It is a large step culturally and intellectually to decide that poetry, stories, philosophy, history need to be transcribed—for a written culture, it is the invention of literature. The first things we can recognize as books were scrolls and the smaller rolls, or *rotuli*. This was a satisfactory system for over a thousand years, and in certain ritual contexts

---

[6] In fact, Matisse did not even really illustrate *Ulysses*. In 1935 he was commissioned to do illustrations for a Limited Editions Club edition of Joyce's novel. But Matisse did not read the book, assuming that it was an English version of Homer, and produced illustrations for scenes from *The Odyssey*. Nevertheless, the book was issued, and this conjunction of two modernist icons produced what has become the most valuable of the Limited Editions Club volumes. See Willard Goodwin, "'A Very Pretty Picture M. Matisse But You Must Not Call It Joyce': The Making of the Limited Editions Club Ulysses," *Joyce Studies Annual* 10 (summer, 1999), pp. 85–103.

continues to be so—for example, the Megillah (literally "scroll"), the brief biblical story of Esther, about fifteen modern pages, that takes less than an hour to recite on the holy day of Purim; and the Torah (literally "teaching" or "law"), a large double scroll comprising in a modern edition about 450 pages. The biggest problem with scrolls is that their physical construction makes anything except consecutive reading very difficult; but this never seemed a significant issue until very late antiquity—Martial tried publishing collections of his epigrams as codices, what we call books, but the idea was unpopular, and he went back to the scroll.[7]

Biblical texts are rendered especially problematic by being written on scrolls. Rabbinic exegesis depends on elaborate comparisons of widely separated passages in the scriptures, and there is no way of flipping back and forth in the Torah; which means that religious education from the beginning depended not only on literacy but also on the development of a capacious memory. Memory training was an essential element in all literacy from ancient times. Histories of literature, and of literacy, really ought to include histories of the changing involvement of, and conception of, memory. The reason the Torah has continued to be a scroll until the present is that in its ritual use it is read aloud consecutively from beginning to end in stipulated portions throughout the year—every year, that is, for more than 2000 years, it has been read consecutively in synagogues throughout the world from beginning to end; and the scroll is a perfectly functional technology for such a use. The codex (literally a tree trunk or block of wood), with double-sided pages attached at one edge, starts to become the norm of the book only around the fourth century AD, specifically for Christian texts. And though this seems an improvement in obvious ways, it has not always been felt to be desirable. Martial's readers did not like it, presumably simply because it was not what they were used to.

Books started being printed to look like manuscripts, and indeed, since the whole point of printing is to find a better way to produce manuscripts, this makes perfect sense, but it was not an easy transition. A great many disparate technologies had to be mobilized to work together: type had to be designed and cast in large numbers, new oil-

---

[7] See L. D. Reynolds and N. G. Wilson, *Scribes and Scholars*, 3rd edn. (Oxford: Oxford University Press, 1993), p. 34.

based ink had to be invented, a press had to be designed and constructed, paper had to be produced in the right size and specially treated to accept the ink clearly and uniformly, and a great many work-men had to be trained in the new technology. It is also worth reminding ourselves that for many cultures, printing was not self-evidently superior to manuscript. Although printing was in use in Asia before it was in Europe, works in Asian societies continued to be produced in manuscript well into the nineteenth century; and even in Europe, scribal publication was still active throughout the seventeenth century.[8]

Books are material objects. We tend to think of printed books as products and multiples, the first instance of the work of art in the age of mechanical reproduction. This is not at all correct until the nineteenth century, with the invention of stereotyping, in which molds were made from the pages set in type, from which plates were cast, and new editions could be printed from these which were identical to the originals.

The creation of the book

The author was the creator of his or her literary work, but until quite late, not the creator of his or her manuscript; the manuscript was in general the work of a professional scribe. Cicero dictated his orations and letters; Montaigne dictated many of his essays. You had a secretary precisely because, if you were a poet, essayist, philosopher, author, you were in the business of thinking, reasoning, inventing (*auctor* is literally a creator), not writing. Writing was a craft, and in classical times, even if you were literate, for the most part you had a slave to do it for you. Reading was a craft too: in the Platonic dialogue *Theaetetus*, a student of Socrates named Eucleides says that he has a complex discourse of Socrates in written form—in this case he wrote it down himself, ensuring its accuracy, continually checking with Socrates to make

[8] For richly detailed accounts, see Harold Love, *Scribal Publication in Seventeenth-Century England* (Oxford: Oxford University Press, 1993), and Arthur F. Marotti, *Manuscript, Print, and the English Renaissance Lyric* (Ithaca: Cornell University Press, 1995).

sure he was remembering it correctly. His interlocutor Terpsion proposes that they go home and read it. Here is the exchange:

> EUCLEIDES. Come, let us go, and while we are resting, the boy shall read to us.
> TERPSION. Very well.
> EUCLEIDES. Here is the book, Terpsion.... Come, boy, take the book and read.[9]

As this suggests, even the relation between books and readers was not direct and unmediated.[10] There was a very active book trade in Athens, but apparently educated Athenians generally did not read the books themselves, but had them read aloud by a literate slave. In the *Phaedrus* Socrates makes fun of a student he detects carrying a scroll under his cloak. The composition of the book was equally mediated, strikingly in the case of Socratic philosophy. Clearly Plato cannot be thought of merely as Socrates's scribe; but how much more is he than that? There is a modern analogue to Socrates in Wittgenstein, many of whose published philosophical works were assembled from his notebooks and from notes taken by students; nevertheless, the philosopher is Wittgenstein, not his editors Elizabeth Anscombe and Rush Rhees.

The scribe who produced the ancient book, of course, could not be simply a slave who could write. He had to have a legible hand, and that meant that scribal hands had to be standardized. And by the same token, when printing was invented, the type started as a copy of somebody's very legible handwriting, handwriting designed to be legible by anyone who could read. When Aldus Manutius set out to print a series of classical texts in an easily portable format, to make the humanist classics readily available, he designed a type based on an italic hand, the hand that letters were written in—the Aldine classics were in the familiar humanist handwriting of the age. The font is beautifully

---

[9] *Theaetetus* in Plato [*Works*], trans. Harold N. Fowler (Cambridge, MA: Harvard University Press, 1921) Vol. 12, 143a–c.

[10] Reading was still the business of servants two millennia later, in *Twelfth Night*: when Olivia is shown the love letter she has supposedly written to Malvolio, she examines the letter closely enough to declare the handwriting to be Maria's, but then instructs one of the servants to read it aloud. Feste clowns up the letter, which is finally read by Fabian. This, indeed, is almost his only dramatic function in the play.

legible, but it is significant that it is designed to look informal, like handwriting. These books assume a community of scholars.

Unique copies

Renaissance books are not multiples in the sense that modern books (or photographs, or any mass-produced objects) are. Consider Ben Jonson's and his publisher William Stansby's mode of operation in the printing of the Jonson folio, a very grand book that took about three years to print. Stansby's printers would set up the type and begin printing. Jonson would come to the printing house regularly and read the sheets, on which he would make changes—in some cases to correct errors, but in others because he had a new idea.[11] These changes would be incorporated into the type, and printing would continue; but the pages already printed were not discarded—paper was expensive. When the book was finally assembled, any copy would include both original and revised pages indiscriminately. What this means is that there was no notion that the book represented the final, correct version of a work, or that all copies of a book had to be identical.

Print culture is now regularly claimed to aspire to the invariable—the technology is presumed to have been designed to produce books that are replications, a potentially infinite number of exact copies. But this is incorrect: what early modern culture wanted from printing was not exact replication, it was dissemination, the ability to produce five hundred or a thousand copies of a book (or, far more often, a broadsheet, edict, injunction, indulgence, advertisement, or polemical pamphlet), rather than five or ten or fifty. The fact that for more than three centuries after the invention of printing there were routinely variations in those copies merely shows how much less of a change print culture represented from manuscript culture than we want it to represent. When Charlton Hinman produced his Norton facsimile of the

[11] Herford and Simpson in the Oxford edition assume that Jonson was constantly in attendance and went to the printing house daily. The Cambridge editors show, however, that his involvement in the production of the volume was less constant, and that many of the folio's routine emendations are the work of the typographers. See the Cambridge Ben Jonson, vol. 1, pp. lxix–lxxi.

Shakespeare folio, he reproduced only pages that were in their final, corrected form. The book in this state was a notional ideal, corresponding to no surviving copy of the original book—it is not an exaggeration to say that every copy of the Shakespeare folio differs from every other copy to some extent. Randall McLeod and Cyndia Clegg have shown that in the case of Holinshed's Chronicles, the censors were at work while the book was in the press: here again, both revised and unrevised pages appear in practically every copy of the work, if not in all.[12] These are not exceptional cases.

Such examples have significant bearing on assumptions about the book, on the very idea of what a book is. It would have been perfectly simple for the publisher of the Shakespeare folio to produce the folio that Charlton Hinman produced. All that was necessary was to print a proof sheet and wait till it was proofread to continue printing—two folio pages, say ten minutes. There was an idea of ultimate correctness for the book—early modern books often have lists of errata at the end—but the text did not have to embody it. The final, correct text, if there was to be one, was the work of the reader, who as he or she made the corrections, was also encouraged to watch for other "faults escaped in the printing." Both Sir John Harington's translation of Ariosto's *Orlando Furioso* (1591) and George Sandys's Ovid's *Metamorphoses* (1632) include substantial lists of errata; these are often found corrected in an early hand.[13]

The purchaser was actively involved in the completion of the book in other ways as well. Though books could be bought in a simple publisher's binding, usually of vellum, books were often sold unbound. The sheets were sent from the printer to the bookseller in barrels, the bookseller folded a few copies and sewed them loosely together, and the purchaser decided how the assembled volume was to be bound. So for books like this, all bindings are special bindings. We are used to thinking of grand medieval manuscripts in this way (the bindings of books of hours in royal and aristocratic collections are typically very

---

[12] See the Introduction to Cyndia Clegg and Randall McLeod, *The peaceable and prosperous regiment of blessed Queene Elisabeth: A Facsimile from Holinshed's Chronicles (1587)* (San Marino, CA: Huntington Library Press 2005).

[13] For Harington's close involvement with the printing of his *Orlando* translation, see Gerard Kilroy, "Advertising the Reader: Sir John Harington's 'Directions in the Margent'," *English Literary Renaissance* 41.1 (winter, 2011), pp. 64–110.

splendid) but until quite late in the history of the book it could be true of any book. It is not until the late seventeenth century that all books start to be issued in bindings by the publisher, and the binding becomes, finally, a marketing strategy. Nineteenth-century books, especially children's books, have highly decorated bindings; the only surprise is how long it took publishers to realize the possibilities inherent in bindings.

But also, books are property, on which their owners impose themselves in ways that extend beyond the binding. They write their names in them and paste bookplates into them, and write things in the margins and on the flyleaves. This is an essential part of the book's history; and one of the strangest bits of bibliophilic and curatorial pathology is the desire for pristine copies of books and the consequent attempt to erase evidence of any previous ownership.

The ascent of drama

The most valuable book in English is a collection of plays, the Shakespeare first folio—the equally iconic original edition of the King James Bible is, in the marketplace, far less valuable, though it is in fact more rare. Let us then, in conclusion, return to the ascent of drama from play to book to Work, from performance to quarto to folio. Play texts, even printed ones, start as performing scripts. In this form, the only people who will read them are the actors and the censor. The actors, moreover, did not receive the whole script, but only their individual parts with their cue lines. So to begin with, the play was its performance, and the earliest printed plays acknowledged that. For three decades in the mid-sixteenth century, published plays characteristically solicited performance by announcing, either on the title page or in the cast list, how many actors were required and how the parts were to be multiplied. "Foure may playe it easely," says the printed text of *The Longer Thou Livest the More Foole Thou Art*, published around 1569, and even supplies a chart dividing the fifteen roles among four players. The assumption behind such advertising would seem to be that there is nothing to do with a play but perform it. But not entirely, because this is also a book; and even in those cases where the book seems specifically to address actors, a larger, and different, group is also being courted.

A thoughtful audience of readers is solicited by the title page of *The Longer Thou Livest*, which characterizes the play as "a myrrour very necessarie for youth, and specially for such as are likely to come to dignitie and promotion." Thus audiences are urged to become readers.

But the reading audience for plays did not define itself. Before the readership could be solicited, it had to be imagined. The problems publishers faced in imagining who might want to read plays are visible like stigmata throughout the texts of early modern drama. Consider the two earliest printed incarnations of *Gorboduc*, published in 1565 by William Griffith and in 1570 by John Day. In this play Gorboduc, a descendent of King Lear, recapitulates his story: in his old age he divides his kingdom between his two sons Ferrex and Porrex, as a way of precluding future dissension, but the division of the kingdom has the opposite effect, and the two sons are soon at war. Day's preface to the 1570 version claims that his new edition corrects the unauthorized version of 1565. The first of his changes is the title itself: the play is now not *The Tragedy of Gorboduc*, but *The Tragedy of Ferrex and Porrex*. Purchasers of the earlier edition might reasonably be expected to want to replace, or augment, their copies with a more correct or more complete version, but the change of title is not likely to have been the correction of an error. *Gorboduc* had already been registered with the Stationers' Company by Griffith, and changing the name gave the impression that the new edition was a different literary property—in fact, if Day had not changed the title, he could have been accused of piracy. Moreover, the new title may have served as an advertising strategy: perhaps a play about murderous sibling rivalry seemed more likely to attract new purchasers than a play about a superannuated royal autocrat. If this was the point, it must be relevant that the next edition, in 1590, returned to the title of the supposedly corrupt, inauthentic text, and that the play has been known as *Gorboduc* ever since.[14]

Whatever Day intended, however, most of his claims appear to be false. There is nothing corrupt about the 1565 text; Day's version is better printed, but Griffith's contains few errors, and the textual differences between the two editions are insignificant. Both claim to present the play as it was performed before the queen, but there is a manuscript

---

[14] With the mysterious exception of W. W. Greg, who in his *Bibliography of English Printed Drama* lists the play as *Ferrex and Porrex (Gorboduc)*.

account of the original performance that differs significantly from the published text, which was evidently revised to remove politically sensitive material relating to the queen's marriage. Neither edition, therefore, can have been the play as it was performed before the queen.[15] The only notable change in Day's quarto is the omission, possibly on political grounds, of eight lines in V.i. (The suppressed lines assert that there are no grounds for rebellion against a legitimate monarch. The position is perfectly orthodox, but it may have been felt to raise an issue that itself was dangerous.) Day's edition, then, is *less* complete and accurate than Griffith's, not more. Day's version was, moreover, clearly set up not from a new manuscript, but from a copy of the 1565 volume, lightly marked up—the basis for Day's text was the allegedly incorrect one. Finally, though there is a Stationers' Register entry for Griffith's book, there is none for Day's. Considering the number of unregistered books in the period this was certainly a minor infraction, though Day is an odd person to be breaking the rules: he was a charter member of the Company (so was Griffith), and subsequently became its Master; and he registered several other books for publication in the same year. Was the failure to register, like the change of title, another attempt to conceal both the infringement of a fellow Stationer's property and the true source of the text? In any case, if either edition is at all surreptitious, it is the later one.

We have here, then, a specially clear case of a publisher inventing a narrative designed to create a market and an audience. The two title pages employ competing strategies as well. Griffith gives a great deal of information, and constitutes our only source for the division of authorial labor:

> The TRAGEDIE of GORBODUC, whereof three Actes were wrytten by *Thomas Norton*, and the two laste by *Thomas Sackvyle*. Sett forthe as the same was shewed before the *QUENES* most excellent Maiestie, in her hignes Court of Whitehall, the xviii. day of Ianuary, *Anno Domini* 1561. By the Gentlemen of Thynner Temple in London.

Day reveals much less:

---

[15] See Henry James and Greg Walker, "The Politics of *Gorboduc*," *English Historical Review* 110.435 (February, 1995), pp. 109–21.

> The Tragidie of Ferrex and Porrex, set forth without addition or alteration but altogether as the same was shewed on stage before the Queenes Maiestie, about nine yeares past, *vz.* the xviii day of Ianuary. 1561. by the gentlemen of the Inner Temple.

The authors Norton and Sackville are discreetly mentioned only in a preface, and the details of composition are suppressed. The focus is on the aristocratic venue, the noble patrons, the audience, the performers. Curiously, moreover, though the text has in fact been somewhat improved (the changes involve not only the deletion of the politically sensitive passage but also some amendment of metrics and clarifications of sense), this is not conceived to be a selling point: on the contrary, the work is represented as "set forth without addition or alteration"—the most desirable text is assumed to be the one closest to the original performance. Both title pages claim to offer the reader direct access to that theatrical event, not to the true or final intentions of the authors. The fact that the claim is entirely false indicates where the priorities lie.

Illustration

One way of retaining the performative aspects of the play-book is to illustrate it. Humanist printers began doing this with classical drama very early, though for the most part only in editions of Terence, not Plautus or Seneca. This probably reflects the fact that Terence alone of the three was actually performed in schools, but the illustrations are in general more bookish than theatrical.

The title page to a 1496 Strasbourg edition of Terence, in Figure 6.3, has visually more to do with the Nuremberg Chronicle than with the performance of plays, and illustrations in the same edition (Figure 6.4) combine characters from more than one play, obviously not on a stage, even providing schematic guidelines to indicate what characters belong together. The title page of the 1497 Venetian edition in Figure 6.5, however, does give a real sense of theater in action, and focuses, interestingly, on the academic audience rather than the performers. Many Terence editions include miniature scenes, for the most part in contemporary dress, but again give little sense of an actual performance.

FIGURE 6.3 Terence, *Terentius Comico Carmine*, Strasbourg, 1496, title page.

FIGURE 6.4 Illustrations for *Adelphi* and *Heautontimorumenos* from Terence, *Terentius Comico Carmine*, Strasbourg, 1496.

COLISEVS SI VE THEATRVM

FIGURE 6.5 Terence, *Terentius cum quinque commentis*, Venice, 1497, title page.

Those in Figure 6.6 are from the 1497 edition; the fact that they were still being imitated in a Paris edition of 1552 indicates how much more this sort of illustration has to do with the history of the book than with the history of theater. There are a few notable variations: a 1567 Paris edition, in Figure 6.7, puts the plays on a Renaissance perspective stage, and even includes an audience. But in a sense this is archeology: the point of the perspective settings is that they are classical, not that they represent contemporary theatrical practice. As for modern plays, they were most commonly illustrated not as if taking place on a stage, but with a conspectus of scenes and characters, as narrative poems were illustrated in the period. A characteristic plate in the 1602 edition of Guarini's drama *Il Pastor Fido* (Figure 6.8) shows not a scene, but a summary of a whole act. Virgil, Ovid, Ariosto, and Tasso were imagined in the same way: the pictures represented not scenes but epitomes.

On the other hand, when it was the occasion, not the drama, that was important, the illustrations gave a very detailed and specific sense of performance: masques, *balets de cour*, royal entries, were often issued with splendid plates that provide a vivid particularity. The best known of these is the *Balet Comique de la Royne*, performed at the French court in 1581.

The frontispiece (Figure 6.9) shows not only the scene in progress, in a great hall with dispersed settings, but also the disposition of the audience, with the royal party on the floor of the hall and the rest of the spectators in a gallery. Other illustrations in the volume show costumes and pageants, and the text also includes music, which the book reproduces arranged for the lute, so that musically literate readers could perform it for themselves. Festival books, records of courtly spectacles, were among the most elaborately produced publications in the period; and in these, though scenery and costumes were often lavishly depicted, a principal attraction for the original readers would have been the sense the volumes gave of the royal patrons and the aristocratic venue.

Such books were regularly produced in France and Italy, but not in England. For plays, English publishers from the 1590s on occasionally provided, as a frontispiece or on the title page, a scene from the play, generally as if in performance. There are twenty-eight of these, out of a total of about 700 titles printed. The images rarely accord with the text.

Samnio leno.Efchinus adolefcens.

Ctefipho.Syrus.

FIGURE 6.6 Illustrations from Terence, *Terentius cum quinque commentis*, Venice, 1497.

Trimetri .

PHÆDRIA adolefcens, PARMENO feruus .

Vi d igitur faciam ? non eã ?
ne nunc quidem,
Cum accerfor vltro ? an po-
tius ita me comparem,

FIGURE 6.7   Illustration from Terence, *Comœdiæ*, Paris, 1567.

The image in Figure 6.10 on the title page of a relatively late edition of *The Spanish Tragedy* is not a scene from the play. It is rather a summary of the central action, conflating two separate moments. In the drama, Hieronymo is alone when he discovers his son Horatio's body; the murder of Horatio, his lover Bel-Imperia's cries for help, and her kidnapping by the villains Lorenzo and Balthazar, have all taken place before he enters. Moreover, the dialogue that comes in ribbons from the characters' mouths—"Alas it is my son Horatio / Murder, help, Hieronymo / Stop her mouth"—is nowhere in the text; it has been invented for the picture. Despite the fact that this illustrates a printed version of the play, the action here departs from its script—the scene depicted has been improvised by the artist, as if the play were not a text but a scenario. The sources of this kind of representation are images that, however dramatic, have no connection with plays or

FIGURE 6.8 Giovanni Battista Guarini, *Il Pastor Fido*, 1602, frontispiece to Act 2.

FIGURE 6.9 Baltasar de Beaujoyeulx, *Balet Comique de la Royne*, 1582, frontispiece.

FIGURE 6.10   Thomas Kyd, *The Spanish Tragedy*, 1615, title page. British Library C.117.b.36.

theater—early Annunciation scenes, for example, in which "Ave gratia plena" emanates from the angelic messenger. And nothing in the *Spanish Tragedy* image suggests a theater.

For comparison, Figure 6.11 shows how Italian publishers were illustrating plays in the same period. A Florentine extravaganza called

FIGURE 6.11   G. C. Coppola and Alfonso Parigi, *Le Nozze degli Dei*, 1637, frontispiece to Scene 5 (Stefano della Bella after Alfonso Parigi).

Le Nozze degli Dei, published in 1637, included double-page etchings of the stage sets and characters by Stefano della Bella—the stage designer was Alfonso Parigi. These are scenically detailed, lavish and wildly imaginative. This is a spectacular hell scene in the last act, a conflagration including flying devils and a cloud chariot. Illustrations like these have become classics in the history of scenography. The publishers in such examples were certainly interested in producing a lavishly illustrated book, but the close alliance of book with performance was of the essence.

The English had very little interest in this sort of thing, though the architect and stage designer Inigo Jones was creating stage sets as elaborate as Alfonso Parigi's for English court masques. The only English theatrical text issued in this format before the eighteenth century was Elkanah Settle's heroic tragedy *The Empress of Morocco*, 1673.

The volume was a real attempt to locate Settle's text in the theater: it had as a frontispiece the façade of the London theater where the play was performed, and it included five engravings of stage settings and action (Figure 6.12). The scenes look, however, much more like book

FIGURE 6.12 Elkanah Settle, *The Empress of Morocco*, 1673, illustration for the masque (William Dolle, engraver).

illustrations than theatrical performances; even at their most imaginative their decorative frames overwhelm them. The stage, for this artist,
is clearly constrained by the page. Dryden, who called the play "a
rhapsody of nonsense," was especially contemptuous of its publication
with illustrations, and in fact, the second edition, thirteen years later,
was published without the plates. The play was a success, but London
publishers clearly felt that play texts would do well enough on their
own. When publishers did issue elegant and expensive books of plays,
collected (and usually memorial) volumes, they embellished them not
with dramatic scenes, but with portraits of the author—Shakespeare,
Jonson, Killigrew, Fletcher (the publisher said he could find no portrait
of Beaumont). So plays become literature, visualizing the author rather
than the stage.

BIBLIOGRAPHY

Primary Sources

Anon., *Wits recreations. Selected from the finest fancies of moderne muses*, 1640.

Aristotle, *Opera*. Venice, 1483.

Augustine, *The City of God*, trans. Marcus Dods. Edinburgh: T. and T. Clark, 1871.

Beaujoyeulx, Baltasar de, *Balet Comique de la Royne*, 1582.

Beaumont, Francis, and John Fletcher, *Comedies and Tragedies Written by Francis Beaumont and John Fletcher*. London, 1647.

Burton, Robert, *The Anatomy of Melancholy*, 1621.

Burton, Robert, second edition, 1624.

Burton, Robert, third edition, 1628.

Burton, William, *The Most Delectable and Pleasaunt History of Clitophon and Leucippe ... newly translated into English by W. B.*, 1597.

Byrd, William, *Psalmes, Sonets, & songs of sadnes and pietie*, 1588.

Campion, Thomas, *Observations in the Art of English Poesie*, 1602.

Chaucer, Geoffrey, *Canterbury Tales*, ed. William Caxton, 1477.

Chaucer, Geoffrey, *Canterbury Tales*, ed. William Caxton, 1483.

Chaucer, Geoffrey, *Canterbury Tales*, ed. Wynkyn de Worde, 1498.

Chaucer, Geoffrey, *Workes*, ed. John Stowe, 1561.

Chaucer, Geoffrey, *Workes*, ed. Thomas Speght, 1598.

Chaucer, Geoffrey, *Workes*, ed. Thomas Speght, 1602.

Chester, Robert, *Loves Martyr or, Rosalins Complaint*, 1601.

Colonna, Francesco, *Hypnerotomachia Poliphili*, 1499.

Coppola, Giovanni Carlo, *Le Nozze degli Dei*, 1637.

Crooke, Helkiah, *Mikrokosmographia*, 1615.

Daniel, Samuel, *A Defence of Ryme*, [?]1603.

Day, John, *Pandectae Locorum Communium*, 1572.

Donne, John, *Letters to Severall Persons of Honour*, 1651.

Donne, John, *Poems by J.D. With Elegies on the Authors Death*, 1633.

Donne, John, *Poems &c.*, 1669.

Erasmus, Desiderius, *De Recta Latini Graeque Sermonis Pronuntiatione Dialogus* (*The Correct Pronunciation of Latin and Greek Speech*), trans. Maurice Pope, *Collected Works of Erasmus*, ed. J. K. Sowards. Toronto: University of Toronto Press, 1985, vol. 26., 347–475.

Feltham, Owen, *Resolves*, 1623.

Florio, John, *A Worlde of Wordes*, 1598.

Fraunce, Abraham, *The Countess of Pembrokes Yvychurch*, 1591.

Fraunce, Abraham, *The Third Part of the Countess of Pembrokes Yvychurch*, 1592.

Gerard, John, *Herbal or generall historie of Plantes*, 1633.

Golding, Arthur (Ovid), *The xv. Bookes of P. Ovidius Naso, Entituled, Metamorphosis*, 1567.

Greene, Robert, *Menaphon*, 1589.

Guarini, Giovanni Battista, *Il Pastor Fido*, 1602.

Halle, Edward, *The Union of the Two Noble and Illustre Families of Lancastre and Yorke*, 1550.

Harington, Sir John, *Orlando Furioso in English Heroical Verse*, 1591.

Hariot, Thomas, *A Briefe and True Report of the New Found Land of Virginia*, 1590.

Herbert, George, *The Temple*, 1633.

Herbert, George, *Works*, ed. F. E. Hutchinson. Oxford: Clarendon Press, 1941.

Herbert, George, *The Williams Manuscript of George Herbert's Poems*, ed. Amy M. Charles. Scholars' Facsimiles & Reprints, Delmar, New York, 1977.

Heywood, Thomas, *An Apology For Actors*, 1612.

Higden, Ranulph, *Polychronicon*, 1480.

Hind, John, *The Most Excellent Historie of Lysimachus and Varrona*, 1604.

Hobbes, Thomas, *Leviathan*, 1651.

Hoby, Thomas, *The Courtyer of Count Baldessar Castilio*, 1561.

Holinshed, Raphael, *The First, Second, and Third Volumes of the Chronicles of England, Scotlande, and Irelande*, 1586.

Horace, *Satires, Epistles and Ars Poetica*, ed. and trans. H. R. Fairclough. Cambridge, MA: Harvard University Press, 1929.

Hortus Sanitatis, 1491.

Jonson, Ben, *Workes*, 1616.

Jonson, Ben, *Workes*, 1640–1.

Jonson, Ben, eds. C. H. Herford, Percy and Evelyn Simpson, *Ben Jonson*, 11 vols., Oxford: Oxford University Press, 1925–52.

Jonson, Ben, *Poems*, ed. Ian Donaldson. London: Oxford University Press, 1975.

Jonson, Ben, *The Cambridge Edition of the Works of Ben Jonson*, eds. David Bevington, Martin Butler, and Ian Donaldson. Cambridge: Cambridge University Press, 2012.

Kyd, Thomas, *The Spanish Tragedy*, 1592.

Liber Cronicarum (The Nuremberg Chronicle), 1493.

Locke, John, *A New Method of Making Common-Place-Books*, 1706.

Locke, John, *A Paraphrase and Notes on the Epistles of St. Paul,* 1733.

Marlowe, Christopher, ed. Stephen Orgel, *The Complete Poems and Translations*. New York: Penguin, 1980.

Meres, Francis, *Palladis Tamia Wits Treasury*, 1598.

Milton, John, *Areopagitica*, 1644.

Nashe, Thomas, *The Unfortunate Traveller. Or the Life of Jack Wilton*, 1594.

Norton, Thomas, and Thomas Sackville, *The Tragedie of Gorboduc*, 1565.

Norton, Thomas, and Thomas Sackville, *The Tragidie of Ferrex and Porrex*, 1570.

Plato [*Works*], trans. Harold N. Fowler. Cambridge, MA: Harvard University Press, 1921.

Plutarch, trans. Sir Thomas North, *The Lives of the Noble Grecians and Romanes Compared*, 1579.

Robinson, Thomas, *The Anatomy of the English Nunnery at Lisbon in Portugall*, 1622.

Sandys, George, *Ovid's Metamorphosis Englished, Mythologiz'd, and Represented in Figures*, 1632.

Settle, Elkanah, *The Empress of Morocco*, 1673.

Shakespeare, William, *The Tragicall Historie of Hamlet . . .*, 1603 [i.e., *Hamlet* Q1].

Shakespeare, William, *The Famous Historie of Troylus and Cresseid*, 1609.

Shakespeare, William, ed. Kenneth Muir, *Troilus and Cressida*. The Oxford Shakespeare, Oxford: Clarendon Press, 1982.

Shakespeare, William, ed. Stephen Orgel, *The Tempest*. The Oxford Shakespeare, Oxford: Clarendon Press, 1987.

Shakespeare, William, ed. Charlton Hinman, *The Norton Facsimile of the First Folio of Shakespeare*, 2nd edn. New York: W. W. Norton, 1996.

Shakespeare, William, ed. Colin Burrow, *The Complete Sonnets and Poems*. Oxford: Oxford University Press, 2002.

Shakespeare, William, ed. Suzanne Gossett, *Pericles*. Arden 3. London: Bloomsbury, 2004.

Terence, *Terentius Comoediae*. Strasbourg, 1496.

Terence, *Terentius cum quinque commentis*. Venice, 1497.

Thévenot, Melchisédec, *The art of swimming*, 1699.

Wager, William, *The Longer Thou Livest the More Fool Thou Art*, [?]1569.

Wilson, Thomas, *Arte of Rhetorick*, 1567.

Wilson, Thomas, *Arte of Rhetorick*, 1584.

Secondary Sources

Alexander, Gavin, "Sir Philip Sidney's *Arcadia*," in Andrew Hadfield, ed., *The Oxford Handbook of English Prose 1500–1640*. Oxford, 2013, 219–34.

Allen, W. Sidney, *Vox Latina: A Guide to the Pronunciation of Classical Latin*. Cambridge: Cambridge University Press, 1965.

Attridge, Derek, *Well-Weighed Syllables: Elizabethan Verse in Classical Metres*. Cambridge: Cambridge University Press, 1974.

Barish, Jonas, *The Anti-Theatrical Prejudice*. Berkeley: University of California Press, 1981.

Belsey, Catherine, "Tarquin Dispossessed: Expropriation and Consent in 'The Rape of Lucrece,'" *Shakespeare Quarterly*, 52.3 (autumn, 2001), 315–35.

Bland, Mark, "William Stansby and the Production of *The Workes of Beniamin Jonson*, 1615–16," in *The Library*, 20 (March, 1998), 1–33.

Bourne, Claire M. L., *Typographies of Performance in Early Modern England*. Oxford: Oxford University Press, 2020.

Bourus, Terri, *Young Shakespeare's Young Hamlet*. London: Palgrave Macmillan, 2014.

Cairncross, Andrew, *The Problem of Hamlet: A Solution*. London: Macmillan, 1936.

Chambers, E. K., *William Shakespeare*. Oxford: Clarendon Press, 1930.

Clegg, Cyndia, and Randall McLeod, *The peaceable and prosperous regiment of blessed Queene Elisabeth: A Facsimile from Holinshed's Chronicles (1587)*. San Marino, CA: Huntington Library Press 2005.

Clubb, Louise George, "Commedia Erudita: Birth and Transfiguration," in Michele Marrapodi, ed., *The Routledge Research Companion to Anglo-Italian Renaissance Literature and Culture*. Abingdon: Routledge, 2019, 101–18.

Crawford, John W., "Revisiting Shakespeare's Lucrece: A Social Reason for Her Suicide," *CEA Critic*, 59.3 (spring/summer, 1997), 65–9.

Darnton, Robert, "What is the History of Books?" *Daedalus* 111.3 (1982), 65–83.

Dobson, Michael, "Whatever You Do, Buy," *London Review of Books*, 23.22 (November, 2001). Online at https://www.lrb.co.uk/the-paper/v23/n22/michael-dobson/whatever-you-do-buy

Dowden, Ernest, *Shakespeare*. London: Macmillan 1877.

Duncan, Dennis, *Index: A History of the*. London: Allen Lane, 2021.

Duncan, Dennis, and Adam Smyth, eds., *Book Parts*. Oxford: Oxford University Press, 2019.

Edmond, Mary, "It Was For Gentle Shakespeare Cut," *Shakespeare Quarterly*, 42.3 (1991), 339–44.

Eisenstein, Elizabeth, *The Printing Press as an Agent of Change*. Cambridge: Cambridge University Press, 1979.

Elliott, Ward E. Y., and Robert J. Valenza, "And Then There Were None: Winnowing the Shakespeare Claimants," *Computers and the Humanities,* 30.3 (1996), 191–245.

Elliott, Ward E. Y., and Robert J. Valenza, "Glass Slippers and Seven-League Boots," *Shakespeare Quarterly,* 48.2 (summer, 1997), 177–207.

Elliott, Ward E. Y., and Robert J. Valenza, "So Much Hardball, So Little of it Over the Plate," https://www1.cmc.edu/pages/faculty/welliott/hardball.htm.

Elliott, Ward E. Y., and Robert J. Valenza, "So Many Hardballs, So Few over the Plate: Conclusions from Our 'Debate' with Donald Foster," *Computers and the Humanities,* 36.4 (November, 2002), 455–60.

Else, Gerald, *Aristotle's Poetics: The Argument.* Cambridge, MA: Harvard University Press, 1963.

Erne, Lukas, *Shakespeare as Literary Dramatist.* Cambridge: Cambridge University Press, 2003.

Erne, Lukas, "'Enter the Ghost of Andrea': Recovering Thomas Kyd's Two-Part Play," *English Literary Renaissance,* 30.3 (November, 2008), 339–72.

Frampton, Stephanie Ann, *Empire of Letters.* Oxford: Oxford University Press, 2019.

Genette, Gérard, *Seuils.* Paris: Editions du Seuil, 1987. English trans. Jane E. Lewin, *Paratexts: Thresholds of Interpretation.* Cambridge: Cambridge University Press, 1997.

Goldberg, Jonathan, "Hamlet's Hand," *Shakespeare Quarterly,* 39.3 (Autumn, 1988), 307–32.

Goodwin, Willard, "'A Very Pretty Picture M. Matisse But You Must Not Call It Joyce': The Making of the Limited Editions Club *Ulysses,*" *Joyce Studies Annual,* 10 (summer, 1999), 85–103.

Grazia, Margreta de, *Shakespeare Verbatim.* Oxford: Oxford University Press, 1991.

Greg, W. W., *A Bibliography of the English Printed Drama to the Restoration.* London: The Bibliographical Society/Oxford University Press, 1957.

Greg, W. W., "Hamlet's Hallucination," *The Modern Language Review,* 12.4 (October, 1917), 393–421.

Greg, W. W., *The Shakespeare First Folio.* Oxford: Clarendon Press, 1955.

Halliwell, Stephen, *Aristotle's Poetics.* London: Duckworth, 1986.

Hawkins, Thomas, *The Origin of the English Drama,* 1773.

Higbie, Carolyn, "Divide and Edit: A Brief History of Book Divisions," *Harvard Studies in Classical Philology*, 105 (2010), 1–31.

Higgins, Ben, *Shakespeare's Syndicate: The First Folio, Its Publishers, and the Early Modern Book Trade*. Oxford: Oxford University Press, 2022.

Hinman, Charlton, *The Printing and Proof-Reading of the First Folio of Shakespeare*, Oxford: Clarendon Press, 1963.

James, Henry, and Greg Walker, "The Politics of *Gorboduc*," *English Historical Review*, 110.435 (February, 1995), 109–21.

Kesson, Andy, *John Lyly and Early Modern Authorship*. Manchester: Revels Plays Companion Library, Manchester University Press, 2014.

Kilroy, Gerard, "Advertising the Reader: Sir John Harington's 'Directions in the Margent'," *English Literary Renaissance*, 41.1 (winter, 2011), 64–110.

Kirschbaum, Leo, "The Date of Shakespeare's 'Hamlet'," *Studies in Philology*, 34.2 (April, 1937), 168–75.

Kiséry, András, "An Author and a Bookshop: Publishing Marlowe's Remains at the Black Bear," *Philological Quarterly*, 91.3 (summer, 2012), 361–92.

Lerer, Seth, "'A Scaffold in the Marketplace': Bad *Hamlet*, Good Romans, and the Shakespearean Idiom," *Anglia*, 122 (2004), 373–87.

Lesser, Zachary, *Renaissance Drama and the Politics of Publication*. Cambridge: Cambridge University Press, 2004.

Love, Harold, *Scribal Publication in Seventeenth-Century England*. Oxford: Clarendon Press, 1993.

McCray, W. D., *Annals of the Bodleian Library, Oxford, A.D. 1598–A. D. 1867*. London: Rivington, 1868.

McLeod, Randall (as Random Cloud), "FIAT *f* LUX", in Randall McLeod, ed., *Crisis in Editing: Texts of the English Renaissance*. New York: AMS Press, 1994, 61–172.

McKenzie, D. F., *Bibliography and the Sociology of Texts*. The Panizzi Lectures, The British Library, 1986.

McKitterick, David, *The Invention of Rare Books*. Cambridge: Cambridge University Press, 2018.

Marino, James J., *Owning William Shakespeare*. Philadelphia: University of Pennsylvania Press, 2011.

Marotti, Arthur, *Manuscript, Print, and the English Renaissance Lyric*. Ithaca, NY: Cornell University Press, 1995.

Matthews, Peter D., "Leather Cover of the Bodleian First Folio," https://www.academia.edu/30971029/Leather_Cover_of_the_Bodleian_First_Folio.

Meskill, Lynn S., "Ben Jonson's 1616 Folio: A Revolution in Print," *Études Épistémè* [*sic*] 14 (2008), https://doi.org/10.4000/episteme.736.

Munro, Lucy, "Young Shakespeare/Late Shakespeare: The Case of *Pericles*," *Actes des congrès de la Société française Shakespeare*, 34|(2016). http://journals.openedition.org/shakespeare/3668; DOI:10.4000/shakespeare.3668.

Orgel, Stephen, *Impersonations*. Cambridge: Cambridge University Press, 1996.

Orgel, Stephen, *The Authentic Shakespeare*. New York: Routledge, 2002.

Orgel, Stephen, "Measuring Verse, Measuring Value in English Renaissance Poetry," in Martin McLaughlin, Ingrid D. Rowland, and Elisabetta Tarantino, eds., *Authority, Innovation and Early Modern Epistemology*. Leeds: Legenda, 2015, 97–103.

Orgel, Stephen, *The Reader in the Book*. Oxford: Oxford University Press, 2015.

Orgel, Stephen, *Wit's Treasury: Renaissance England and the Classics*. Philadelphia: University of Pennsylvania Press, 2021.

Orgel, Stephen, *The Invention of Shakespeare and Other Essays*. Philadelphia: The University of Pennsylvania Press, 2022.

Pearson, David, *Books as History*. London: British Library, 2008.

Pebworth, Ted-Larry, "John Donne, Coterie Poetry, and the Text as Performance," *Studies in English Literature, 1500–1900*, 29.1 (winter, 1989), 61–75.

Pitcher, John, "'After the Manner of Horace': Samuel Daniel in the Bodleian in 1605," *Papers of the Bibliographical Society of America*, 13.2 (June, 2019), 149–86.

Preiss, Richard, *Clowning and Authorship in Early Modern England*. Cambridge: Cambridge University Press, 2014.

Rasmussen, Eric, *A Textual Companion to* Doctor Faustus. Manchester: Manchester University Press, 1993.

Rasmussen, Eric, and Anthony James West, eds., *The Shakespeare First Folios: A Descriptive Catalogue*, Basingstoke: Palgrave Macmillan, 2012.

Reynolds, L. D., and N. G. Wilson, *Scribes and Scholars*, 3rd edn. Oxford: Oxford University Press, 1993.

Schuckman, Christian, "The Engraver of the First Folio Portrait of William Shakespeare," *Print Quarterly*, 8.1 (1991), 40–3.

Schuman, Sharon, "Sixteenth-Century English Quantitative Verse: Its Ends, Means, and Products," *Modern Philology*, 74.4 (May, 1977), 335–49.

Smith, Bruce, "Shakespeare's Sonnets and the History of Sexuality: A Reception History," in Jean Howard and Richard Dutton, eds.,

The Blackwell Companions to Shakespeare: The Poems, Problem Come-dies, Late Plays. Oxford: Blackwell, 2003, 4–26.

Smith, G. Gregory, *Elizabethan Critical Essays*. Oxford: Oxford University Press, 1904.

Sparshott, Francis, "The Riddle of Katharsis," in Eleanor Cook et al., eds., *Centre and Labyrinth*. Toronto: University of Toronto Press, 1983, 14–37.

Stallybrass, Peter, "Books and Scrolls," in Jennifer Anderson and Elizabeth Sauer, eds., *Books and Readers in Early Modern England*. Philadelphia: University of Pennsylvania Press, 2002.

Steevens, George, and Samuel Johnson, *Supplement to the Edition of Shak-speare's Plays Published in 1778 by Samuel Johnson and George Steevens*. London, 1780.

Stewart, Alan, *Philip Sidney: A Double Life*. London: Chatto and Windus, 2000.

Stoddard, Roger E., "Morphology and the Book from an American Per-spective," *Printing History* 9.1 (1987), 2–14.

Taylor, Gary, "Some Manuscripts of Shakespeare's Sonnets," *Bulletin of the John Rylands Library*, 68.1 (1985), 210–46.

Taylor, Gary, *Reinventing Shakespeare*. New York: Weidenfeld and Nicolson, 1989.

Trettien, Whitney, "Title Pages," in *Book Parts*, eds. Dennis Duncan and Adam Smyth. Oxford: Oxford University Press, 2019, 39–50.

Trimpi, Wesley, "The Meaning of Horace's *Ut Pictura Poesis*," *Journal of the Warburg and Courtauld Institutes*, 36 (1973).

Wakelin, Daniel, "Humanism and Printing," in Vincent Gillespie and Susan Powell, eds., *A Companion to the Early Printed Book in Britain, 1476–1558*. Cambridge: D. S. Brewer, 2014, 227–47.

Weimann, Robert, *Author's Pen and Actor's Voice*. Cambridge: Cambridge University Press, 2000.

West, Anthony James, *The Shakespeare First Folio: The History of the Book*, Oxford: Oxford University Press, 2001.

Wilson, J. Dover, "The Parallel Plots in 'Hamlet'," *The Modern Language Review*, 13.2 (April, 1918), 129–56.

Woudhuysen, H. R., "Editors and Texts, Authorities and Originals," in Lukas Erne and Margaret Jane Kidnie, *Textual Performances*. Cam-bridge: Cambridge University Press, 2004, 36–48.

Zirin, Ronald A., *The Phonological Basis of Latin Prosody*. The Hague: Mouton, 1970.

INDEX

For the benefit of digital users, indexed terms that span two pages (e.g., 52–53) may, on occasion, appear on only one of those pages.